Luxury sedan

Super car

Roadster

Sports car

F1 racer

Off-road racing car

Hybrid car

Off-road car

Recreational vehicle

Heavy truck

Luxury coach

Structure of car

 Mercedes-Benz 梅塞德斯－奔驰	 BMW 宝马	 Audi 奥迪	 Volkswagen AG 大众
 Opel 欧宝	 Porsche 保时捷	 GM 通用	 Chevrolet 雪佛兰
 Buick 别克	 Cadillac 凯迪拉克	 Pontiac 庞蒂克	 Saturn 土星
 Oldsmobile 奥兹莫比尔	 Chrysler 克莱斯勒	 Dodge 道奇	 Viper 蝰蛇
 Eagle 鹰	 Plymouth 普利茅斯	 Ford 福特	 Cougar 美洲狮

 Lincoln 林肯	Mustang 野马	 Mercury 水星	 Panoz 帕诺兹
 Mack 马克	Jeep 吉普	Land Rover 路虎	Hummer 悍马
 Toyota 丰田	Lexus 凌志	 Nissan 尼桑	 Infiniti 无限
 Honda 本田	 Acura 讴歌	 Mitsubishi 三菱	 Mazda 马自达
Isuzu 五十铃	Daihatsu 大发	 Subaru 富士斯巴鲁	Suzuki 铃木

 Hino 日野	 Tommykaira 龟牌	 Peugeot 标致	 Citroen 雪铁龙
 Renault 雷诺	 Venturi 文图瑞	 Fiat 菲亚特	 Ferrari 法拉利
 Iveco 依维柯	 Maserati 玛莎拉蒂	 Lamborghini 兰博基尼	 Lancia 蓝旗亚
 Pininfarina 平尼法尼那	 Abarth 阿巴斯	 Bugatti 布加蒂	 Piaggio 比亚乔
Alfa-Romeo 阿尔法罗密欧	 Rolls-Royce 劳斯莱斯	 Jaguar 捷豹	 Mini 迷你

 Lotus 莲花	 Leyland 利兰	 Marcos 玛柯斯	 Bentley 宾利
 Rover 罗孚	 MG 名爵	 Aston Martin 阿斯顿马丁	 Hyundai 现代
 Kia 起亚	 Daewoo 大宇	 Volvo 沃尔沃	 Saab 萨博
 Scania 斯堪尼亚	 SEAT 西特	 Skoda 斯柯达	 Smart 精灵
 Dacia 达西亚	 Proton 宝腾	 Polonez 波罗乃兹	 Lada 拉达

实用汽车英语

（第2版）

PRACTICAL AUTOMOBILE ENGLISH

(2nd Edition)

主编　刘　璇　于秀敏
参编　郭建华　樊　华
　　　刘艳莉　程　鸣

北京理工大学出版社
BEIJING INSTITUTE OF TECHNOLOGY PRESS

内容简介

本书共13个单元，每单元由以下3个部分构成：

Section A：介绍汽车各主要系统的构造及工作原理。附有课后练习，旨在帮助学生巩固所学内容，主要包括词汇、短语、专业术语练习，以及英汉互译练习。

Section B：涉及汽车主要系统或部件的维修保养、故障检测。附有课后练习，旨在帮助学生掌握一些常用汽车缩略语及熟悉一些外国汽车品牌。

Section C：单课：口语练习——汽车职场对话。双课：阅读练习——汽车文化。

本书既可作为高等院校汽车、交通类专业的英语教材，也可用做高等教育自学考试、成人教育、职业培训等汽车相关专业的本、专科生的英语教材，还可供从业人员自学使用。

版权专有　侵权必究

图书在版编目（CIP）数据

实用汽车英语／刘璇，于秀敏主编．—2 版．—北京：北京理工大学出版社，2012.7（2023.10重印）

ISBN 978 - 7 - 5640 - 6203 - 3

Ⅰ.①实… Ⅱ.①刘…②于… Ⅲ.①汽车工程 - 英语 - 高等学校 - 教材 Ⅳ.①H31

中国版本图书馆 CIP 数据核字（2012）第 141402 号

出版发行／北京理工大学出版社
社　　址／北京市海淀区中关村南大街5号
邮　　编／100081
电　　话／（010）68914775（办公室）　68944990（批销中心）　68911084（读者服务部）
网　　址／http：／／www.bitpress.com.cn
经　　销／全国各地新华书店
印　　刷／北京虎彩文化传播有限公司
开　　本／787 毫米×1092 毫米　1/16
印　　张／14.25
彩　　插／4
字　　数／308 千字
版　　次／2012 年 7 月第 2 版　2023 年 10 月第 12 次印刷
定　　价／42.00 元

责任编辑／梁铜华
责任校对／周瑞红
责任印制／王美丽

图书出现印装质量问题，本社负责调换

前 言

△ 实用汽车英语（第2版）

随着我国汽车业的迅猛发展及大量的汽车新技术的引进，对汽车人才英语水平的要求越来越高，因此全面提高汽车专业学生及汽车行业人员的实用英语水平已成为当务之急。本书是在新形势下注重应用型学科的实用性而编写的。在课文内容的编写上注重从传统知识向新技术的过渡，以使学生对汽车各主要系统有全面了解。

本书共13个单元，每单元由以下3个部分构成：

Section A：介绍汽车各主要系统的构造及工作原理。本部分附有课后练习，旨在帮助学生巩固所学内容，主要包括词汇、短语、专业术语练习，以及英汉互译练习。

Section B：涉及汽车主要系统或零部件的维修保养、故障检测。本部分附有课后练习，旨在帮助学生掌握一些常用汽车缩略语及熟悉一些外国汽车品牌。

Section C：单课：口语练习——汽车职场对话。涉及汽车买卖、询价、付款方式、汽车美容、汽车维修、汽车保险及电话回访等七大职场话题。口语话题的引入，旨在打破专业英语传统教学中的英汉互译法，提高学生的口语表达能力，以满足未来职业岗位的需求。双课：阅读练习——汽车文化。涉及世界汽车发展史上著名人物及著名汽车厂家的发展历程，使学生在提高英语阅读能力的同时，受到汽车文化的熏陶。

使用者可以根据培养目标、学习兴趣等对本书内容进行取舍。例如：汽车营销专业可选学Section A和Section C，而汽车售后技术服务专业可选学Section A和Section B。

书末附录提供课后练习答案、常用汽车缩略语及外国汽车车名，以方便使用者查阅。

本书既可作为高等院校汽车、交通类专业的英语教材，也可用做高等教育自学考试、成人教育、职业培训等汽车相关专业的本、专科生的英语教材，还可供从业人员自学使用。

本书由吉林大学刘璇、于秀敏主编。吉林大学郭建华、樊华、刘艳莉以及西安工程大学程鸣参与了编写工作。

在编写本书的过程中，得到了吉林大学汽车学院的大力支持，编者在此对其表示衷心的感谢！

在编写本书的过程中，参考了大量的国内外书籍和资料，以及一些相关网站，有些内容引自其中，在此对原作者表示诚挚的谢意！

由于编者水平有限，书中难免存在一些缺点和错误，恳请广大师生、读者及各位专家不吝指教，以使教材不断完善。

编 者

Contents

△ 实用汽车英语（第 2 版）

▶ **Unit One** 1

Section A Basic Structure of an Automobile 1
Section B History of Automobile Industry 7
Section C Dialogue   At the 4S Store 10

▶ **Unit Two** 14

Section A Components and Operation of the Engine 14
Section B Troubles and Maintenance of Engines 21
Section C Karl Benz 25

▶ **Unit Three** 29

Section A Engine Fuel System 29
Section B Fuel Injector and Its Maintenance 35
Section C Dialogue   Price Discussion 38

▶ **Unit Four** 41

Section A Engine Exhaust System 41
Section B Emission Control System 46
Section C BMW 49

▶ **Unit Five** 53

Section A Engine Cooling System 53
Section B Cooling System Troubleshooting 59
Section C Dialogue   Terms of Payment 62

▶ **Unit Six** 65

Section A Engine Lubrication System 65

Section B　Engine Lubricating Oil ……………………………………………… 70
Section C　Henry Ford ……………………………………………………………… 74

▶ **Unit Seven** ……………………………………………………………………………… 78

Section A　Engine Ignition System ……………………………………………… 78
Section B　Battery and Its Maintenance ……………………………………… 84
Section C　Dialogue　At the Auto Beauty Shop …………………………… 88

▶ **Test（Unit 1 – Unit 7）** ……………………………………………………………… 92

▶ **Unit Eight** ……………………………………………………………………………… 97

Section A　Clutch …………………………………………………………………… 97
Section B　Clutch Troubleshooting …………………………………………… 103
Section C　General Motors Corporation ……………………………………… 107

▶ **Unit Nine** ……………………………………………………………………………… 112

Section A　Transmission ………………………………………………………… 112
Section B　Checking and Servicing the Automatic Transmission …… 120
Section C　Dialogue　In the Auto Repair Shop …………………………… 124

▶ **Unit Ten** ………………………………………………………………………………… 127

Section A　Suspension System ………………………………………………… 127
Section B　Leaf Spring Maintenance ………………………………………… 133
Section C　Toyota …………………………………………………………………… 136

▶ **Unit Eleven** …………………………………………………………………………… 140

Section A　Steering System ……………………………………………………… 140
Section B　Causes of Steering Troubles ……………………………………… 147
Section C　Dialogue　Auto Insurance ………………………………………… 150

▶ **Unit Twelve** …………………………………………………………………………… 153

Section A　Brake System ………………………………………………………… 153
Section B　Antilock Brake System（ABS） …………………………………… 158
Section C　FAW-VW ……………………………………………………………… 161

▶ **Unit Thirteen** ·· 166

    Section A   Automobile Navigation System ·· 166
    Section B   Types of Vehicles ·· 171
    Section C   Dialogue   A Return Call Visit ··· 176

▶ **Test (Unit 8 – Unit 13)** ·· 178

▶ **Final Exam** ·· 183

▶ **Appendix** ·· 188

    I. Key to the Exercises ··· 188
    II. Abbreviations ·· 208
    III. Names of Cars ··· 213

References ··· 217

Unit One

Section A Basic Structure of an Automobile

Automobiles are basically the same in structure although they are quite different in style and design. In other words, any automobile is composed of four sections, such as the engine, chassis, body and electrical system (See Fig. 1 – 1).

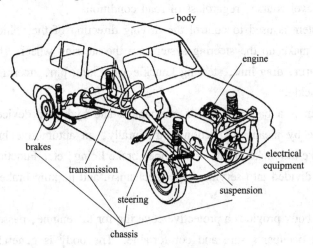

Fig. 1 – 1 Layout of an automobile

Engines

The engine is the power source of an automobile. The most common type is the internal combustion engine, which burns fuel within the cylinders and converts the expanding force of the combustion or "explosion" into rotary force used to propel the vehicle.

All engines have fuel, exhaust, cooling, and lubrication systems. Gasoline engines also have ignition systems.

The fuel system plays a vital part in the power-producing process since it supplies the gasoline to the cylinders of the engine.

The exhaust system is used to conduct the burned gases to the rear of a vehicle and into the air, quiet the exhaust noise, and, in most cases, reduce the pollutants in the exhaust.

The cooling system removes excessive heat from the engine components.

The lubrication system is important in keeping the engine running smoothly. Motor oil is the lubricant used in the system.

The ignition system supplies the electric spark needed to ignite the air-fuel mixture in the cylinders, which initiates the power stroke.

Chassis

The chassis is a framework used to assemble auto components on it. The chassis includes the power train, suspension, steering, and brake system.

The power train system consists of mechanisms and units which transmit torque from the engine to the drive wheels and change torque and rpm in magnitude and direction. Among these mechanisms and units are the transmission (gearbox), clutch, propeller shaft, rear axle, differential and the wheels.

The primary purpose of the suspension system is to support the weight of the vehicle. The basic job of the suspension system is to absorb the shocks caused by irregular road surfaces, which would otherwise be transmitted to the vehicle and its occupants, thus helping to keep the vehicle on a controlled and level course, regardless of road conditions.

The steering system is used to control the driving direction of the vehicle as it moves. The key components that make up the steering system are the steering wheel, steering shaft, worm, gear sector, pitman arm, drag link, steering knuckle arm, king pin, steering arm, tie rod, front axle and steering knuckle.

The brake system is a balanced set of mechanical and hydraulic devices used to retard the motion of the vehicle by means of friction. Structurally, an automotive brake system contains several major parts like the brake drum, brake shoe, brake lining, etc. Functionally, an automotive brake system can be divided into service brake mechanism and parking brake mechanism.

Bodies

The automobile body provides a protective covering for the engine, passenger and cargo. It is designed to keep the occupants safe and comfortable. The body is generally divided into four sections — the front, the upper or top, the rear and the underbody. These sections can further fall into a lot of assemblies and parts, such as the hood, the fender, the roof panel, the door, the instrument panel, the bumper and the luggage compartment.

Electrical Systems

The electrical system supplies lighting and driving power for the automobile. The electrical system of a modern automobile is composed of four main circuits and a number of branch circuits. The four main circuits are the generating circuit, the starting circuit, the ignition circuit and the lighting circuit. All the main circuits are connected together and linked to the battery which is necessary in electric services on any vehicle.

New Words

structure	[ˈstrʌktʃə]	n.	构造
chassis	[ˈʃæsi]	n.	底盘
cylinder	[ˈsilində]	n.	汽缸
convert	[kənˈvəːt]	v.	转变
propel	[prəˈpel]	v.	推进
exhaust	[igˈzɔːst]	n.	排气,废气
		v.	排气,耗尽
lubrication	[ˌljuːbriˈkeiʃən]	n.	润滑
ignition	[igˈniʃən]	n.	点燃,点火
component	[kəmˈpəunənt]	n.	成分,部件,零件
ignite	[igˈnait]	v.	点燃,点火
initiate	[iˈniʃieit]	v.	发动,开始
stroke	[strəuk]	n.	冲程,行程
assemble	[əˈsembl]	v.	装配,安装
		n.	组件
suspension	[səsˈpenʃən]	n.	悬挂
steer	[stiə]	v.	驾驶
		n.	(车辆)转向机构
brake	[breik]	n.	制动器,刹车
		v.	制动
mechanism	[ˈmekənizəm]	n.	机械机构
transmit	[trænzˈmit]	v.	传动,传送
torque	[tɔːk]	n.	转矩,扭矩
magnitude	[ˈmægnitjuːd]	n.	大小,数量;(数)量值
transmission	[trænzˈmiʃən]	n.	变速器,传动装置
clutch	[klʌtʃ]	n.	离合器
differential	[ˌdifəˈrenʃəl]	n.	差速器
worm	[wəːm]	n.	蜗杆
balance	[ˈbæləns]	v.	使平衡
hydraulic	[haiˈdrɔːlik]	a.	液压的,水力的
retard	[riˈtɑːd]	v.	使减速,阻止,妨碍
friction	[ˈfrikʃən]	n.	摩擦,摩擦力
hood	[hud]	n.	引擎罩,车篷
fender	[ˈfendə]	n.	挡泥板,防护物
bumper	[ˈbʌmpə]	n.	汽车保险杠,缓冲器
circuit	[ˈsəːkit]	n.	电路,线路,回路
battery	[ˈbætəri]	n.	电池

Phrases and Expressions

electrical system	电器系统
internal combustion engine	内燃发动机
fuel system	燃料系统
exhaust system	排气系统
cooling system	冷却系统
lubrication system	润滑系统
ignition system	点火系统
air-fuel mixture	可燃混合气
power stroke	做功冲程
power train	传动系统
suspension system	悬架系统
steering system	转向系统
brake system	制动系统
propeller shaft	传动轴
rear axle	后桥,后轴
steering wheel	方向盘
steering shaft	转向轴
gear sector	扇形齿轮
pitman arm	转向摇臂
drag link	直拉杆
steering knuckle arm	转向节臂
king pin	主销
steering arm	转向臂
tie rod	转向横拉杆
front axle	前轴
steering knuckle	转向节
by means of	用,依靠
brake drum	制动鼓
brake shoe	制动蹄片
brake lining	制动器摩擦衬片,制动衬片
service brake	行车制动器,主制动器
parking brake	驻车制动器
roof panel	(车身)顶板,顶盖
instrument panel	仪表(安装)板
luggage compartment	行李舱,行李间

Notes to the Text

1. In other words, any automobile is composed of four sections, such as the engine, chassis, body and electrical system.
   换言之,任何汽车都是由 4 部分组成的,如发动机、底盘、车身以及电器系统。
2. All engines have fuel, exhaust, cooling, and lubrication systems. Gasoline engines also have ignition systems.
   发动机都有燃料系统、排气系统、冷却系统和润滑系统。汽油发动机还有点火系统。
3. The chassis includes the power train, suspension, steering and brake system.
   底盘包括传动系统、悬架系统、转向系统及制动系统。
4. The basic job of the suspension system is to absorb the shocks caused by irregular road surfaces, which would otherwise be transmitted to the vehicle and its occupants, thus helping to keep the vehicle on a controlled and level course, regardless of road conditions.
   悬架系统的基本作用是吸收路面不平引起的冲击和振动,使其不会传递给车辆和乘客。这样,不管路况如何,都能使车辆具有可控制的、水平的行驶路线。

Exercises on the Text

I. Answer the following questions according to the text.
   1. What are the four basic sections of an automobile?
   2. What's the function of the exhaust system?
   3. What's the function of the cooling system?
   4. What's the function of the power train?
   5. What's the function of the electrical system?

II. Fill in the table below (Tab. 1 – 1).

Tab. 1 – 1

English	Chinese
	差速器
propeller shaft	
	方向盘
rear axle	
	离合器
cylinder	
	转矩
internal combustion engine	
	传动系统
power stroke	

III. Fill in the blanks with the words or phrases given below, and change the form where necessary.

| conduct | retard | provide | supply |
| assemble | remove | control | be composed of |

1. The fuel system _____ the gasoline to the cylinders of the engine.
2. The cooling system _____ excessive heat from the engine.
3. The exhaust system is used to _____ the burned gases to the rear of a vehicle and into the air.
4. The chassis is a framework used to _____ auto components on it.
5. The brake system is used to _____ the motion of the vehicle by means of friction.
6. The steering system is used to _____ the driving direction of the vehicle as it moves.
7. The automobile body _____ a protective covering for the engine, passenger and cargo.
8. The electrical system of a modern automobile _____ four main circuits and a number of branch circuits.

IV. Reading comprehension: Read the following passage carefully and fill in the blanks with the words given below.

| framework | design | case | chassis | requirements |
| functions | engine | body | forces | engineers |

An automobile is composed of four sections such as the engine, __1__, body and electrical system. The __2__ is the power source of an automobile. The chassis is a __3__ on which the body is seated. In the __4__ of a collision, the body __5__ to provide lifesaving protection. The __6__ of an automobile body is therefore governed by various __7__ from safety researchers and structural __8__. Passenger comfort had always been one of the propelling __9__ in the development of the automobile __10__. It is expected that future cars will have less interior noise, better vibration isolation and better air-conditioning.

V. Translate the following paragraph into Chinese.

The primary purpose of the suspension system is to support the weight of the vehicle. The basic job of the suspension system is to absorb the shocks caused by irregular road surfaces that would otherwise be transmitted to the vehicle and its occupants, thus helping to keep the vehicle on a controlled and level course, regardless of road conditions.

VI. Translate the following sentences into English.
1. 虽然汽车在设计方面有所不同,但在构造上是基本相同的。
2. 发动机的类型有多种,但最常见的是内燃机。

3. 转向系统被用来控制车辆的驾驶方向。
4. 底盘包括传动系统、悬架系统、转向系统以及制动系统。
5. 电器系统向汽车提供照明和驱动的电力。

Section B　　History of Automobile Industry

　　It is already over one hundred years since the first automobile was invented in the world. The origin of the automobile cannot be attributed to one person. On January 29, 1886, Karl Benz from Germany applied for a patent for his tricycle. This is officially considered the birth of the first car invented. From then on, the transportation on land shifted from the age of coaches to the age of automobiles.

　　Soon after the invention of the first automobile, auto manufacturers from other countries immediately made great investments in auto design and production. As a result, the world auto industry has been developed by leaps and bounds.

　　Germany was the birthplace of the automobiles. Karl Benz, who had experience with railway locomotives, and Gottlieb Daimler, who had been a mechanic with the firm of Otto and Langen, both produced workable gasoline vehicles in 1886 and continued to do so. Daimler's great contribution was to recognize that an internal combustion engine for a motor vehicle had to operate at high speed, at least 1,000 rpm, and he set out to design and build such an engine. Benz introduced spark ignition.

　　In spite of their priority, neither Daimler nor Benz made cars in any significant numbers for many years. Indeed their companies did not get into large scale production until they were merged to form Daimler-Benz in 1926. Today this corporation enjoys an enviable reputation as the maker of Mercedes-Benz cars. Its undisputed German competitor is BMW (Bavarian Motor Works).

　　During the first half of the twentieth century, the United States established the leadership position in automobile production because Henry Ford introduced the assembly line of mass production in the automobile industry. The adoption of mass production techniques can be seen as a revolution in car making history.

　　The massive market of the automobiles in America was dominated by the Big Three motor manufacturers. Up until the 1920s, Ford had been the market leader and owned the prestigious Lincoln marque. By the 1930s, the Big Three were headed by American General Motors with its batch of makes which included the Buick, Chevrolet, Oldsmobile and Cadillac names. Chrysler, the last of the Big Three to be established, had Plymouth as its high volume, low cost arm.

　　The early 1950s witnessed some development of the motor industry in Japan. Before the war, Japan's carmakers consisted, in essence, of Toyota and Nissan, which produced the Datsun. From 1960, the Nissan name appeared on some models sold on the home market. Those built for export were called Datsun but this practice only lasted until 1983. Since then, the company has only manufactured Nissan cars. With a great export drive first targeted at America and then Europe, Japan has emerged as the international community's major manufacturing force. Not only are Japan's products seen on almost every road on the globe, but its car makers have also taught the rest of the motoring world how to build its automobiles more cost-effectively.

China was totally an agricultural country with almost no industries before liberation. It was not until the 1900s that the first automobiles were introduced to China. In 1913, the first highway in China was built between Changsha and Xiangtan and the year 1918 witnessed the official issue of the first driving licenses in China. Then, between the 1930s and the 1940s, the auto transportation was somewhat developed but the vehicles driven then were all made in other developed countries. The auto industry in China did not start until the 1950s. In 1956, the No. 1 Auto Plant was established in Changchun, and turned out the first batch of *liberation* automobiles for our country. After that, several other auto plants were set up one after another in Nanjing, Beijing, Jinan and Sichuan. In the early 1980s, the No. 2 Auto Plant designed and equipped by ourselves was put into massive production. In the late 1980s and the late 1990s, the Shanghai Auto Industry Corporation established joint ventures with German Volkswagen and American General Motors, marking a new stage in the development of auto industry in China.

Over the ensuing century, the automobile has evolved from a hand-crafted, three-wheeled motorized coach into a high-tech product without which our life would be unimaginable.

New Words

attribute	[əˈtribju(ː)t]	v.	把……归因于,认为……是某人所有
Germany	[ˈdʒəːməni]	n.	德国
patent	[ˈpeitənt]	n.	专利(权),专利证
		v.	给予……专利证(权),取得……专利证(权)
tricycle	[ˈtraisikl]	n.	三轮车
transportation	[ˌtrænspɔːˈteiʃən]	n.	交通
shift	[ʃift]	v.	转移,转变
coach	[kəutʃ]	n.	(旧时的)四轮大马车,长途公共汽车,(铁路上的)客车
manufacturer	[ˌmænjuˈfæktʃərə]	n.	制造商
locomotive	[ˌləukəˈməutiv]	n.	火车头,机车
mechanic	[miˈkænik]	n.	技工,机械工
priority	[praiˈɔriti]	n.	先,前,优先(权)
merge	[məːdʒ]	v.	使(企业等)合并,使并入
enviable	[ˈenviəbl]	a.	值得羡慕的,引起嫉妒的
competitor	[kəmˈpetitə]	n.	竞争者
dominate	[ˈdɔmineit]	v.	支配,统治

marque	[mɑːk]	n.	汽车的型号或式样
batch	[bætʃ]	n.	一次生产量,一批
witness	['witnis]	v.	目睹,目击
ensue	[in'sjuː]	v.	接着而来,接着发生
evolve	[i'vɔlv]	v.	使发展,使逐渐形成,使进(演)化
craft	[krɑːft]	n.	工艺,手艺
		vt.	(一般以过去分词形式出现)(以手工)精巧地制作
motorized	['məutəraizd]	a.	摩托化的,机动化的

Phrases and Expressions

Karl Benz	卡尔·本茨(奔驰汽车公司创始人)
apply for	申请
by leaps and bounds	非常迅速地
set out	出发,开始
Henry Ford	亨利·福特(美国福特汽车公司的创始人)
assembly line	装配线,总装线
Ford	(美国)福特汽车公司
Lincoln	林肯
American General Motors	美国通用汽车公司
Buick	别克
Chevrolet	雪佛兰
Oldsmobile	奥兹莫比尔
Cadillac	凯迪拉克
Chrysler	克莱斯勒(美国第三大汽车制造企业)
Plymouth	普利茅斯
in essence	实质上
Toyota	(日本)丰田汽车公司
Nissan	(日本)日产汽车公司
driving license	驾驶执照
No. 1 Auto Plant	第一汽车制造厂
turn out	生产,制造
put into production	投入生产
joint venture	合资企业
German Volkswagen	德国大众汽车公司

Notes to the Text

1. The massive market of the automobiles in America was dominated by the Big Three motor manufacturers.

   巨大的美国汽车市场被三大汽车制造商所占据。

2. ... the year 1918 witnessed the official issue of the first driving licenses in China.

   ……1918年中国正式发行了第一批驾驶执照。

Exercises

I. Translate the following names of cars into Chinese.

1. Benz　　_____
2. Volkswagen　　_____
3. Golf　　_____
4. BMW　　_____
5. Grace　　_____
6. Porsche　　_____
7. Audi　　_____
8. Opel　　_____

II. Translate the following abbreviations into corresponding Chinese terms.

1. CYL（cylinder）　　_____
2. ASSY（assembly）　　_____
3. A/C（air conditioning）　　_____
4. ANT（antenna）　　_____
5. DIFF（differential）　　_____
6. VIN（vehicle identification number）　　_____

Section C　Dialogue　At the 4S Store

The following dialogues took place at a 4S store (See Fig. 1-2).

Fig. 1-2　At the 4S store

Dialogue One:

Salesclerk(S): Good morning, Sir. Can I help you?
Customer(C): I'd like to buy a car. Recommend one for me?
S: Is it for personal or business use?
C: It's for personal use. Would you tell me some more details?
S: With pleasure. Why not go to the showroom? I'll show you around. We have many models displayed there.
C: Great! Let's go!
...
S: Look! All our new models are here. I think there is one type that suits you.
C: I hope so.
S: Sir, how about this one? This car has excellent safety features, like the dual air bags and ABS brakes. Compared with the old types, this type is improved in exterior design and tint. It offers high level of comfort and eye-catching styling. And some pieces of optional equipment are also offered.
C: It looks really nice! But it's a little more than I want to pay.
S: Oh, how about that yellow one? It has the characteristics of small volume, stable property, safety and reliability, low fuel consumption, long life in service. Besides, the price is moderate.
C: It's quite good. But I prefer the white color.
S: Oh, the white ones of this type are out of stock. Can you wait?
C: OK if not waiting for a long time.
S: It would not keep you waiting for more than one week. Please fill in this form, and I'll call you as soon as possible.
C: All right! Thank you for your help.
S: My pleasure.

Dialogue Two:

Salesclerk(S): Good afternoon, madam. Welcome to our 4S store.
Customer(C): Good afternoon. I'm planning to buy a car.
S: What make are you interested in? We have many for you to choose from.
C: I like Toyota Camry.
S: Alright, madam. You are making a good choice. Toyota has made a lot of design improvement in the new Camry.
C: What does it come with standards?
S: Well, the standards include: air conditioning, anti-lock brakes, anti-theft electric lock, air bags, an AM/FM stereo with a CD player and cruise control.
C: That sounds good. What colors does the new Camry come in?

S: We have this new model in white, black, grey and silver. These are the standard colors. Of course you could specially order from various other colors too.

C: Oh, No. I'll take the silver one. I think it is just OK for me.

Useful Expressions and Sentences

1. At the 4S Store
   在4S店(4S店是一种以"四位一体"为核心的汽车特许经营模式,包括整车销售"Sale"、零配件销售"Spare parts"、售后服务"Service"、信息反馈"Survey"等。)

2. I'd like to buy a car. Recommend one for me?
   我想买一辆汽车。给我介绍一辆好吗?
   recommend [ˌrekə'mend] v. 推荐,介绍,建议

3. Is it for personal or business use?
   是私用还是商用?

4. Would you tell me some more details?
   您能多给我介绍一些情况吗?

5. With pleasure. Why not go to the showroom? I'll show you around. We have many models displayed there.
   很乐意。我们到展厅去好吗?我可以带你看一看,那儿陈列有我们很多车型。
   Why not do... 表示建议某人去做某事。
   show sb. around 带某人参观
   display [dis'plei] v. 陈列,展览

6. I think there is one type that suits you.
   我想总有一款适合你。

7. Sir, how about this one? This car has excellent safety features, like the dual air bags and ABS brakes. Compared with the old types, this type is improved in exterior design and tint. It offers high level of comfort and eye-catching styling. And some pieces of optional equipment are also offered.
   先生,这辆怎么样?这辆车的安全性能是一流的,有两个安全气囊和ABS刹车。与老款相比,这款在外观设计和色泽上有所改进。这款车提供高标准的乘坐舒适感和乘客视野,还提供一些附加配置。
   How about... (你认为)……怎么样?
   tint [tint] n. 色泽,色调
   style [stail] n. 风格,作风,类型,式样
             v. 使符合某种式样,设计

8. But it's a little more than I want to pay.
   但是价格有点贵。

9. It has the characteristics of small volume, stable property, safety and reliability, low fuel consumption, long life in service. Besides, the price is moderate.

它(这款车)具有体积小,性能稳定,安全可靠,低油耗,使用寿命长等特点。此外,其价格适中。
moderate [ˈmɔdərit] *a.* 中等的,适度的

10. But I prefer the white color.
    但我更喜欢白色。

11. The white ones of this type are out of stock.
    这款车白色的已脱销。
    out of stock 已脱销,已不在贮存中   in stock 有库存量

12. Please fill in this form.
    请填写这张表格。

13. My pleasure. 我乐意,不用谢。

14. What make are you interested in? We have many for you to choose from.
    您喜欢什么牌子的车?我们有很多牌子的车供您选择。

15. I like Toyota Camry. 我喜欢丰田凯美瑞。

16. Toyota has made a lot of design improvement in the new Camry.
    丰田在新款凯美瑞的设计上做了很多改进。

17. What does it come with standards?
    它的标准配置都有什么?

18. Well, the standards include: air conditioning, anti-lock brakes, anti-theft electric lock, air bags, an AM/FM stereo with a CD player and cruise control.
    啊,(它的)标准配置包括空调、防抱死制动系统、防盗电子锁、安全气囊、短波/调频收音机、CD 播放器以及巡航控制系统。

19. What colors does the new Camry come in?
    新款凯美瑞都有什么颜色?

20. Of course you could specially order from various other colors too.
    当然,您还可以专门订购其他颜色的。

21. Oh, No. I'll take the silver one. I think it is just OK for me.
    啊,不用。我买银色的。我觉得银色车刚好适合我。

Unit Two

Section A   Components and Operation of the Engine

Components of the Engine

The various components of an engine are assembled together during being manufactured and most of them are secured by means of bolts, nuts and other types of fasteners. Some parts are internal and others are attached to the outside of the engine.

The engine block forms the main framework or foundation of the engine. The block is made of cast iron or aluminum. The other parts of the engine are either cast into the block or attached to it.

The lower part of the block is known as the crankcase and this has bearings that carry the crankshaft.

The cylinders, which contain the pistons, are cast into the block.

The water jackets, filled with coolant, are also cast into the block.

Many parts are attached by fastening devices to the block. These items include the water pump, the oil pan, the flywheel or clutch housing, the ignition distributor, the oil and fuel pump, and the cylinder head.

The piston is a cylindrical shaped hollow part that moves up and down inside the engine cylinder, which converts the potential energy of the fuel into the kinetic energy that turns the crankshaft. The piston is composed of the piston head, piston ring, piston land, piston skirt and piston pin hole.

The piston head or "crown" is the top surface against which the explosive force is exerted. It may be in various shapes to promote turbulence or help control combustion.

The piston rings carried in the ring grooves are of two basic types: compression rings and oil-control rings. The upper compression rings are used to prevent compression leakage; the lower oil-control rings control the amount of oil being deposited on the cylinder wall.

The piston lands are parts of the piston between the ring grooves. The lands provide a seating surface for the sides of the piston rings.

The main section of a piston is known as the skirt. It forms a bearing area in contact with the cylinder wall.

The piston pin hole in the piston also serves as a bearing for the piston pin, which is used to connect the connecting rod.

The connecting rod is attached to the crankshaft at one end (big end) and to the piston at the other end (small end). It transmits force and motion from the piston pin. The power from the combustion in the cylinders powers the piston to push the connecting rods to turn the crankshaft.

The crankshaft revolves in bearings located in the engine crankcase. It provides a constant turning force to the wheels. The function of the crankshaft is to change the reciprocating motion of the piston to rotary motion to drive the wheels and handle the entire power output. The crankshaft is made of alloy steel or cast iron. The crankshaft is actually made up of various parts such as the main bearing journal, rod journal, crank arm bearing, counter-balanced weight and flywheel end. In order to reduce or eliminate vibration, a crankshaft must be provided with counter balanced weights that extend radially from the crankshaft centerline in the opposite direction of the crank arms. The rod journals are bored hollow in order to reduce the crankshaft inertia. Drilled diagonally through the crank arms are oil holes to supply oil to the rod journals (See Fig. 2-1).

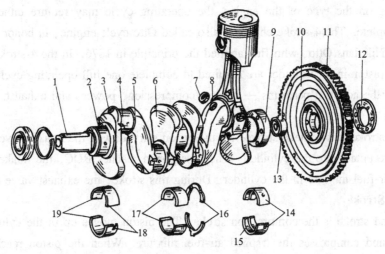

Fig. 2-1 A crankshaft

1—crankshaft front end; 2—front main journal; 3—oil passage hole; 4—crank pin; 5—crank web;
6—counter weight; 7—oil passage plug; 8—oil passage; 9—crankshaft collar; 10—flywheel;
11—flywheel gear ring; 12—flywheel lock plate; 13—clutch shaft bearing; 14—rear main bearing half shell;
15—oil groove; 16—crankshaft thrust; 17—central main bearing half shell;
18—bearing half shell; 19—front main bearing half shell

A flywheel is attached to the rear of the crankshaft with bolts. The function of the flywheel is to keep the engine running smoothly between power strokes. Its inertia tends to keep the flywheel rotating at a constant speed. In some engines, the flywheel also serves as a mounting surface for the clutch. The outer rim of the flywheel has a large ring attached with gear teeth cut into it. The teeth of the starting motor engage these teeth and spin the flywheel to crank the engine. When an automatic transmission is used, the torque converter assembly works with the flywheel.

In conclusion, each component of the engine has its own functions in producing power for vehicles.

Operation of the Engine

There are various types of engines such as electric motors, steam engines, and internal combustion engines. But most automobile engines are internal combustion, reciprocating 4-stroke gasoline engines.

The internal combustion engine, as its name indicates, burns fuel within the cylinders and converts the expanding force of the combustion into rotary force used to propel the vehicle.

Reciprocating means "up and down" or "back and forth." It is the up and down action of a piston in the cylinder that produces power in a reciprocating engine.

The term "stroke" refers to piston movement within the cylinder. The upper limit of piston movement is called top dead center (TDC). The lower limit of piston movement is called bottom dead center (BDC). A stroke occurs when the piston moves from TDC to BDC or from BDC to TDC. The piston completes a stroke each time it changes the direction of motion.

Depending on the type of the engine, the operating cycle may require either two or four strokes to complete. The 4-stroke engine is also called Otto cycle engine, in honor of the German engineer, Dr. Nikolaus Otto, who first applied the principle in 1876. In the 4-stroke engine, four strokes of the piston in the cylinder are required to complete one full operating cycle. Each stroke is named after the action it performs — intake, compression, power, and exhaust.

Intake Stroke

The first stroke is the intake stroke. As the piston starts down, the intake valve opens and the air-fuel mixture enters into the cylinder. When the piston reaches BDC, the intake valve closes, trapping the air-fuel mixture in the cylinder. During this stroke, the exhaust valve stays closed.

Compression Stroke

The second stroke is the compression stroke. The piston moves up in the cylinder with both valves closed and compresses the trapped air-fuel mixture. When the piston reaches TDC, the pressure rises.

Power Stroke

The third stroke is the power stroke. Near the end of the compression stroke, the spark plug fires, igniting the compressed air-fuel mixture that produces a powerful explosion. The combustion process pushes the piston down the cylinder with great force turning the crankshaft to provide the power to drive the car.

Exhaust Stroke

The fourth stroke is the exhaust stroke. With the piston at BDC, the exhaust valve opens, and the piston moves up again and forces the burned gases out of the cylinder. The piston travels up to the top of the cylinder pushing all the exhaust out before closing the exhaust valve in preparation for starting the four-stroke process over again.

This 4-stroke cycle is continuously repeated in every cylinder as long as the engine remains running (See Fig. 2-2).

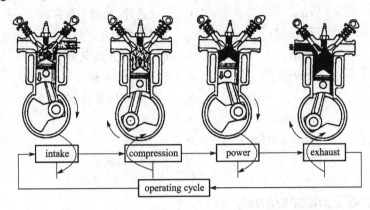

Fig. 2-2 The operation of a 4-stroke-cycle engine

New Words

secure	[si'kjuə]	v.	紧固
bolt	[bəult]	n.	螺栓
		v.	用螺栓连接
nut	[nʌt]	n.	螺帽,螺母,螺套
fastener	['fɑːsənə]	n.	紧固件,钩扣
cast	[kɑːst]	v.	铸造
aluminum	[ə'ljuːminəm]	n.	铝
crankcase	['kræŋkkeis]	n.	曲柄箱
bearing	['bɛəriŋ]	n.	轴承
crankshaft	['kræŋkʃɑːft]	n.	曲轴
piston	['pistən]	n.	活塞
coolant	['kuːlənt]	n.	冷却液,冷却剂
flywheel	['flaiwiːl]	n.	飞轮
turbulence	['təːbjuləns]	n.	紊流,涡流
leakage	['liːkidʒ]	n.	渗漏,泄漏
deposit	[di'pɔzit]	v.	沉积,淤积
vibration	[vai'breiʃən]	n.	振动,震动,颤动
revolve	[ri'vɔlv]	v.	旋转,转动
reciprocate	[ri'siprəkeit]	v.	往复,做往复运动
eliminate	[i'limineit]	v.	消除,除去
radially	['reidiəli]	adv.	径向地
centerline	['sentəlain]	n.	中心线轴线
bore	[bɔː]	n.	内径
		v.	钻孔

inertia	[iˈnəːʃjə]	n.	惯性,惯量
rim	[rim]	n.	边缘,轮缘,齿圈
engage	[inˈgeidʒ]	v.	连接,啮合
spin	[spin]	v./n.	(使)快速旋转
crank	[kræŋk]	n.	曲柄,曲轴
		v.	用曲柄启动(转动)
intake	[ˈinteik]	n.	进气
compression	[kəmˈpreʃən]	n.	压缩
valve	[vælv]	n.	气门,阀门,阀

Phrases and Expressions

be attached to	把……装于……上
cylinder block	汽缸体
water jacket	水套,冷却水套
water pump	水泵
oil pan	油底壳,油盆
clutch housing	离合器壳
ignition distributor	分电器,点火分电器
cylinder head	汽缸盖,汽缸头
kinetic energy	动能
piston head	活塞顶部
piston ring	活塞环
piston land	活塞环槽岸
piston skirt	活塞裙部
piston pin hole	活塞销孔
ring groove	环槽
compression ring	压缩环,气环
oil-control ring	控油环,油环
cylinder wall	汽缸壁
connecting rod	连杆
bearing journal	支撑轴颈
rod journal	连杆轴颈
crank arm	曲柄臂
counter balanced weight	平衡重量,平衡块
flywheel end	曲轴的飞轮端
gear teeth	轮齿
starter 或 starting motor / SM	起动机
torque converter	液力变矩器

English	Chinese
electric motor	电动机
steam engine	蒸汽机
in honor of	以纪念……，向……表示敬意
intake valve	进气阀
exhaust valve	排气阀
spark plug	火花塞
TDC	上止点
BDC	下止点

Notes to the Text

1. The engine block forms the main framework or foundation of the engine.
   发动机汽缸体组成了发动机的主要框架或基础。

2. A crankshaft must be provided with counter balanced weights that extend radially from the crankshaft centerline in the opposite direction of the crank arms.
   曲轴必须装有平衡块，而且平衡块应径向地从曲轴中心线向曲柄臂相对的方向延伸安装。

3. The connecting rod is attached to the crankshaft at one end (big end) and to the piston at the other end (small end).
   连杆的一端（大头）与曲轴连接，另一端（小头）与活塞连接。

4. In the 4-stroke engine, four strokes of the piston in the cylinder are required to complete one full operating cycle.
   在四冲程发动机中，需要汽缸中活塞的4个冲程来完成一个完整的工作循环。

Exercises on the Text

I. Answer the following questions according to the text.
   1. What is the use of the engine block?
   2. Which component is the connecting rod attached to?
   3. What is the function of the flywheel?
   4. What does the internal combustion engine mean?
   5. Can you list the strokes in a 4-stroke-cycle engine in their proper order?

II. Fill in the table below (Tab. 2-1).

Tab. 2-1

English	Chinese
	汽缸体
oil pan	
	活塞环
ignition distributor	

To be continued

English	Chinese
	自动变速器
connecting rod	
	排气阀
water jacket	
	压缩行程
spark plug	

III. Fill in the blanks with the words or phrases given below, and change the form where necessary.

| reciprocating | crankshaft | stroke | coolant |
| convert...into | crankcase | be made of | secure |

1. The piston _____ the potential energy of the fuel _____ the kinetic energy.
2. Many components of an engine _____ by means of bolts and nuts.
3. The lower part of the block is known as the _____.
4. The water jacket is filled with _____.
5. The crankshaft is to change the _____ motion of the piston to rotary motion.
6. A flywheel is attached to the rear of the _____ with bolts.
7. The term _____ is used to describe the movement of the piston within the cylinder.
8. The cylinder block _____ cast iron or aluminum.

IV. Reading comprehension: Read the following passage carefully and fill in the blanks with the words given below.

| four-stroke | reciprocating | piston | process | spark |
| compression | applications | petrol | exhaust | vast |

The __1__ majority of car engines are of the __2__ piston type and utilize __3__ ignition to initiate the combustion __4__ in the cylinders. They also operate on the __5__ principle in which the __6__ travels one complete stroke for each of the successive events of induction, __7__, combustion and __8__. There are also some __9__ of two-stroke engines. Familiar applications of the two-stroke principle to the __10__ engine include motor-cycle engines, especially those used in smaller machines and small industrial stationary engines.

V. Translate the following paragraph into Chinese.

Depending on the type of engine, the operating cycle may require either two or four strokes to complete. The 4-stroke engine is also called Otto cycle engine, in honor of the German engineer, Dr. Nikolaus Otto, who first applied the principle in 1876. In the 4-stroke engine, four strokes of the piston in the cylinder are required to complete one full operating cycle. Each stroke is named after the action it performs — intake, compression, power and exhaust.

VI. Translate the following sentences into English.
1. 发动机汽缸体构成了发动机的主要框架或基础。
2. 活塞由活塞顶部、活塞环、活塞环槽岸、活塞裙部以及活塞销孔组成。
3. 连杆的一端(大头)与曲轴连接,另一端(小头)与活塞连接。
4. 有各种各样的发动机,如电动机、蒸汽机和内燃机。
5. 内燃机在汽缸内燃烧燃料,并把内燃所产生的膨胀力转变成旋转力,用以推动车辆前进。

Section B　Troubles and Maintenance of Engines

The engine is generally considered the "heart" of an automobile. A sound engine should develop full power to maintain the tractive effort and consume fuel and oil within the established limits.

The symptoms indicative of some troubles with the engine are the excessive fuel and oil consumption, smoky exhaust, loss of power, and knocking in the engine.

Excessive fuel and oil consumption and smoky exhaust (the oil level in the crankcase being normal) are usually attributed to the sticking or wear of the piston rings. Worn valve guides are also a frequent cause of excessive fuel and oil consumption. When oil is being consumed by passing through the engine, it usually causes heavy blue smoke to come from the exhaust, particularly after the engine has idled for several minutes.

Sticking can be remedied by mixing equal parts of denatured alcohol and kerosene and pouring 20g of the mixture into each cylinder through the spark plug hole, leaving it there overnight. In the morning, start the engine, run it for 10 to 15 minutes, shut down and change the oil.

Loss of engine power resulted from the drop of compression which may occur when the cylinder block head nuts are tightened nonuniformly or insufficiently, or the head gasket is damaged; the piston rings are stuck in the grooves owing to carbon or lacquer deposit; the rings are worn, broken or lose their resilience; the cylinders are worn.

Noises and knocks in the engine are caused by the following factors:
- A distinct metallic knocks appear if the piston and the cylinder are worn and the clearance

between them is excessive. The knocks are most vivid when the engine runs cold.

• An abnormal sound originates from some forms of piston-ring problems during engine acceleration, and not frequently from a piston ring striking the ring ridge at the top of the cylinder.

• A piston-pin knock is noticeable most of the time when an engine is idling, which is usually the result of a worn piston pin, piston-pin boss, piston pin bushing, or a lack of oil.

• An abnormal noise is usually the result of loose connecting-rod bearings, when the engine is running at speeds above 35 miles per hour (mph) without a load; and of a loose crankshaft main bearing or crankshaft thrust bearing upon engine acceleration under load. A loose vibration damper or flywheel can also cause abnormal engine noises.

• Excessive clearance in the valve train produces a noise that is usually more apparent during engine idle rpm than any other time.

In order to eliminate noises and knocks in an engine, it is necessary to rebore the cylinders, to service the engine with oil, to replace some worn parts like pistons, rings, sleeves, piston pins and connecting rod bearings, etc. Besides replacement, it is also necessary to realign, service, resize or adjust some faulty or loose parts.

Engine Overheating

Overheating may cause serious engine problems, such as oil leakage, engine sludging, blown head gaskets, burnt through pistons, warped engine heads, and blown radiators, etc. The degree of overheating is indicated by the temperature gauge on the instrument panel. Overheating is usually affected by the following factors:

• Low coolant level, coolant leakage;
• Faulty cooling fan;
• Clogged radiator;
• Loose water pump or thermostat.

If the engine is overheating, check the coolant level. It should be between the "Low" and "Full" marks in the coolant expansion tank. If it is too low, add the coolant. But remember: Never open the radiator or the expansion tank cap when the engine is hot!

If the engine is overheating, check the cooling system. The cooling system can be cleaned with special chemicals designed for the purpose. The procedure is to fill the system with water, then put in the chemical. The chemical, after dissolving the rust and scale, is flushed from the system. In severe cases of clogged radiators, it is necessary to remove them and have them cleaned by specialized equipment. For the loose parts, it will be necessary to replace or tighten them.

To keep the engine in good working trim, to reduce the wear of parts, and to identify and eliminate any defects in time, the engine should undergo regular maintenance.

New Words

tractive   ['træktiv]   a.   牵引的

symptom	['simptəm]	n.	迹象，症候
knock	[nɔk]	n./v.	敲击，撞击
sticking	['stikiŋ]	n.	卡住，黏附
denature	[di'neitʃə]	v.	使变性，除去……之特性
kerosene	['kerəsi:n]	n.	(美)煤油
gasket	['gæskit]	n.	垫，垫圈
resilience	[ri'ziliəns]	n.	弹跳，弹性，回弹
clearance	['kliərəns]	n.	间隙，空隙
abnormal	[æb'nɔ:məl]	a.	反常的，异常的
originate	[ə'ridʒineit]	v.	起因，发源
noticeable	['nəutisəbəl]	a.	显而易见的，值得注意的
rebore	[ri'bɔ:(r)]	v.	重新镗缸，镗大(内燃机汽缸的)孔径
service	['sə:vis]	v.	修理，提供服务
realign	[ri:ə'lain]	v.	(使)重新排列，(使)重新对准
faulty	['fɔ:lti]	a.	出差错的，不正确的
sludging	['slʌdʒiŋ]	n.	油泥，油垢
warp	[wɔ:p]	v.	扭曲，使翘起，弄弯
gauge	[geidʒ]	n.	规格，量规，量表
dissolve	[di'zɔlv]	v.	溶解，解散
scale	[skeil]	n.	水锈，水垢
clog	[klɔg]	v.	阻塞，障碍
radiator	['reidieitə]	n.	散热器，冷却器
thermostat	['θə:məstæt]	n.	恒温器，温度自动调节器
flush	[flʌʃ]	v./n.	冲洗，冲出
identify	[ai'dentifai]	v.	认识，识别，检验
defect	[di'fekt]	n.	缺点，故障
undergo	[ˌʌndə'gəu]	v.	经受，经历，承受
maintenance	['meintənəns]	n.	维修，保养

Phrases and Expressions

established limit	规定范围
be indicative of	表现出，有……的征兆
valve guide	气门导管
denatured alcohol	变性酒精
head gasket	汽缸盖衬垫，汽缸垫
ring ridge	活塞环槽
piston pin	活塞销
piston-pin boss	活塞销座

piston pin bushing	活塞销衬套
crankshaft main bearing	曲轴主轴承
crankshaft thrust bearing	曲轴推力轴承
vibration damper	减振器
valve train	配气机构
the coolant level	冷却液液面
instrument panel	仪表安装板,仪表板

Notes to the Text

1. The symptoms indicative of some troubles with the engine are the excessive fuel and oil consumption, smoky exhaust, loss of power, and knocking in the engine.
   显示发动机有一些故障的特征是耗油过量,有烟排气,功率损失大以及敲缸。

2. Excessive clearance in the valve train produces a noise that is usually more apparent during engine idle rpm than any other time.
   配气机构间隙过大会产生噪声,这种噪声在发动机怠速下更为明显。

3. It should be between the "Low" and "Full" marks in the coolant expansion tank.
   它(冷却液的液面高度)必须保持在冷却液罐的标记"LOW"和"FULL"中间.

4. To keep the engine in good working trim, to reduce the wear of parts, and to identify and eliminate any defects in time, the engine should undergo regular maintenance.
   为了保持发动机良好的工作状态,减少零部件磨损,及时发现并消除故障,应该定期保养发动机。

Exercises

I. Translate the following names of cars into Chinese.

1. General Motor　　＿＿＿＿　　2. General　　＿＿＿＿
3. Cadillac　　＿＿＿＿　　4. Saturn　　＿＿＿＿
5. Buick　　＿＿＿＿　　6. Pontiac　　＿＿＿＿
7. Chevrolet　　＿＿＿＿　　8. Oldsmobile　　＿＿＿＿

II. Translate the following abbreviations into corresponding Chinese terms.

1. E/G (engine)　　＿＿＿＿＿＿
2. EM (engine maintenance)　　＿＿＿＿＿＿
3. ECS (engine control system)　　＿＿＿＿＿＿
4. ECT (engine coolant temperature)　　＿＿＿＿＿＿
5. ECL (engine coolant level)　　＿＿＿＿＿＿
6. EMD (engine monitor display)　　＿＿＿＿＿＿

Section C Karl Benz

Karl Friedrich Benz (See Fig. 2-3) was a German engine designer and automobile engineer. He designed and built the world's first practical automobile powered by an internal combustion engine. Other German contemporaries, Gottlieb Daimler and Wilhelm Maybach, also worked independently on the same type of invention, but Benz patented his work first.

Fig. 2-3 Karl Friedrich Benz

Karl Friedrich Benz was born in 1844 in Baden Muehlburg, Germany. He was the son of an engine driver. When he was two years old, his father died from pneumonia caused by a railway accident. Despite living near poverty, his mother strove to give him a good education. At the age of fifteen, he passed the entrance exam for mechanical engineering at the University of Karlsruhe, which he subsequently attended. Benz graduated on July 9, 1864, at nineteen.

During these years, while riding his bicycle through muddy roads, and getting frustrated while doing so, he started to envision concepts for a vehicle that would eventually become the horseless carriage. Between 1864 and 1870, he worked for a number of different firms as a draughtsman, designer and works manager before founding his first firm, the "Iron Foundry and Machine Shop," a supplier of building materials, in 1871 in Mannheim, with August Ritter.

But the economic convulsions of the 1870s caused difficulties for the young company and Ritter turned out to be unreliable. The difficulty was overcome when Benz's fiancée, Bertha Ringer, bought out Ritter's share in the company. To get more revenues, in 1878 he began to work on new patents. He concentrated all his efforts on creating a reliable gas two-stroke engine. After two years' work, his first engine finally sprang to life on New Year's Eve, 1879. He took out various patents on this machine.

Equally important were the contacts with new business associates, with whose assistance Benz founded a gas engine factory in Mannheim. But after only a short time, he withdrew from this company since it did not give him a free enough hand for his technical experiments. Benz found two new partners and with them founded "Benz & Cie., Rheinische Gasmotorenfabrik" in 1883 in Mannheim (Fig. 2-4).

Fig. 2-4 Logo with laurels used on Benz & Cie automobiles after 1909

Business was good and soon the production of industrial engines was being stepped up. With this new financial security, Karl Benz could set about designing a "motor carriage," with an engine based on the Otto four-stroke cycle. Unlike Daimler, who installed his engine in an ordinary carriage, Benz designed not only

Fig. 2 – 5 An 1886 Benz Motorwagen (Photo taken at the Motorshow 2000, UK)

his engine, but the whole vehicle as well(See Fig. 2 – 5). On 29th January, 1886, he was granted a patent on it and on 3rd July, 1886, he introduced the first automobile in the world to the astonished public.

In 1888, Benz started to advertise his 3-wheeler, but the public refused to buy it. It was after his family (his wife and two sons) stole the car one night and drove it from Mannheim to Pforzheim (approximately 65 miles) that the public became fascinated by it and the car started to be sold. In 1893, the Benz Velo became the world's first inexpensive, mass-produced car.

In 1894, Benz improved this design in his new Velo model, which may be considered the first automobile of mass production and it also participated in the first automobile race(See Fig. 2 – 6). The next year Benz designed the first truck in history(See Fig. 2 – 7). Karl Benz was granted a patent for his design of the first flat engine in 1896 and this design continues to be used.

Fig. 2 – 6 The Velo introduced in 1894, the first mass-produced automobile

Fig. 2 – 7 First bus in history: a Benz truck modified by Netphener Company (1895)

By 1898, Benz was beginning to face competition from (for instance) Panhard et Lavassor or Louis Renault. Although Gottlieb Daimler died in March of 1900 — and there is no evidence that Benz and Daimler knew each other nor about each other's early achievements — eventually, competition with Daimler Motors (DMG) began to challenge the leadership of Benz & Cie.

Without consulting Benz, the other directors hired some French designers. France was a country with an extensive automobile industry. Because of this action, after difficult discussions, Karl Benz announced his retirement from design management on January 24, 1903, although he remained as director on the Board of Management through its merger with DMG in 1926 and remained on the board of the new Daimler-Benz corporation until his death in 1929.

New Words

contemporary	[kən'tempərəri]	n.	同代的人，同时期的人，同辈
pneumonia	[njuː'məunjə]	n.	肺炎
strive (strove, striven)	[straiv]	vi.	努力
muddy	['mʌdi]	a.	泥泞的

frustrate	[frʌˈstreit]	v.	挫败，破坏，使失望
envision	[inˈviʒən]	v.	想象，预见，展望
concept	[ˈkɔnsept]	n.	观念，思想，概念
draughtsman	[ˈdrɑːftsmən]	n.	起草人，打样人，制图员
convulsion	[kənˈvʌlʃən]	n.	震动，骚动
fiancée	[fiˈɑːnsei]	n.	未婚妻
merger	[ˈməːdʒə]	n.	（企业等的）合并，结合

Phrases and Expressions

engine driver	火车司机
step up	逐步增加，提升，提高
spring to life	苏醒，活跃起来
take out	取得(专利权等)，领取(执照等)
buy out	收购……的股份(股权)，买下……的全部产权
flat engine	平置式发动机，卧式发动机

Proper Names

Gottlieb Daimler	戈特利布·戴姆勒(1834—1900)（德国工程师和发明家，现代汽车工业的先驱者之一。戴姆勒设计出四冲程发动机，发明了摩托车，并创造了第一辆戴姆勒汽车。）
Wilhelm Maybach	威廉·迈巴赫(1846—1929)（被誉为"设计之王"，不但是戴姆勒－奔驰公司(梅赛德斯－奔驰公司前身)的3位主要创始人之一，更是世界首辆梅赛德斯－奔驰汽车的发明者之一。他一生最大的传奇在于创造了两个举世闻名的豪华品牌，即梅赛德斯与迈巴赫，分别在豪华车的不同领域演绎着各自的辉煌。）
University of Karlsruhe	卡尔斯鲁厄大学（创办于1825年，是德国历史最悠久的理工科院校，特别是计算机信息专业在全德国名列第一。）
Louis Renault	路易斯·雷诺(1877—1945)（法国雷诺公司的创始人。）
Mannheim	曼海姆（德国城市）
Pforzheim	波茨海姆（德国城市）

Notes to the Text

1. Other German contemporaries, Gottlieb Daimler and Wilhelm Maybach, also worked independently on the same type of invention, but Benz patented his work first.
   与本茨同时代的其他德国人，比如戈特利布·戴姆勒和迈巴赫也独立地进行着同样的发明，但本茨先申请了专利。

2. Although Gottlieb Daimler died in March of 1900 — and there is no evidence Benz and Daimler knew each other nor about each other's early achievements — eventually, competition with Daimler Motors (DMG) began to challenge the leadership of Benz & Cie.

戈特利布·戴姆勒于1900年3月去世,虽然没有证据表明本茨和戴姆勒相识,他们也不知道对方的早期成就,但此后戴姆勒公司却成为挑战奔驰在汽车领域领导地位的最大劲敌。

Questions for Discussion:
1. Who was Karl Benz?
2. When did Karl Benz start to conceive a horseless carriage?
3. How did Benz's first firm overcome the financial difficulties?
4. When did Benz invent his first engine?
5. How was Benz's first car accepted by the public?

Unit Three

Section A Engine Fuel System

The function of the fuel system is to store and supply fuel to the cylinder chamber where it can be mixed with air, vaporized, and burned to produce energy. Different components are used in a fuel system (See Fig. 3 – 1).

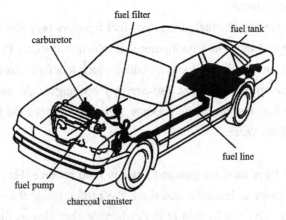

Fig. 3 – 1 The fuel system

Fuel Tank

The fuel tank is used to store the fuel needed by the engine. It is usually located at the rear of the vehicle and is attached to the vehicle frame with metal traps. In order to strengthen the tank as well as to prevent surging of fuel when the vehicle rounds a curve, rapidly starts or suddenly stops, baffle plates are attached to the inside of the tank.

The fuel cap on the fuel tank is used to keep the fuel from splashing out, release the vacuum created by the fuel removing, and prevent vapors from escaping directly into the atmosphere.

Fuel Line

Metallic tubes or synthetic rubber hoses used are called fuel lines. The fuel lines carry the fuel from the tank to the fuel pump, from the pump to the carburetor, return excess fuel to the tank, and carry fuel vapors.

Fuel Pump

A fuel pump draws the fuel from the tank through fuel lines and delivers it through a fuel filter to either a carburetor or a fuel injector, then delivers it to the cylinder chamber for combustion.

There are two types of gasoline engine pumps: mechanical fuel pumps and electric fuel pumps. All fuel injected cars today use electric fuel pumps, while most carbureted cars use mechanical fuel pumps.

The mechanical fuel pump is driven by the camshaft. There is a cam or an eccentric lobe on the camshaft. As the camshaft turns, the lobe lifts a lever up and down, causing a pumping action. Fuel is drawn from the tank by a vacuum and sent to the carburetor.

An electric fuel pump is quite efficient. It fills the carburetor merely by turning on the key. Another feature is the electric pump's adaptability to most locations. The electric pump uses an electromagnet (a magnet produced by electricity flowing through a coil) to operate a metal bellows that alternately forms a vacuum and then pressure. Some electric pumps use an electromagnet to work a regular diaphragm. Other models drive either a vane or an impeller type pump with a small electric motor.

Fuel systems that have electric fuel pumps and fuel injectors may use a fuel pressure regulator to keep the fuel pressure constant. In a multipoint fuel injection system, the fuel pressure regulator has an inlet connection from the fuel rail and an outlet which lets fuel return to the tank. A control diaphragm and a pressure spring determine the exposed opening of the outlet and the amount of fuel that can return. So the strength of the pressure spring determines the fuel pressure in the fuel rail, and keeps it at a fixed value.

Fuel Filter

The job of the fuel filter used on gasoline engines is to remove dirt, rust, water, and other contamination from the gasoline before it can reach the carburetor or the injection system. It can protect not only the float-valve mechanism of the carburetor, but also its fuel-metering devices and internal passages.

Several different types of fuel filters are used, and some systems may contain two or more. Filters can be located either between the fuel pump and carburetor or in the fuel lines. The useful life of the filters is limited. If fuel filters are not cleaned or replaced according to the manufacturer's recommendations, they will become clogged and restrict fuel flow.

Many diesel engines used in automotive applications have only one filter, which is called the primary filter. On some engines, a secondary filter is adopted and combined with the primary one to build into a single filter.

Electronic Fuel Injection System

Because of the need to comply with exhaust emission regulations (EER), the modern gasoline engine requires a fuel system of extreme accuracy and long-term reliability. This is achieved by electronic fuel injection.

Electronic fuel injection (EFI), like carburetion, is a way of delivering the correct air-fuel mixture to the engine at the correct time under different operating conditions. Electronic fuel injection, however, is much simpler, more precise, and more reliable because it is controlled electronically rather than mechanically.

Electronic fuel injection systems use the same principle of pressure differential used in a carbureted system, but in a slightly different way. It is the difference in pressure between the inside and the outside of the engine that forces fuel out of the carburetor fuel bowl. In EFI systems, the airflow or air pressure sensor determines the pressure difference and informs the computer. The computer evaluates the air sensor's input along with that of other sensors to decide how much fuel is required for the engine operation, then controls injector operation to provide the correct fuel quantity. The computer makes it possible for the fuel injectors to do all the functions of the main systems used in a carburetor.

An EFI system generally uses one or more solenoid-operated injectors to spray fuel in timed pulses, either into the intake manifold or near the intake port. EFI systems are operated intermittently.

The most common type of the EFI system is a single point fuel injection system, more commonly called the throttle body fuel injection (TBI) system. In the TBI system, it combines a single (or twin) fuel injection nozzle, fuel pressure regulator, throttle valve, throttle switch and idle speed regulator into a compact throttle body unit. This unit is mounted directly on the intake manifold, in a similar manner to a conventional carburetor. Fuel is injected into the area around the throttle valve, where air velocity is at a maximum; thus ensuring fuel droplets are thoroughly atomized and will be distributed throughout the air mass.

A multipoint fuel injection system, also called the port fuel injection (PFI) system, has one injector for each engine cylinder. The injectors are mounted in the intake manifold near the cylinder head where they can inject fuel as close as possible to the intake valve. This eliminates the need for fuel to travel through the intake manifold, improving cylinder to cylinder distribution. An EFI system supplies an accurate air-fuel ratio to the engine no matter what operating conditions are encountered. This provides better drive-ability, fuel economy, and emissions control.

New Words

store	[stɔː]	v.	储存
vaporize	[ˈveipəraiz]	v.	(使)蒸发
trap	[træp]	n.	夹子
surging	[ˈsəːdʒiŋ]	n.	浪涌,冲击,波动
splash	[splæʃ]	v.	溅,泼,使飞溅
synthetic	[sinˈθetik]	a.	合成的,人造的
hose	[həuz]	n.	软管
carburetor	[ˈkɑːbjuretə]	n.	化油器
injector	[inˈdʒektə]	n.	喷油器,喷(注)射器

camshaft	[ˈkæmʃɑːft]	n.	凸轮轴,偏心轴
cam	[kæm]	n.	凸轮
eccentric	[ikˈsentrik]	a.	离心的,偏心的
lobe	[ləub]	n.	凸轮凸台,凸角
adaptability	[əˌdæptəˈbiliti]	n.	适应性,改编
electromagnet	[iˌlektrəuˈmægnit]	n.	电磁体(铁)
bellows	[ˈbeləuz]	n.	波纹管,真空膜盒
diaphragm	[ˈdaiəfræm]	n.	膜片,薄膜,振动膜
vane	[vein]	n.	叶片,轮叶
impeller	[imˈpelə]	n.	(驱动)叶轮,驱动涡轮
atomization	[ˌætəmaiˈzeiʃən]	n.	雾化
comply	[kəmˈplai]	v.	服从,依从,遵从
sensor	[ˈsensə]	n.	传感器
solenoid	[ˈsəulinɔid]	n.	电磁阀,电磁线圈,螺线管
nozzle	[ˈnɔzəl]	n.	喷嘴
throttle	[ˈθrɔtl]	v.	(使)节流,(使)减速,调节
		n.	节流阀(或杆)
velocity	[viˈlɔsiti]	n.	速度,速率
atomize	[ˈætəmaiz]	v.	把……喷成雾状,使雾化

Phrases and Expressions

fuel tank	燃油箱
baffle plate	油箱隔板,挡板
fuel cap	油箱盖
fuel line	油管,燃油输送管路
synthetic rubber hose	(人造)合成橡胶软管
fuel pump (FP)	输油泵
fuel filter	燃油滤清器
fuel injector	喷油器
fuel pressure regulator	燃油压力调节器
fuel rail	燃油管路(燃油喷射)
intake manifold	进气歧管
combustion chamber	燃烧室
electronic fuel injection (EFI)	电子燃油喷射
exhaust emission	废气排放,排气污染
exhaust emission regulation (EER)	废气排放法规
intake port	进气口,进气道
single point fuel injection	单点燃油喷射

throttle body fuel injection (TBI)　　　节气门体燃油喷射
throttle valve (TV)　　　节流阀,节气门(化油器),油门
multipoint fuel injection　　　多点燃油喷射
port fuel injection (PFI)　　　(汽油机)进气口燃油喷射,进气道燃油喷射(将汽油连续或间断地喷入进气道内)
air-fuel ratio　　　空燃比

Notes to the Text

1. Fuel is drawn from the tank by a vacuum and sent to the carburetor.
   燃油被一真空装置从油箱中吸入并送到化油器。
2. An EFI system supplies an accurate air-fuel ratio to the engine no matter what operating conditions are encountered.
   在发动机的所有工况下,电子燃油喷射系统均能提供一个准确的空燃比。

Exercises on the Text

I. Answer the following questions according to the text.
  1. What's the function of the fuel system?
  2. Please name the major parts that make up the fuel system.
  3. What's the function of the fuel pump?
  4. What's the function of the carburetor?
  5. What's the advantage of TBI over the conventional carburetor?

II. Fill in the table below (Tab. 3-1).

Tab. 3-1

English	Chinese
	燃料系统
fuel injector	
	传感器
throttle valve	
	化油器
fuel pressure regulator	
	燃油滤清器
combustion chamber	
	燃油箱
multipoint fuel injection	

III. **Fill in the blanks with the words or phrases given below, and change the form where necessary.**

camshaft	clog	injector	splash
fuel lines	constant	protect	spray

1. A multipoint fuel injection system has one _____ for each engine cylinder.
2. The mechanical fuel pump is driven by the _____.
3. Fuel systems that have electric fuel pumps and fuel injectors may use a fuel pressure regulator to keep the fuel pressure _____.
4. If fuel filters are not cleaned or replaced in time, they will become _____ and restrict fuel flow.
5. A fuel filter can _____ not only the float-valve mechanism of the carburetor, but also its fuel-metering devices and internal passages.
6. In the fuel system, metallic tubes or synthetic rubber hoses used are called _____.
7. One function of the fuel cap on the fuel tank is to keep the fuel from _____ out.
8. An electronic fuel injection system generally uses one or more injectors to _____ fuel.

IV. **Reading comprehension: Read the following passage carefully and fill in the blanks with the words given below.**

prevent	created	from	store	atmosphere
rounds	needed	with	rear	splashing

The fuel tank is used to __1__ the fuel __2__ by the engine. It is usually located at the __3__ of the vehicle and is attached to the vehicle frame __4__ metal traps. In order to strengthen the tank as well as to __5__ surging of fuel when the vehicle __6__ a curve, rapidly starts or suddenly stops, baffle plates are attached to the inside of the tank. The fuel cap on the fuel tank is used to keep the fuel from __7__ out, release the vacuum __8__ by the fuel removing, and prevent vapors __9__ escaping directly into the __10__.

V. **Translate the following passage into Chinese.**

Fuel systems that have electric fuel pumps and fuel injectors may use a fuel pressure regulator to keep the fuel pressure constant. In a multipoint fuel injection system, the fuel pressure regulator has an inlet connection from the fuel rail and an outlet which lets fuel return to the tank. A control diaphragm and a pressure spring determine the exposed opening of the outlet and the amount of fuel that can return. So the strength of the pressure spring determines the fuel pressure in the fuel rail, and keeps it at a fixed value.

VI. Translate the following sentences into English.
1. 燃料系统的主要部件包括燃油箱、输油泵、燃油滤清器、化油器以及油管等。
2. 燃油箱用以储存燃油。
3. 输油泵的作用是把燃油从燃油箱输送至化油器。
4. 汽油机的输油泵有两种：机械输油泵和电子输油泵。
5. 在发动机的所有工况下，电子燃油喷射系统均能提供一个准确的空燃比。

Section B Fuel Injector and Its Maintenance

Fuel Injector

A fuel injector is nothing but an electronically controlled valve. The function of the fuel injector is to deliver finely atomized fuel under high pressure to the combustion chamber of the engine.

In older vehicles, the sensing, control, and fuel metering functions were all performed by the carburetor. In EFI-equipped engines, fuel delivery is done with injectors. The fuel delivery pipe serves to secure the injector in place. The injector is supplied with pressurized fuel by the fuel pump in the vehicle, and it is capable of opening and closing many times per second.

When the injector is energized, an electromagnet moves a plunger that opens the valve, allowing the pressurized fuel to squirt out through a tiny nozzle. The nozzle is designed to atomize the fuel — to make as fine a mist as possible so that it can burn easily. The nozzle comprising a nozzle body and nozzle needle valve is the main part of the injector.

The injector always opens the same distance, and the fuel pressure is maintained at a constant value by the pressure regulator. The amount of fuel delivered by the injector depends on the amount of time when the nozzle is open. This is the injector pulse width: the time in milliseconds when the nozzle is open.

The pulse width is varied to supply the amount of fuel that an engine needs at a specific moment. A long pulse width delivers more fuel, while a short pulse width delivers less fuel.

The injectors are mounted in the intake manifold so that they spray fuel directly at the intake valves. A pipe called the fuel rail supplies pressurized fuel to all of the injectors.

To reduce the possibility of vapor lock, which tends to occur during high temperature operation, a side feed injector is used in engines.

Maintenance of Fuel Injector

The fuel injector plays an important role in the electronic fuel injection system. Even a small amount of injector clogging can affect the engine's performance. So proper maintenance of fuel injectors is necessary. There are several methods to test the operation of fuel injectors.

Electrical Test

Remove the harness connector from each injector and use an ohmmeter to test the resistance across the injector terminals. The resistance depends on whether there is a separate set of series resistors in the system or not. Check the manual for the correct specifications. If the resistance is incorrect, replace the injector.

Vibration Test

When the fuel injector is opening and closing — while the engine is idling, a buzzing or clicking sound can be heard. No vibration or a different pitch of vibration in one versus the others, indicates a bad injector or harness connection. Interchange connectors with an injector on the same circuit from the control unit (check the wiring diagrams). If the same injector is still faulty, then replace the injector; if the injector now works, check the wiring.

Leak Test

Fuel injector leaks can occur at the seams around the body of the fuel injector and bleed off fuel pressure, causing hot-start problems. Clean off the injector and look closely for seepage. The injectors usually leak most when they are cold.

The injector pintles should also be checked for leakage. Remove the injectors and the fuel rail with the injectors still attached. Run the fuel pump without running the engine to build up fuel pressure. If any of the injectors leaks at the rate of more than two drops per minute, the injector may be clogged. Clean the injectors as described below. If that does not help, replace the injector.

Clogging Test

A clogged fuel injector can be indicated by rough, idle hesitation during acceleration, or a failed emission test. The fuel injector clogging is caused by a buildup of carbon and other deposits on the injector pintle. This reduces the flow of gasoline through the injectors and results in a poor spray pattern.

The fuel injector clogging is caused by a number of factors: high underhood temperatures on smaller cars, fuel being metered at the tip of the injector, short driving cycles followed by hot-soak periods, and low-detergent fuels with a high carbon content and low hydrogen content.

The first step towards solving the problem of fuel injector clogging is to determine whether one or more injectors are indeed clogged. The injector leak test described above gives one indication of a possible clogged injector. There are also a number of tests that any good repair shop can perform. One is called a pressure-balance test, where each injector is triggered with a fixed pulse and the pressure drop in the system is measured. If one has a greater pressure drop, it's most likely clogged.

The tendency to form injector deposits varies considerably depending on the fuel. Many cases of injector clogging can be cured by using premium fuels where manufacturers advertise more detergent additives. Most regular unleaded fuels probably have enough detergent to keep unclogged injectors clean, but they won't dissolve deposits on clogged injectors.

New Words

pressurize	[ˈpreʃəraiz]	v.	对(给)……加压
energize	[ˈenədʒaiz]	v.	通以电流,供能,施力
plunger	[ˈplʌndʒə]	n.	柱塞,(电磁铁的)插棒式铁芯
squirt	[skwəːt]	v.	喷出
seam	[siːm]	n.	缝,裂缝,接缝,接口
bleed	[bliːd]	v.	渗出,流出
pintle	[ˈpintl]	n.	针阀
orifice	[ˈɔrifis]	n.	孔,流孔,喷嘴(口)

Phrases and Expressions

nothing but	仅仅,只不过
pulse width	脉冲宽度,脉冲持续时间
fuel rail	油轨
driving cycle	驾驶操作循环,行驶工况循环
premium fuel	高级(优质)燃料

Notes to the Text

1. When the injector is energized, an electromagnet moves a plunger that opens the valve, allowing the pressurized fuel to squirt out through a tiny nozzle. The nozzle is designed to atomize the fuel — to make as fine a mist as possible so that it can burn easily.
   当喷油器通电时,电磁铁把柱塞吸起,将喷油器打开,让高压油通过细小的喷嘴喷出。这种专门设计的喷嘴能使燃油雾化——使燃油尽可能雾化成细小的油雾,以便易于燃烧。

2. The amount of fuel delivered by the injector depends on the amount of time when the nozzle is open.
   喷油器的供油量是由喷油器的喷嘴开启的时间长短决定的。

Exercises

I. Translate the following names of cars into Chinese.

1. Chrysler　_____　2. Eagle　_____
3. Dodge　_____　4. Viper　_____
5. Plymouth　_____　6. Jeep　_____
7. Mustang　_____　8. Mercury　_____

II. Translate the following abbreviations into corresponding Chinese terms.

1. TV (throttle valve)　　　　　　　_____
2. A/F (air/fuel ratio)　　　　　　　_____
3. EFI (electronic fuel injection)　　_____
4. FP (fuel pump)　　　　　　　　_____
5. MFI (multipoint fuel injection)　_____
6. TBI (throttle body injection)　　_____

Section C Dialogue Price Discussion

The following dialogues are about price discussion (See Fig. 3 - 2).

Fig. 3 - 2 Price discussion

Dialogue One:

Customer(C): I want to buy a new car. Would you please give me a price list?
Salesclerk(S): Yes. Here is the price inquiry of our company.
　　　　C: Oh, your price is higher than I expected. Would you allow me a special discount?
　　　　S: We usually allow 2% discount. In order to popularize the new models, all the catalogue prices of the new types are subjected to a special discount of 10% during the month of April only. This is really a bargain.
　　　　C: It is really an attractive price to me. I'm considering buying one.

Dialogue Two:

Customer(C): I want to buy this car. Can you give me a discount for it?
Salesclerk(S): Here are our latest price sheets. Our price is without further discounts.
　　　　C: Come on. Bring down the price just a little. You know, I can buy this car in another store, but I prefer to buy it with you if you will lower the price a little for me.

S: Well, I do have to meet a quota in order to get my commission. OK. I'll take off five hundred yuan. How does that sound?

C: Oh, no. I was thinking maybe more than that. Something like two thousand?

S: Please. That's too much. Reducing one thousand yuan is our bottom line. This quote has minimized our room for profits.

C: OK. I can settle for that.

Useful Expressions and Sentences

1. price　价格,价钱
   price list　价格表,价目单
   lowest (floor, bottom) price　底价,最低价格
   current price　现行价格
   cost price　成本价格
   net price　实价,净价
   gross price　毛价
   fixed (set) price　固定价格
   quoted price　报价
   unit price　单价
   buying (selling) price　买(售)价
   price sheet　价格单
   price tag　价格标签
   wholesale (retail) price　批发(零售)价格
   competitive (attractive) price　具有竞争力(吸引力)的价格
   reasonable (moderate, favorable, workable) price
   合理的(公道的,优惠的,可行的)价格
   reduce (raise) a price　减(提)价
   make a price　开价,定价

2. Would you please give me a price list?
   您能给我一份价格表吗?

3. Here is the price inquiry of our company.
   这是我们公司的询价。
   inquiry [inˈkwaiəri] n. 询问,打听

4. Your price is higher than I expected. Would you allow me a special discount?
   你的价格比我想象的高。可以打个特别折扣吗?
   discount [ˈdiskaunt] n. 折扣　v. 打去(若干)折扣,打折扣卖

5. We usually allow 2% discount.
   我们通常给打2%的折扣。

6. In order to popularize the new models, all the catalogue prices of the new types are subjected to

a special discount of 10% during the month of April only.

为了推销新车型,目录上所列的新款车的价格在 4 月份内均打 10% 的特别折扣。

popularize [ˈpɔpjuləraiz] v. 使普及,推广

catalogue [ˈkætəlɔg] n. 目录

subject [səbˈdʒekt] v. 使隶属,使服从

7. This is really a bargain.

这才叫价格低廉。

bargain [ˈbɑːgin] n. (经讨价还价后)成交的商品,廉价货 v. 议价,讨价还价

8. It is really an attractive price to me. I'm considering buying one.

对我来说,这的确是个具有吸引力的价格。我在考虑买一辆。

9. Here are our latest price sheets.

这是我们的最新价格单。

10. Our price is without further discounts.

我们的价格不再打折扣。

11. Come on. Bring down the price just a little. You know, I can buy this car in another store, but I prefer to buy it with you if you will lower the price a little for me.

别这样,只要把价格降低一点点。你明白,我可以在另一家店买这辆车,如果你能把价格降低点儿,我还是愿意在你们这儿买。

12. Well, I do have to meet a quota in order to get my commission. OK. I'll take off five hundred yuan. How does that sound?

嗯,为了拿到佣金,我必须卖出一定的配额。好吧,我就减价 500 元,你觉得如何?

quota [ˈkwəutə] n. 定额,分配额,限额

commission [kəˈmiʃən] n. 佣金

13. Please. That's too much. Reducing one thousand yuan is our bottom line.

拜托,那太多了。减价 1 000 元是我们的底线。

14. This quote has minimized our room for profits.

这个报价已经最大限度地压缩了我们的利润空间。

15. OK. I can settle for that.

好吧,我就接受那个价格。

Unit Four

Section A Engine Exhaust System

The exhaust system is an assembly in a vehicle's engine that takes care of the burned gases that the engine produces. The main function of the exhaust system is to conduct the burned gases to the rear of a vehicle and into the air. This system also serves to silence the exhaust noise; and, in most cases, reduce the pollutants in the exhaust.

Major parts of the exhaust system include the exhaust manifold, exhaust pipe, muffler, resonator and tail pipe, etc. A catalytic converter is also used in the exhaust system, which converts the pollutant gases produced during combustion into less harmful substances (See Fig. 4-1).

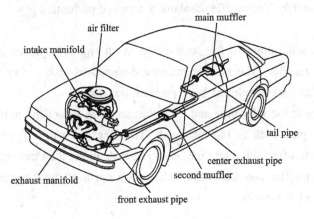

Fig. 4-1 The exhaust system

Exhaust Manifold

The exhaust manifold is bolted to the cylinder head and conducts exhaust gases from the exhaust ports in the head to the exhaust system. In some engines a gasket is positioned between the cylinder head and the exhaust manifold. On other engines a gasket is not required. On these applications, the manufacturer may suggest the use of a sealer between the exhaust manifold and the cylinder head. The exhaust manifold is made of cast iron or steel piping that can withstand rapid increases in temperature and expansion. And it has smooth curves in it for improving the flow of exhaust.

Many exhaust manifolds contain such emission devices as the exhaust-gas recirculation (EGR) valve, air pipe fittings, and heated air-inlet stove and tube. Most engines with computer-controlled carburetors have an oxygen sensor threaded into the exhaust manifold.

Heat Riser Valve

Some engines have a heat riser valve located in the exhaust manifold. The heat riser valve is used to restrict the exhaust gases during starting and warm-up periods. The restriction tends to raise the engine to operating temperature more quickly, which aids in the vaporization of fuel.

Exhaust Pipe

The exhaust pipe is the bent-up or convoluted pipe that you will notice underneath your car. It is the connecting pipe between the exhaust manifold and the muffler or catalytic converter.

Many types of exhaust pipes are used on vehicles. Some are shaped to go over the rear axle, allowing the rear axle to move up and down without bumping into the exhaust pipe; some are shaped to bend around under the floor of the vehicle, connecting the catalytic converter with the muffler. The shape depends on the configuration and size of the engine, and undercarriage of the vehicle. It can also be of single or dual design. The bigger the exhaust pipes of an exhaust system are, the better, because exhaust gases can take their exits more freely that way.

Exhaust Muffler

The purpose of the muffler is to reduce engine exhaust noise to an acceptable level. It is made of metal and is located underneath the body of the vehicle. It is connected between the tail pipe and the catalytic converter. The muffler contains a series of perforated pipes, baffles and chambers that absorb noise.

In order to reduce the noise of the combustion of an engine, exhaust gases from the engine are passed through a muffler. The muffler must be designed in such a way that the gases expand slowly and there is the least amount of back pressure developed.

Exhaust gases enter the inlet pipe and go to the opposite end of the muffler, turn around and flow through another pipe back to the inlet end. Then the gases turn again and exit through an outlet pipe. On most mufflers the inlet pipe has a larger diameter than the outlet pipe. The exhaust flow capacity of the muffler and the entire exhaust system must be adequate for the cubic inch displacement (CID) of the engine.

Resonator

In some exhaust systems, a smaller muffler is connected after the main muffler. This smaller muffler is referred to as a resonator, which is used to absorb excessive sound vibration. Most of the noise from an exhaust system is sound vibration. The vibration causes louder noise. Resonators provide additional sound protection at critical points in the exhaust flow.

Tail Pipe

The tail pipe is a long metal tube attached to the muffler, which is used to carry the exhaust gases from the muffler or resonators to the rear of the vehicle, and then into the air.

Dual Exhaust System

The exhaust system is vital to any vehicle because the life and performance of the vehicle's engine depend on it. So, some vehicles run on dual exhaust systems. In a dual exhaust system, the engines of such vehicles can give off exhaust gases more freely, thereby lowering the back pressure which is inherent in an exhaust system. An engine cannot function well if there is back pressure trapped in it. Trapped exhaust gases choke an engine and stop it from doing productive work. As a result, the vehicle cannot run smoothly and silently, or in the worst cases, will not run at all. With a dual exhaust system, a sizable increase in engine horsepower can be obtained because the "breathing" capacity of the engine is improved, leaving less exhaust gases in the engine at the end of each exhaust stroke.

New Words

silence	[ˈsailəns]	v.	消除(噪声)
muffler	[ˈmʌflə]	n.	消声器
resonator	[ˈrezəneitə]	n.	共振系统,(汽车)辅助消声器
convolute	[kɔnvəˈluːt]	v.	回旋,卷绕
configuration	[kənfigjuˈreiʃən]	n.	构造,外形
undercarriage	[ˈʌndəkæridʒ]	n.	下部构造,底架
choke	[tʃəuk]	v.	阻塞,堵塞,塞满,塞住

Phrases and Expressions

back pressure	回压,背压力
exhaust manifold	排气歧管
exhaust pipe	排气管
tail pipe	排气尾管
catalytic converter	(排气净化的)催化转化器,催化净化器
exhaust port	排气孔,排气口
exhaust-gas recirculation (EGR) valve	排气再循环阀
pipe fitting	管连接件
heat riser valve	(进气)预热阀(使发动机的排气只在冷机时加热进气管进行预热,在热机时不再加热进气管的控制阀)
crossover pipe	交叉管
inlet pipe	进入管,进气管
cubic inch displacement (CID)	立方英寸排量(发动机排量以立方英寸作单位)
dual exhaust system	双排气系统

Notes to the Text

1. The exhaust system of a vehicle is used to conduct the burned gases to the rear of the vehicle and into the air.
   车辆的排气系统用以把已燃气体传导至车辆后部并排放到空气中去。
2. The heat riser valve is used to restrict the exhaust gases during starting and warm-up periods.
   进气预热阀用以在冷起动热机时限制废气。

Exercises on the Text

I. Answer the following questions according to the text.
   1. What's the function of the exhaust system?
   2. Please name the major parts that make up the exhaust system.
   3. What's the function of the exhaust manifold?
   4. Which component is the tail pipe attached to?
   5. What's the function of the exhaust muffler?

II. Fill in the table below (Tab. 4 – 1).

Tab. 4 – 1

English	Chinese
	排气系统
catalytic converter	
	排气管
burned gas	
	排气尾管
back pressure	
	消声器
crossover pipe	
	排气歧管
resonator	

III. Fill in the blanks with the words or phrases given below, and change the form where necessary.

muffler	assembly	exhaust pipe	performance
depend on	absorb	exhaust	silence

1. The exhaust system is an _____ in a vehicle's engine that takes care of the burned gases that the engine produces.
2. The exhaust system also serves to _____ the sounds of exhaust.
3. In order to reduce the noise of the combustion of an engine, exhaust gases from the engine are passed through a _____.
4. In a dual exhaust system, the engine can _____ more freely.
5. The resonator is used to _____ excessive sound vibration.
6. The exhaust manifold conducts the exhaust gases from the combustion chambers to the _____.
7. The shape of the exhaust pipe _____ the configuration and size of the engine.
8. The life and _____ of the vehicle's engine depend on the exhaust system.

IV. Reading comprehension: Read the following passage carefully and fill in the blanks with the words given below.

absorb	function	body	amount	noise
slowly	passed	made	pipe	reduce

The __1__ of the muffler in the exhaust system is to __2__ engine exhaust noise to an acceptable level. It is __3__ of metal and is located underneath the __4__ of the vehicle. It is connected between the tail __5__ and the catalytic converter. The muffler contains a series of perforated pipes, baffles and chambers that __6__ noise.

In order to reduce the __7__ of the combustion of an engine, exhaust gases from the engine are __8__ through a muffler. The muffler must be designed in such a way that the gases expand __9__ and there is the least __10__ of back pressure developed.

V. Translate the following passage into Chinese.

Many types of exhaust pipes are used on vehicles. Some are shaped to go over the rear axle, allowing the rear axle to move up and down without bumping into the exhaust pipe; some are shaped to bend around under the floor of the vehicle, connecting the catalytic converter with the muffler. The shape depends on the configuration and size of the engine, and undercarriage of the vehicle. It can also be of single or dual design. The bigger the exhaust pipes of an exhaust system are, the better, because exhaust gas can take their exits more freely that way.

VI. Translate the following sentences into English.
1. 排气系统的主要作用是把已燃气体传导至车辆后部并排放到空气中去。
2. 排气系统主要由排气歧管、排气管、催化式净化器、消声器以及尾管等组成。
3. 排气系统不但起着排放废气的作用，而且还起着消除排放噪声的作用。
4. 消声器连接在排气尾管和催化式净化器之间。

5. 在双排气系统中，发动机排气更加通畅，因此降低了单排气系统中固有的背压。

Section B Emission Control Systems

Approximately 99.9 percent of the exhaust from the average car engine (gasoline powered) consists mostly of water, nitrogen, carbon dioxide, and carbon monoxide. About 0.1 percent of the exhaust is made up of hydrocarbons (unburned gasoline). Some of these emissions, such as water, oxygen, nitrogen, and carbon dioxide are of little concern. Others, such as hydrocarbons, oxides of nitrogen, and carbon monoxide can pose health problems for the people if uncontrolled.

Pollutants are given off not only from the exhaust pipe of the exhaust system but also from the fuel tank and the engine crankcase. So the emission controls on a modern automobile are not a separate system, but a part of an engine's fuel, ignition, and exhaust systems. The total automotive emission control system contains three different types of controls. Various emission control systems and devices are designed on all vehicles to reduce pollution of the atmosphere from incompletely burned and evaporating gases and to maintain good drive-ability and fuel economy.

Crankcase Emission Control

The positive crankcase ventilation (PCV) system controls hydrocarbon emissions from the engine crankcase. The PCV system uses a hose connected between the engine and the intake manifold. The purpose of the PCV system is to take the vapors produced in the crankcase during the normal combustion process, and redirect them into the air-fuel intake system to be burned during combustion. These vapors dilute the air-fuel mixture, and they have to be carefully controlled and metered so as not to affect the performance of the engine. This is the job of the PCV valve. The PCV system operates when intake vacuum is high. The PCV valve draws blow-by gases from the valve cover into the intake manifold. Blow-by gases are drawn through a metered PCV valve and routed back to the intake manifold to be burned in the combustion chamber.

Evaporative Emission Control

The evaporative emission control (EEC or EVAP) system (also called evaporation control system) is designed to control the evaporation of hydrocarbon vapors from the fuel tank, pump, and carburetor or fuel injection system.

Gasoline evaporates quite easily. Twenty percent of all hydrocarbon emissions from the automobile are from the fuel tank. The evaporation control system keeps vapors inside the fuel tank from escaping into the atmosphere. This closed system separates fuel vapors and routes them back into the engine to be burned. When the engine is not running, a charcoal canister is used to store fuel vapors. Once the engine starts, the engine vacuum draws vapors out of the canister and into the engine intake manifold.

Exhaust Emission Control

Various systems and devices are used to control hydrocarbon, oxides of nitrogen, and carbon monoxide emissions from the engine exhaust.

All vehicles are equipped with **exhaust gas recirculation (EGR) systems** to reduce the amount of oxides of nitrogen produced during the combustion process. With this system, exhaust gas is partially recirculated from an exhaust port of the cylinder head into a port that is located at the intake manifold. Exhaust gases will mix with the air-fuel mixture to lower combustion temperature. At lower combustion temperatures, very little of the nitrogen in the air will combine with oxygen to form oxides of nitrogen. Most of the nitrogen is simply carried out with the exhaust gases. Normally, the EGR system operates when the engine is at high speed.

The amount of the exhaust gas that is recirculated can be controlled by an EGR valve. Such valves are widely used as they can be designed to admit carefully controlled amounts of exhaust gases into the intake air stream. The exact amount will vary according to the engine speed and loading.

The **air injection (AIR) system** provides additional air to the exhaust system to help burn up hydrocarbon and carbon monoxide in the exhaust and to aid catalytic conversion.

The air injection system pushes fresh air into the exhaust ports of the cylinder head or the catalytic converter. Additional air helps complete combustion and lower hydrocarbon and carbon monoxide emissions. Some models use air management systems that divert air between exhaust ports and the catalytic converter.

The **catalytic converter** is installed in the exhaust line, between the exhaust manifold and the muffler, and makes use of chemicals that act as a catalyst. The catalytic converter is designed to cause a desirable chemical reaction to take place in the exhaust emission. In other words, the catalytic converter is used to complete the oxidation process for hydrocarbon and carbon monoxide. In addition, it reduces oxides of nitrogen back to simple nitrogen and carbon dioxide.

Much progress has been made in the development of a number of emission control systems and devices. These units, when properly installed, serviced and maintained, do an excellent job of reducing harmful emissions. Ongoing research and development in this vital area will undoubtedly bring about further reductions.

New Words

nitrogen	['naitrədʒen]	n.	氮
hydrocarbon	[ˌhaidrəu'kɑːbən]	n.	碳氢化合物
pose	[pəuz]	v.	造成,形成,提出
evaporate	[i'væpəreit]	v.	蒸发,挥发
evaporation	[iˌvæpə'reiʃən]	n.	蒸发,挥发
divert	[dai'vəːt]	v.	转移,转向
catalyst	['kætəlist]	n.	催化剂
oxidation	[ɔksi'deiʃən]	n.	氧化,氧化作用
ongoing	['ɔnˌgəuiŋ]	a.	不断前进(发展)中的

Phrases and Expressions

carbon dioxide	二氧化碳
carbon monoxide	一氧化碳
oxides of nitrogen	氮氧化合物
give off	散发，放出（液体、气体、气味等）
positive crankcase ventilation (PCV) system	强制式曲轴箱通风系统（PCV系统）
blow by	漏气，窜气（发动机燃烧室内的燃气经汽缸与活塞间的间隙窜入曲轴箱），渗漏
charcoal canister	活性炭罐
exhaust gas recirculation (EGR) system	排气再循环系统（EGR系统）
take place	发生
bring about	带来，造成

Notes to the Text

1. The purpose of the PCV system is to take the vapors produced in the crankcase during the normal combustion process, and redirect them into the air-fuel intake system to be burned during combustion.
   强制式曲轴箱通风系统（PCV系统）的作用是将正常燃烧过程中曲轴箱产生的油气改道引入可燃混合气的进气系统中以便燃烧。
2. The catalytic converter is installed in the exhaust line, between the exhaust manifold and the muffler, and makes use of chemicals that act as a catalyst.
   催化转化器安装在排气管内，位于排气歧管和消声器之间，利用化学制品作为催化剂。

Exercises

I. Translate the following names of cars into Chinese.

1. Ford _____   2. Lincoln _____
3. Cougar _____   4. King _____
5. Cobra _____   6. Phoenix _____
7. Mack _____   8. Thunderbird _____

II. Translate the following abbreviations into corresponding Chinese terms.

1. EX (exhaust) _____
2. EGR (exhaust gas recirculation) _____
3. EGOS (exhaust gas oxygen sensor) _____
4. PCV (positive crankcase ventilation) _____
5. EEC (evaporative emission control) _____
6. EP (exhaust pipe) _____

Section C BMW

Bayerische Motoren Werke AG (BMW) (Its logo is shown in Fig. 4 – 2.) is a German manufacturer of automobiles, motorcycles, and aircraft engines. Based in Munich, Germany, the company is the leading auto exporter in Europe (See Fig. 4 – 3).

The company traces its origins to 1913, when a Bavarian named Karl Rapp began an aircraft-engine shop in Munich named Rapp Motoren Werke. In 1917 Rapp resigned because of financial troubles.

Fig. 4 – 2 Logo

The company was taken over by two Austrian engineers Franz-Josef Popp and Max Fritz, who changed its name to BMW — Bayerische Motoren Werke in 1918. In the same year, the chief engineer Max Friz designed the company's first aircraft engine, the six-cylinder Type IIIa, which created a strong demand for BMW engines. When the 1919 Treaty of Versailles prohibited German companies from producing aircraft and aircraft engines, BMW switched to making air brakes for railway cars.

In 1923 Friz developed the company's first motorcycle, the R32 motorcycle, which was the first BMW bike. The BMW R32 motorcycle made a strong impression at its world premiere at the Berlin Automobile Show in 1923. With the R32, BMW succeeded in moving into vehicle construction even before the development of automobiles. This was the moment when the history of the BMW boxer engine began and would continue until the present day. It held world speed records for motorcycles during most of the 1930s. In 1925 R37 motorcycle provided the basis for the BMW racing machines and made the brand well known throughout the whole motorcycle world.

Fig. 4 – 3 BMW's Headquarters in Munich, Germany

1928 marked the beginning in terms of the BMW car. BMW bought a car factory at Eisenach and built a small car called the Dixi 3/15 (See Fig. 4 – 4). The first Dixis used an open roof and were powered by a 4-cylinder engine producing 15 horsepower with a top of 80 km/h. The 1929 Dixi was the first vehicle to carry the famous BMW logo, the blue-and-white logo which is in fact based on the shape of a propeller, not on an auto component.

In the 1930s BMW began producing a line of larger touring cars and sports cars, introducing its highly successful model — the 328 sports car in 1936 (See Fig. 4 – 5). This car is a legend in the racing history, one of the best and the most beautiful cars that BMW has ever created. As recognition, the 328 roadster was nominated for the Car of the Century.

In 1941, all motorcycle production facilities and design documentation were transferred to Eisenach due to the war. The production of the BMW cars was stopped. The first post war car model, 501 luxury sedan equipped with the V8 engine, was produced in 1951 (See Fig. 4 – 6). The 500-series cars may not have been BMW's most glamorous products, but these big and sturdy middle-class machines were the mainstay of the company's car division from 1951 up until 1964.

In the 1960s, the company turned its fortunes around by focusing on sports sedans and compact touring cars, and it began to compete with Mercedes-Benz in the luxury-car markets of Europe and the United States. BMW's sales in the U.S.A. peaked in 1986 but then dropped steeply, partly due to competition from two new luxury cars — Lexus, made by Toyota Motor Corporation, and Infiniti, made by Nissan Motor Co., Ltd. The 1989 collapse of the Berlin Wall led to a boom in car sales in Europe, and in 1992 BMW outsold Mercedes-Benz in Europe for the first time.

Fig. 4 – 4　The first BMW car — the Dixi 3/15 in 1928　　Fig. 4 – 5　The beautiful lines of the 328 roadster　　Fig. 4 – 6　501

In 1990 BMW formed a joint venture with the British aerospace company Rolls-Royce PLC to produce aircraft engines for business jets. In 1992 BMW broke ground for a major automobile plant in Spartanburg, South Carolina, its first automobile plant in the United States. In 1994 BMW acquired 80 percent of the Rover Group, a British manufacturer of small cars, luxury cars, and Land Rover sport-utility vehicles. The ＄1.2 billion acquisition brought the company into new markets.

In 2004, BMW introduced the new K1200S Sports Bike which marked a new stage for BMW. It is both powerful and significantly lighter than previous K models. It was BMW's latest attempt to keep up with the pace of development of sports machines from the likes of Honda, Kawasaki, Yamaha, and Suzuki.

BMW was one of the earliest manufacturers to offer anti-lock brakes on production motorcycles starting in the late 1980s. The generation of anti-lock brakes available on the 2006 and later BMW motorcycles paves the way for the introduction of sophisticated electronic stability control.

BMW has become a globally renowned brand and is associated with powerful and sporty cars in the minds of most auto fans. Its advanced and refined engine technology has helped it become the world's leading premium carmaker. BMW says it will continue to offer "sheer driving pleasure" as the global auto industry moves to lower fuel consumption and emissions. The company has pledged to maintain or even enhance the impressive performance of its cars while at the same time making them more efficient through its "Efficient Dynamics" strategy, which it views as its core competitiveness for the future.

New Words

trace	[treis]	n.	踪迹,痕迹,足迹
		v.	跟踪,追踪,追溯
resign	[ri'zain]	v.	放弃(工作、权利),辞去(职务)
premiere	['premiə]	n.	首次公演
roadster	['rəudstə]	n.	双座敞篷轿车,跑车
nominate	['nɔmineit]	v.	任命,提名
glamorous	['glæmərəs]	a.	迷人的,富有魅力的
sturdy	['stə:di]	a.	结实的,强健的,坚决的,不屈的
mainstay	['meinstei]	n.	支柱,中流砥柱
peak	[pi:k]	n.	山顶,顶点
		vi.	到达最高点
outsell	[aut'sel]	v.	卖得比……多[快、贵],比……更能推销
sophisticated	[sə'fistikeitid]	a.	复杂的,精密的,老于世故的
premium	['pri:miəm]	a.	优质的,高端的

Phrases and Expressions

take over	接收,接管
the six-cylinder Type IIIa	6缸Ⅲa型
break ground	破土,创办
anti-lock brake	防抱死制动
electronic stability control	电子稳定控制

Proper Names

Munich	慕尼黑
Bavarian	巴伐利亚人
Treaty of Versailles	《凡尔赛条约》(也称《凡尔赛和约》,是第一次世界大战后战胜国(协约国)对战败国(同盟国)的和约,它的主要目的是惩罚和削弱德国。)
Eisenach	爱森纳赫(德国中部城市)
Lexus	凌志
Infiniti	无限

Berlin Wall	柏林墙(是德国首都柏林在第二次世界大战以后,德意志民主共和国(简称"民主德国"或"东德")在己方领土上建立的围墙。目的是隔离东德(含东德的首都东柏林)和德意志联邦共和国(简称"联邦德国"或"西德"),从而阻隔东西柏林之间市民的往来。柏林墙的建立,是第二次世界大战以后德国分裂和冷战的重要标志性建筑。它于1961年建造,于1989年拆除,两德重归统一。)
Rolls-Royce PLC	劳斯莱斯飞机引擎制造商
Spartanburg	斯帕坦堡(它是美国南卡罗来纳州皮德蒙特高原上的城市,是纺织工业及纺织机械中心,还有服装、电机、化学、食品等多种工业。附近有许多独立战争时代的遗迹。)
Honda	本田
Kawasaki	川崎
Yamaha	雅马哈
Suzuki	铃木
Rover Group	陆虎集团(陆虎集团是英国最大的汽车制造商,每年生产约50万辆汽车。该集团设计、制造及销售的汽车包括陆虎中小型和豪华型轿车、MG跑车和越野陆虎特殊用途四轮驱动汽车。)

Notes to the Text

1. The BMW R32 motorcycle made a strong impression at its world premiere at the Berlin Automobile Show in 1923.

   1923年宝马的R32在柏林汽车展览会上的首次亮相就给世人留下了深刻的印象。

2. The 500-series cars may not have been BMW's most glamorous products, but these big and sturdy middle-class machines were the mainstay of the company's car division from 1951 up until 1964.

   500系列也许不是宝马最吸引人的产品,但这些大而结实的中档机器却成为1951年车型分类以来直至1964年宝马公司的中流砥柱。

Questions for Discussion:

1. When was BMW established?
2. Why did BMW switch to making air brakes for railway cars?
3. When did BMW begin to produce automobiles?
4. Which model of BMW's cars was nominated for the Car of the Century?
5. What is viewed as BMW's core competitiveness for the future?

Unit Five

Section A Engine Cooling System

The temperature is quite essential for an engine to produce power. No engine can work well without suitable operating temperatures. If the engine temperature is too low, fuel economy will suffer and emissions will rise; if the temperature is allowed to get too hot for too long, the engine will destroy itself. For optimum engine operation, the cooling system must regulate the engine temperature within a precise and narrow range, so that it is not too hot and not too cold.

As fuel is burned in the engine, about one-third of the heat energy in the fuel is converted into power. Another third goes out through the exhaust pipe unused, and the remaining third must be handled by the cooling system. This means that the engine can work effectively only when the heat energy is equally handled so as to keep the engine temperature in balance. So, a cooling system of some kind is necessary in any internal combustion engine.

Actually, there are two types of cooling systems used on motor vehicles: water-cooling systems and air-cooling systems. But for the most part, automobiles and trucks use water-cooling systems.

Water-Cooling System

A water-cooling system means that water is used as a cooling agent to circulate through the engine to absorb the heat and carry it to the radiator for disposal. The engine is cooled mainly through heat transfer and heat dissipation. The heat generated by the mixture burned in the engine must be transferred from the cylinder to the water in the water jacket. The outside of the water jacket dissipates some of the heat to the air surrounding it, but most of the heat is carried by the cooling water to the radiator for dissipation.

Coolant

The cooling water used in cooling systems is called coolant. Pure water is no longer employed as coolant; today's coolant is a mixture of water (drinking quality), antifreeze (generally ethylene glycol), and various corrosion inhibitors selected for the specific application. An antifreeze concentration of 30% – 50% raises the coolant mixture's boiling point to allow operating temperatures of up to 120℃ at a pressure of 1.4 bar in passenger cars.

Coolant Flow

Engine coolant is forced from the water pump into the engine block. The coolant flows around the outside of the cylinder to cool the cylinder walls. Coolant continues to flow from the engine block through passages in the head gaskets into the cylinder head. The coolant flow through the cylinder head provides cooling for the valves, combustion chambers, and spark plugs. After flowing through the cylinder head, the coolant flows through the thermostat housing and top radiator hose to the inlet tank. As the coolant flows through the radiator, heat is transferred to the air flowing through the radiator. Coolant returns from the outlet tank and lower hose to the water pump.

When the coolant is cold, the thermostat is closed and the coolant flows through the intake manifold and heater core. Under this condition there is no coolant flow through the radiator. Once the engine reaches normal operating temperature, the thermostat opens and the coolant begins to flow through the radiator. When the thermostat is open, the coolant continues to flow through the intake manifold passage and the heater core (See Fig. 5-1).

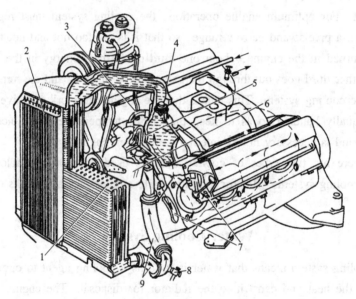

Fig. 5-1 The cooling system
1—radiator; 2—shutters; 3—by-pass hose; 4—thermostat; 5—water pump;
6—fan; 7—cylinder block and head cooling jacket; 8—drain cock; 9—connecting

Water Pump

A water pump is used to circulate the coolant. Coolant passages in the engine are connected to the pump. A drive belt from a crankshaft pulley is connected to the water pump. When the engine is running, the crankshaft turns the drive belt, and the hot coolant is pumped out of the engine and through a radiator. Water pumps are of many designs, but most of them are the centrifugal type which consists of a rotating fan, or impeller, and seldom are of the positive displacement type that uses gears or plungers.

Radiator

A radiator is designed to dissipate the heat which the coolant has absorbed from the engine. It is constructed to hold a large amount of water in tubes or other passages which provide a large area in contact with the atmosphere. The radiator usually mainly consists of the radiator core and radiator tank. Radiator cores are of two basic types: the fin and tube type (fins are placed around the tube to increase the area for radiating the heat) and the ribbon cellular or honeycomb type.

Radiator Cap

A radiator cap mounted on the top of the radiator is used to control the pressure in the cooling system. It is designed to release pressure if it reaches the specified upper limit that the system was designed to handle. This improves cooling efficiency and prevents evaporation of the coolant. Since evaporation is reduced or eliminated, it is not necessary to add coolant as often.

Thermostat

A thermostat is needed to control the temperature of the coolant by its work of opening or closing a valve to control the flow of coolant. It is designed to open and close at predetermined temperatures to maintain efficient engine operating temperatures. The closed thermostat helps the engine warm up rapidly. As soon as the coolant heats up, the thermostat opens and allows coolant to flow to the radiator.

Cooling Fan

The belt-driven fan is usually mounted on an extension of the water pump shaft and is driven by a V-belt from a pulley mounted on the front end of the crankshaft. Usually the alternator is also driven by the same belt. The fan blades are curved so that they pull air through the radiator as they rotate.

Many vehicles have cooling fans which are driven by an electric motor. The electrically driven fan only runs when additional cooling is required. Therefore, this type of fan uses less engine power than a belt-driven fan that rotates continuously. Since less engine power is used to drive the cooling fan, fuel economy and performance is improved. Many fuel-efficient front-wheel-drive cars have electric cooling fans.

Air-Cooling System

The air-cooling system is not commonly used. Air-cooled engines are just found on a few older cars and many modern motorcycles.

An air-cooling system means that air is used as a cooling agent to circulate through the engine to carry the heat away from the moving parts. The system consists of a centrifugal fan, a thermostat, a fan drive belt, radiation fins, baffle plates, an air control ring, etc. When the engine is running, forced air is directed over and through the fins to dissipate the heat.

In order to regulate the engine temperature by controlling the volume of the cooling air, a thermostat is installed inside the metal housing which encloses the engine. The thermostat unit is connected to an air control ring. As the engine becomes hotter, the control ring opens wider to admit more air, and closes when the engine is cold. With the ring closed, air circulation is restricted, and a cold engine warms up more rapidly. Rapid warm-up is one of the characteristics of air-cooled engines, since they do not have heated water in cylinder jackets and radiators.

In conclusion, the engine cooling system is actually a temperature regulation system. It is very critical for the operation of the engine.

New Words

essential	[i'senʃəl]	a.	基本的,本质的,必要的,必不可少的
regulate	['regjuleit]	v.	调节
agent	['eidʒənt]	n.	代理人(商)
disposal	[dis'pəuzəl]	n.	处理,处置,清除
transfer	[træns'fə:]	n./v.	传导,传递
dissipation	[,disi'peiʃən]	n.	分散,消散
antifreeze	['ænti,fri:z]	n.	(汽车水箱)防冻液,(化)防冻剂
pulley	['puli]	n.	滑轮,滑车,带轮
ribbon	['ribən]	n.	带状物,带子
cellular	['seljulə]	a.	多孔的,蜂窝状的
honeycomb	['hʌnikəum]	n.	蜂房(巢),蜂窝结构
alternator	['ɔ:ltəneitə]	n.	交流发电机,振荡器
housing	['hauziŋ]	n.	外壳,外罩
enclose	[in'kləuz]	v.	封入,装入

Phrases and Expressions

operating temperature	工作温度,运转温度
cooling agent	冷却介质
ethylene glycol	乙二醇
heater core	加热器芯子
in contact with	和……接触,跟……保持联系
radiator core	散热器芯
radiator cap	散热器盖
warm up	预热
centrifugal fan	离心式风扇
fan drive belt	风扇皮带
baffle plate	隔板,折流板
air control ring	空气量调节圈

Notes to the Text

1. This means that the engine can work effectively only when the heat energy is equally handled so as to keep the engine temperature in balance.
   这就意味着只有均等地处理热能以保持发动机温度的均衡,发动机才能有效地工作。
2. The outside of the water jacket dissipates some of the heat to the air surrounding it, but most of the heat is carried by the cooling liquid to the radiator for dissipation.
   冷却水套外围将一些热量散发到水套周围的空气中,但大部分热量由冷却水带入散热器散发。
3. A radiator cap mounted on the top of the radiator is used to control the pressure in the cooling system.
   安装在散热器顶部的散热器盖被用来调节冷却系的压力。

Exercises on the Text

I. Answer the following questions according to the text.
   1. What's the function of the cooling system?
   2. What does a water-cooling system mean?
   3. Please name the major components that make up the water-cooling system.
   4. What's the function of the radiator?
   5. What does an air-cooling system mean?

II. Fill in the table below (Tab. 5 -1).

Tab. 5 -1

English	Chinese
	冷却系统
cooling agent	
	水泵
alternator	
	散热器
operating temperature	
	恒温器
coolant	
	冷却水套
centrifugal fan	

III. Fill in the blanks with the words or phrases given below, and change the form where necessary.

convert	coolant	regulation	circulate
essential	radiator	melt	thermostat

1. A cooling system prevents the internal engine parts from _____ from the heat of the burning fuel.
2. As fuel is burned in the engine, about one-third of the heat energy in the fuel _____ into power.
3. The temperature is quite _____ for an engine to produce power.
4. The cooling water used in cooling systems is called _____.
5. A water pump is used to _____ the coolant.
6. A _____ is designed to dissipate the heat which the coolant has absorbed from the engine.
7. A _____ is needed to control the temperature of the coolant.
8. The engine cooling system is actually a temperature _____ system.

IV. Reading comprehension: Read the following passage carefully and fill in the blanks with the words given below.

seizure	efficient	operating	cooling	breakdown
consumption	degrees	combustion	engine	temperature

Excessively high __1__ temperatures would cause __2__ of the lubricating oil films, resulting in undue wearing and possible __3__ of the working parts. For these reasons the engine must be provided with a __4__ system, so that it can be maintained at its most __5__ practicable operating temperature. This generally means that the __6__ of the cylinder walls should not exceed about 250 __7__ centigrade whereas the actual temperature of the cylinder gases during __8__ may reach ten times this figure. Conversely, there is no merit in operating the __9__ too cool since this would reduce thermal efficiency and therefore increase fuel __10__.

V. Translate the following passage into Chinese.

As fuel is burned in the engine, about one-third of the heat energy in the fuel is converted into power. Another third goes out through the exhaust pipe unused, and the remaining third must be handled by the cooling system. This means that the engine can work effectively only when the heat energy is equally handled so as to keep the engine temperature in balance.

VI. **Translate the following sentences into English.**
1. 没有适当的运转温度,发动机就不能正常工作。
2. 车辆上使用的冷却系统有两种:水冷却系统和空气冷却系统。
3. 水冷却系统是指以水作为冷却介质在发动机中循环来吸收热量,并将热量带至散热器散发。
4. 安装在散热器顶部的散热器盖被用来调节冷却系的压力。
5. 空气冷却系统是指以空气作为冷却介质在发动机中循环来带走发动机运动部件的热量。

Section B Cooling System Troubleshooting

The temperature of gases in the cylinders of a running engine averages around 1,000℃. During the engine operation, the gases heat the walls of the cylinders, pistons, and cylinder heads. If the engine had not been cooled properly, the film of lubricating oil between the rubbing components of the engine would have been burnt off, resulting in undue wearing of the components, possible seizure of the pistons because of their excessive expansion, and other troubles. So, proper maintenance of the cooling system is very important to the life of the engine and the trouble free operation of the cooling system in general.

Check Circulation

Cooling system service begins with an inspection of all components for damage and leakage. Be sure to check the water pump drive belt. The water pump creates pressure that causes coolant to circulate. Unwanted restrictions in the radiator, the engine or hoses can block circulation, however.

The basic way to check circulation is to look for cooler spots in the system. Run the engine until it is fully warm and the thermostat is open. Then shut off the engine and run your hand over the radiator core from inlet tank to outlet tank to feel for cool spots. Do the same with all the hoses. The radiator and hoses should be uniformly warm. Any spots cooler than others indicate restrictions, or blockage, in the system.

Check the Thermostat

To test a thermostat while it is still in the engine, start the engine and let it come to the normal operating temperature. If it takes an unusually long time for the engine to warm up or for the heater to begin delivering hot air, the thermostat may be stuck in the open position. If the engine does warm up, shut it off and look for the two radiator hoses that go from the engine to the radiator. Feel them carefully (they could be very hot). If one hose is hot and the other is cold, the thermostat may be stuck closed. Remove the thermostat and test it, if you are still having problems and suspect the thermostat.

Check the Cooling Fan

The radiator cooling fan is an important part of the cooling system operation. If the engine temperature begins rising soon after the vehicle comes to a stop, the first thing to check is the fan operation. If the fan is not turning when the engine is hot, a simple test is to turn the AC on. If the fan begins to work, suspect the temperature sensor in the fan circuit. In order to test the fan motor itself, unplug the two-wire connector to the fan and connect a 12 volt source to one terminal and ground the other. If the fan motor begins to turn, the motor is good. If it does not turn, the motor must be replaced.

Test the Radiator Cap

A radiator cap is designed to maintain pressure in the cooling system at a certain maximum pressure. Pressure loss may occur through a radiator cap that doesn't maintain a proper seal. If the cap should fail, the engine can easily overheat. A pressure test of the radiator cap is a quick way to tell if the cap is doing its job. Remove the cap from the radiator and attach it to a test adapter. Dampen the cap gaskets to help them seal. Slowly operate the pump until the reading on the gauge stops increasing. This is the pressure at which the cap relief valve is opening. Repeat the test two or three times to verify the results. Replace the cap if the relief valve opens below or above the proper pressure. Since the radiator cap is quite cheap, it is better to replace it every 3 years or 36,000 miles. Make sure that you replace it with the one that is designed for your vehicle.

Test External Leaks

Pressure testing the cooling system is a simple process to determine where a leak is located. Once you are sure that the cooling system is full of coolant, a cooling system pressure tester is attached in place of the radiator cap. A gauge on the tester indicates how much pressure is being pumped. Once pressure is applied, you can start to look for leaks. Also watch the gauge on the tester to see if it loses pressure. If the pressure drops more than a couple of pounds in two minutes, there is likely a leak somewhere that may be hidden. It is not always easy to see where a leak is originating from, but one sure sign is the unmistakable odor of antifreeze inside the car. The windshield steaming up with an oily residue is also noticeable.

Test Internal Leaks

If you are losing coolant, but there are no signs of leaks, you could have a blown head gasket. The best way to test for this problem is with a combustion leak test on the radiator. This is accomplished by using a block tester, which is a kit that performs a chemical test on the vapors in the radiator. Blue tester fluid is added to the plastic container on the tester. If the fluid turns yellow during the test, then exhaust gases are present in the radiator. The most common cause for exhaust gases to be present in the radiator is a blown head gasket. Replacing a bad head gasket requires a major disassembly of the engine and can be quite expensive. Other causes include a cracked head or a cracked block.

Refill the Coolant Periodically

When you replace old coolant by draining it out and replacing it with fresh coolant, the best way to properly maintain your cooling system is to have the system power flushed. Power flushing will remove all the old coolant and flush out any sediment and scale along with it. Water, and sometimes, a cleaning agent is pumped through the cooling system in a reverse path from the normal coolant flow. This allows any scale to be loosened and flow out.

The cooling system is refilled with the appropriate amount of antifreeze to bring the coolant to the proper mixture of antifreeze and water. For most vehicles and most climates, the mixture is 50 percent antifreeze and 50 percent water. In colder climates, more antifreeze is used, but must never exceed 75 percent antifreeze. Most antifreeze used in vehicles is green in color and should be replaced every two years or 30,000 miles, which ever comes first. Newer antifreeze formulations which are usually red in color will last for 5 years or 150,000 miles before requiring replacement.

New Words

troubleshooting	[ˈtrʌblʃuːtiŋ]	n.	故障诊断与排除
seizure	[ˈsiːʒə]	n.	卡住,咬住
adapter	[əˈdæptə]	n.	转接器,接合器,适配器
dampen	[ˈdæmpən]	v.	弄湿,使潮湿
verify	[ˈverifai]	v.	证实,核实,确认
odor	[ˈəudə]	n.	气味,名声
windshield	[ˈwindʃiːld]	n.	(汽车上的)挡风玻璃
residue	[ˈrezidjuː]	n.	渣滓,滤渣,剩余物
kit	[kit]	n.	成套的零件,仪表(或工具),工具箱
refill	[riːˈfil]	v.	再填,重新注满
		n.	添补物,新补充物
drain	[drein]	v.	排出,排泄,排水
		n.	排水管,下水道
sediment	[ˈsedimənt]	n.	沉淀物,沉积
appropriate	[əˈprəupriit]	a.	适当的

Phrases and Expressions

undue wearing　　　　　　　　　　　过度磨损,不正常磨损
in place of　　　　　　　　　　　　代替

Notes to the Text

1. If the engine had not been cooled properly, the film of lubricating oil between the rubbing components of the engine would have been burnt off, resulting in undue wearing of the components, possible seizure of the pistons because of their excessive expansion, and other troubles.
   如果发动机冷却不良,发动机摩擦件之间的油膜就会烧掉,结果引起部件的过度磨损,还可

能使活塞急剧膨胀而拉缸,或引起其他故障。

2. Unwanted restrictions in the radiator, the engine or hoses can block circulation, however.
然而,散热器、发动机或软管中一些不必要的约束会阻碍冷却液的循环流动。

3. A gauge on the tester indicates how much pressure is being pumped.
测试仪上的量表显示出正在注入的压力。

4. In colder climates, more antifreeze is used, but must never exceed 75 percent antifreeze.
在较寒冷的气候条件下,可以使用更多的防冻剂,但比例不要超过75%。

Exercises

I. Translate the following names of cars into Chinese.

1. Toyota _____   2. Lexus _____
3. Crown _____   4. Corolla _____
5. Nissan _____   6. Cedric _____
7. Bluebird _____   8. Infiniti _____

II. Translate the following abbreviations into corresponding Chinese terms.

1. CTS (coolant temperature sensor) _____
2. CAC (charge air cooler) _____
3. LLC (long-life coolant) _____
4. CF (cooling fan) _____
5. AC (air cooling) _____
6. DTC (diagnostic trouble code) _____

Section C Dialogue Terms of Payment

The following dialogues are about terms of payment on cars (See Fig. 5 – 2).

Fig. 5 – 2 Negotiating about terms of payment on cars

Dialogue One:

Salesclerk(S): I'm glad to say that we've settled the price of this car. Now what about the terms of payment?

Customer(C): For the five-year loan, how much do I need to pay for this model?

S: 3,250 yuan a month. But I think the five-year loan is not economical. We have a convenient easy-payment installment plan. We require a one-fourth down payment, and you'll pay the balance in a year.

C: That's good. Would you tell me some details, please?

S: It's just a formality. We usually require references if you pay by installments.

C: What kind of reference do you need?

S: Providing a banker's reference would be quite satisfactory.

C: OK. I think I will adopt this kind of payment method. Thanks for your help.

S: You're welcome.

Dialogue Two:

S: Sir, how are you going to pay for this car?

C: What's your regular practice of terms of payment?

S: Generally, you can pay in cash, by credit card, or by installments. If you pay in cash or by credit card, we will give you 2% discount. If you pay by installments, the annual interest is calculated by 7%.

C: Oh, I'd like to pay by credit card. It's the easiest way to pay, I think. Here's my card.

S: Just a minute... Here's your receipt.

Useful Expressions and Sentences

1. terms of payment (or methods of payment)　付款方式
2. I'm glad to say that we've settled the price of this car. Now what about the terms of payment?
   很高兴我们已谈妥了这辆车的价格。现在谈谈付款方式吧？
3. For the five-year loan, how much do I need to pay for this model?
   对于5年期的贷款,买这种型号的车我需要支付多少？
4. But I think the five-year loan is not economical.
   但我认为5年期的贷款不合算。
5. We have a convenient easy-payment installment plan. We require a one-fourth down payment, and you'll pay the balance in a year.
   我们有很方便的分期付款方案。我们要收1/4的首期付款,其余的一年付清。
6. That's good. Would you tell me some details, please?
   好,请您将细则说说好吗？

7. It's just a formality. We usually require references if you pay by installments.
   就是手续问题。如果您分期付款,我们通常是需要担保的。
   formality [fɔː'mæliti] n. 正式手续
   reference ['refərəns] n. 证明文书,介绍信,推荐书
   installment 分期付款,按揭   pay by installments 分期付款
8. What kind of reference do you need?
   您需要什么样的担保呢?
9. Providing a banker's reference would be quite satisfactory.
   提供一份银行证明就可以了。
10. Sir, how are you going to pay for this car?
    先生,对于这辆车您打算如何付款?
11. What's your regular practice of terms of payment?
    Or: What terms of payment do you usually adopt?
    你们通常采用何种方式付款?
12. Generally, you can pay in cash, by credit card, or by installments. If you pay in cash or by credit card, we will give you 2% discount. If you pay by installments, the annual interest is calculated by 7%.
    通常,您可以用现金或信用卡支付,也可分期付款。如果您用现金或信用卡支付,我们将给您打9.8折。如果您采用分期付款,年利息按7% 计算。
    pay in cash   付现金
    in cash   以现金的方式
    cash payment   现金付款
    be short of cash   缺少现款,支付不足
    cash price   现金付款的最低价格
    cash on delivery   货到付款,交货付现
    pay by (with) credit card   用信用卡付款
    credit card   信用卡
    letter of credit   信用证
13. Other useful expressions:
    check/ cheque   支票
    pay by check   用支票付款
    pay by loan   以贷款付款
    pay in advance   预付
    leave a deposit   留下押金
    bank transfer   银行转账
    bill of exchange/draft   汇票
    telegraphic transfer   电汇汇票
    margin   保证金

Unit Six

Section A Engine Lubrication System

Without the aid of friction, an automobile could not move itself. Excessive friction in the engine, however, would mean rapid destruction. Internal friction cannot be eliminated, but it can be reduced to a considerable degree by the use of lubricating oil so that the automobile can move smoothly with proper friction.

The purpose of the lubrication system is to circulate oil between moving engine parts. Oil between the parts prevents metal-to-metal contact which causes friction and wear. The circulating oil has other important jobs. It carries heat away from engine parts, cleans engine parts, and helps the piston rings seal in compression pressures.

Apart from the lubricating oil, the lubrication system also contains other mechanical parts, such as the oil pump, the oil filter, the oil pressure relief valve; also pipes, passages and drillings in various parts of the engine through which the oil can flow. A quantity of oil is held in the oil pan. From this, oil is taken by the oil pump and circulated throughout the engine before returning to the oil pan. The oil cooler is also used in the lubrication system (See Fig. 6 – 1).

The **oil pump** is to induce oil circulation in the engine lubrication system. It is usually bolted to a boss on the lower face of the crankcase or to a crankshaft main bearing cap. Generally, the oil pump is located in the sump of the oil pan.

Oil pumps are of the positive displacement type in several designs. Vanes, plungers, rotors and gears are all used to build up the necessary pressure. The two most widely used are the gear and the rotor types. The pumps of gear and rotor types are always positively driven, usually from the camshaft either by means of gears or cams.

The oil pump in tractor engines is driven from a gear on the nose of the crankshaft, while in automobile engines, it is driven from a gear made integral with the camshaft.

Oil filters are used in the lubrication system to filter dirt and solids out of the oil. As these particles of foreign matter are prevented from entering the engine by oil filters, the rate of wear of engine parts is reduced. Engines of more recent designs generally use full-flow centrifugal oil filters. That is, all oil passes through the filter before it reaches the bearings. However, in the

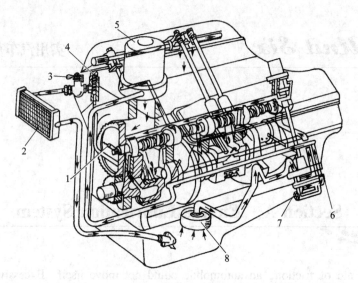

Fig. 6-1 The lubrication system
1—reducing valve; 2—oil cooler; 3—cooler cock; 4—safety valve;
5—centrifugal filter; 6—oil pump; 7—reducing valve; 8—screened intake

event the filter gets clogged, a bypass valve is provided so that oil will continue to reach the bearings.

This full-flow centrifugal oil filter is a reaction-type centrifugal filter with which all of the oil delivered by the oil pump is cleaned in the filter rotor. This filter has an oil outlet pipe fitted inside the hollow spindle of the filter rotor and connected to the oil line that distributes the oil to the various parts of the lubrication system.

Some engines use a new, impulse-reaction centrifugal oil filter. In contrast to the reaction-type centrifugal oil filter, this type of oil filter has no jet nozzles, and the oil used to drive the filter rotor does not drain to the oil pan but goes instead to lubricate the working parts of the engine.

The **oil pressure relief valve** is mainly to act both as a pressure regulator and as a safety device in the lubrication system. As a pressure regulator, the valve prevents the oil pump from building up excessive pressure. When the oil pump is in good condition, the valve will regulate the oil pressure within limits. As a safety device, the valve prevents oil pressure from building up to a dangerous level. The valve can secure the oil circulation through engine parts under proper pressure.

The **oil pan** is bolted to the bottom of the engine. The deep part of the oil pan houses an oil pump and pick-up screen. The pan also collects the oil that runs off engine parts after lubrication. A plug in the bottom of the oil pan is used to drain the oil at required intervals. The oil pan stores and collects the oil. Engines usually have an oil pan that holds 4, 5, or 6 quarts. A pick-up screen in the oil pan is connected by a pipe to the inlet of the oil pump. One end of the pan is lower and forms a reservoir called a sump. The drain plug is placed in the bottom of the sump.

The purpose of the **oil cooler** is to cool the oil in summer time. It is a one-piece unit consisting of a series of steel tubes of a flattened oval section and two tanks: a top tank and a bottom tank. To enlarge the cooling surface area, a spiral of thin steel ribbon is wound around each cooler tube. The oil coolers of some engines have their tubes passing through a large number of flat cooling fins, and their tanks are divided into several compartments by partitions. Welded to the tanks are the inlet and outlet oil pipe connections and mounting lugs. The oil cooler is mounted in front of the cooling system radiator. In air-cooled engines, the oil cooler takes the form of a single tube repeatedly bent in and out and carrying a ribbon spiral wound around it. With the radiator shutter or blind fully open, the oil flowing through the cooler tubes that are exposed to the flow of cooling air on the outside gets colder by 10 ℃ to 12 ℃.

Engines are lubricated in three ways: pump pressure, splashing, or a combination of both. In the pressure system, the oil is fed to the majority of engine parts under the pump pressure, especially to the main bearings and connecting rod bearings.

In the splash system, there are dippers on the lower parts of the connecting rod bearing caps, these dippers enter oil trays in the oil pan with each crankshaft revolution. The dippers splash the oil to the upper parts of the engine. The oil is thrown up as the oil sprays, which provides adequate lubrication to valve mechanisms, cylinder walls, piston rings and bearings.

In modern engine designs, these two methods are often combined. Pressure is developed by the oil pump, which delivers the oil to the filter for cleaning before it is sent to the camshaft and valve train components at the top of the engine. Other components are lubricated by splashing the oil and by a network of passages.

New Words

destruction	[di'strʌkʃən]	n.	毁坏,破坏
lubricate	['ljuːbrikeit]	v.	使润滑,加润滑油
seal	[siːl]	n./v.	密封
filter	['filtə]	n.	过滤器,滤油器
		v.	过滤
pan	[pæn]	n.	槽,盘
induce	[in'djuːs]	v.	诱发,引起,感应
sump	[sʌmp]	n.	油底壳,贮槽
rotor	['rəutə]	n.	转子,涡轮
particle	['pɑːtikl]	n.	微粒
regulator	['regjuleitə]	n.	调节器
screen	[skriːn]	n.	滤网
wind	[waind]	v.	(wound[waund]或 winded)绕,缠绕
partition	[pɑː'tiʃən]	n.	隔板,隔开
weld	[weld]	v.	焊接,熔接

Phrases and Expressions

lubricating oil	润滑油
oil pump	油泵
oil filter	机油滤清器
oil pressure relief valve	机油减压阀
oil cooler	润滑油冷却器,机油散热器
main bearing cap	主轴承盖
positive displacement type	容积式
build up	增大,集结
foreign matter	杂质,异物
rate of wear	磨损率,磨损速度
full-flow type	全流式
bypass valve	分流阀,旁通阀
reaction-type centrifugal filter	反馈式(反作用式)离心过滤器
outlet pipe	排出管(泵的排泄管)
impulse-reaction centrifugal filter	冲击—反击式离心过滤器
jet nozzle	喷(油)嘴
pick-up screen	集滤器
at required intervals	在规定时间
mounting lug	安装用(起重)吊耳
be fed to	向……提供……

Notes to the Text

1. As these particles of foreign matter are prevented from entering the engine by oil filters, the rate of wear of engine parts is reduced.
   由于机油滤清器阻止了杂质微粒进入发动机,因此降低了发动机部件的磨损率。
2. ... in the event the filter gets clogged, a bypass valve is provided so that oil will continue to reach the bearings.
   ……如果机油滤清器被阻塞,就得起用分流阀,以使机油继续流向各轴承。
3. Engines are lubricated in three ways: pump pressure, splashing, or a combination of both.
   发动机的3种润滑方式是油泵压力、飞溅以及复合式。

Exercises on the Text

I. Answer the following questions according to the text.
   1. What's the function of the lubrication system?
   2. Please name the major parts that make up the lubrication system.

3. What's the function of the oil filter?
4. Engines are lubricated in three ways, and what are they?
5. What's the function of the oil pressure relief valve?

II. Fill in the table below (Tab. 6-1).

Tab. 6-1

English	Chinese
	润滑系统
oil cooler	
	调节器
jet nozzle	
	油泵
pick-up screen	
	润滑油
oil pan	
	机油滤清器
oil pressure relief valve	

III. Fill in the blanks with the words or phrases given below, and change the form where necessary.

```
build up       sump        wind        circulate
bypass valve   regulate    drain       wear
```

1. The purpose of the lubrication system is to _____ oil between moving engine parts.
2. Vanes, plungers, rotors and gears are all used to _____ the necessary pressure.
3. To enlarge the cooling surface area, a spiral of thin steel ribbon _____ around each cooler tube.
4. Oil between the parts prevents metal-to-metal contact which causes friction and _____.
5. One end of the pan is lower and forms a reservoir called a _____.
6. When the oil pump is in good condition, the valve will _____ the oil pressure within limits.
7. In the event the filter gets clogged, a _____ is provided so that oil will continue to reach the bearings.
8. A plug in the bottom of the oil pan is used to _____ the oil at required intervals.

IV. Reading comprehension: Read the following passage carefully and fill in the blanks with the words given below.

| filter | circulate | pressure | hold | splash |
| sent | cleaning | lubricated | combined | control |

The lubrication system of an automotive engine consists of an oil pan to __1__ the oil supply, a pump to develop __2__, a filter for __3__, and valves which __4__ flow and pressure.

Two methods are used to __5__ oil through an engine: pressure and __6__. In modern engine designs, these two methods are often __7__. Pressure is developed by the oil pump, which delivers oil to the __8__ for cleaning before it is __9__ to the camshaft, and valve train components are __10__ by splashing oil and by a network of passages.

V. Translate the following passage into Chinese.

Oil filters are used in the lubrication system to filter dirt and solids out of the oil. As these particles of foreign matter are prevented from entering the engine by oil filters, the rate of wear of engine parts is reduced. Engines of more recent designs generally use full-flow centrifugal oil filters. That is, all oil passes through the filter before it reaches the bearings. However, in the event the filter gets clogged, a bypass valve is provided so that oil will continue to reach the bearings.

VI. Translate the following sentences into English.
1. 没有摩擦力的作用,汽车就不能开动。
2. 发动机的润滑系统由机械部件组成,如油泵、机油滤清器、机油减压阀等。
3. 机油滤清器的主要功能是把机油中的杂质微粒过滤掉。
4. 机油减压阀能够确保机油在适当的压力下在发动机各部件间循环。
5. 机油通过油泵压力、飞溅、复合式等润滑方式供向发动机各运动部件。

Section B　Engine Lubricating Oil

Engine Oil Purposes

Lubrication

A very important purpose of the engine oil is to lubricate engine parts to reduce friction and wear. Friction and wear are caused by metal-to-metal contact of the moving parts. Wear is also caused by acidic corrosion, rusting, and the abrasion from the contaminants carried in the oil.

Metal-to-metal contact is controlled by proper viscosity selection and the use of film-forming compounds. Acidic corrosion and rusting are controlled by the formulation of the oil, while the abrasive wear is controlled by air and oil filtration and oil drain intervals.

The lubrication system must supply a continuous flow of oil to all the engine bearings and lubricated surfaces to maintain the oil film of each component and minimize wear. The correct oil viscosity is also essential to reduce friction.

Cooling

The oil carries the heat away from each bearing or component that is lubricated. When the oil is returned to the oil pan, some of the heat is dissipated from the oil by air surrounding the crankcase.

Cylinder walls, pistons, and piston rings may operate at temperatures of several hundred degrees Fahrenheit. The engine oil in contact with these surfaces may break down or burn to some extent and produce carbon. It is important that the oil temperature be kept below the flash point of the oil, which is the temperature at which the oil will ignite and burn. The engine oil must have a high heat-resistance so that carbon formation is kept to a minimum.

Sealing

The engine oil helps the piston rings to form a tight seal between the piston rings and cylinder walls. Microscopic irregularities in the piston rings or cylinder walls are filled by the oil film, which prevents the escape of combustion chamber gases. The engine oil clings to the metal surfaces and resists the tendency of combustion chamber gases to blow by through the piston rings. The oil film also provides lubrication between the rings and the piston ring grooves to allow free movement of the rings and therefore continuous contact between the rings and cylinder walls.

Cleaning

The engine oil has a cleaning effect on all the engine components that it contacts. Carbon formations are cleaned from the pistons and rings by the engine oil. Excessive carbon deposits can cause the piston rings to seize in their grooves, which results in excessive leakage of gases past the rings on the compression and power strokes. This excessive leakage in an engine is called blow-by. When blow-by becomes extreme, engine performance and fuel economy are reduced. Additives in the engine oil help the oil to perform its cleaning operation. Carbon particles will be removed from the oil by the oil filter.

Engine Oil Formulation

The engine oil must function whether the temperature is below zero or above 200 degrees Fahrenheit. This is contrary to the nature of petroleum products since they tend to thicken at low temperatures and thin out at high temperatures. The oil must go through many processes during manufacture to reduce this tendency to change viscosity with changes in temperature.

A satisfactory engine oil must have certain characteristics, or properties. It must have proper viscosity and must resist oxidation, carbon formation, corrosion, rust, extreme pressures, and foaming. Also, it must act as a good cleaning agent, must pour at low temperatures, and must have good viscosity at extremes of high and low temperatures.

Any mineral oil, by itself, does not have all these properties. Manufacturers therefore put a number of additives into the oil during the manufacturing process. The oil for severe service may have many additives as follows: a viscosity-index improver, pour-point depressants, oxidation inhibitors, corrosion inhibitors, rust inhibitors, foam inhibitors, detergent-dispersants, and extreme-pressure agents.

Engine Oil Change

Changing the oil is an easy way to keep an engine working well. Manufacturers set the oil-change intervals for their cars. Follow their recommendations. Recently, the interval between oil changes has been lengthened. With better oil and better engines, the oil can be used longer without damaging the engine. Also, unleaded fuels do not dirty oil the way leaded gasoline does.

Most manufacturers suggest that you change the oil filter with every other oil change, rather than every oil change. They feel that modern oil filters can withstand these longer intervals. But remember, oil filters hold 1 quart of oil at all times. So if you drain the oil but leave the old filter, you are mixing four quarts of fresh oil with one quart of dirty oil. For this reason, it is a good idea to change the filter every time you change the oil.

It's easy to change the oil and replace the filter. Put the car on a hoist or lift. Or, drive the car onto a portable car ramp, and block the wheels. Place a pan under the drain plug in the bottom of the oil pan. Remove the plug to drain the dirty oil into the pan.

Warm the engine before changing the oil because warm oil flows more freely and carries more dirt with it. Be careful! Or you could burn yourself in changing the oil on a hot engine.

Once you have drained the oil, clean the drain plug and replace it in the pan. Do not overtighten the plug. You could damage the oil pan.

Remove the oil filter. Before installing a new filter, make sure the oil-filter mounting pad is clean. Assure a proper seal, coat the rubber seal with a light coating of oil. Be sure that the new filter is the same size and type as the old one. If the oil filter fits onto the engine with the mounting surface up, you can fill the filter with as much oil as it can hold. This keeps the engine from being starved for oil when it first starts.

Tighten the new filter by hand. Pour in the fresh oil through the tube covered by the oil-fill cap. You will find this cap on a valve cover. Remove the cap, pour in the fresh oil, and replace the cap.

Start the engine and check for leaks at the oil filter. After running the engine for a few minutes, shut it off. Check the crankcase dipstick to find if the sump contains enough oil.

Lubricating oil is the lifeblood of the internal combustion engine. Extensive research and in-service field testing are required to develop oils meeting the increasing severity demanded by today's engines.

New Words

abrasion	[əˈbreiʒən]	n.	磨损,磨蚀
contaminant	[kənˈtæminənt]	n.	致污物,污染物
viscosity	[visˈkɔsiti]	n.	黏稠度,黏稠
formulation	[ˌfɔːmjuˈleiʃən]	n.	成分,配方
formulate	[ˈfɔːmjuleit]	v.	制定……的配方,按配方制造(或配制),系统地阐述
abrasive	[əˈbreisiv]	a.	磨蚀的
		n.	腐蚀剂,研磨料
filtration	[filˈtreiʃən]	n.	过滤
additive	[ˈæditiv]	n.	添加物,添加剂
detergent	[diˈtəːdʒnət]	n.	去污剂,去垢剂
		a.	清洁的,净化的
dispersant	[disˈpəːsənt]	n.	分散剂
hoist	[hɔist]	n.	吊起,升起,起重机
portable	[ˈpɔːtəbəl]	a.	可移动的,便携的
ramp	[ræmp]	n.	人造斜坡,坡道,滑行台,梯子,斜梯
coat	[kəut]	v.	给(某物)涂上(覆盖上)一层
coating	[ˈkəutiŋ]	n.	涂层,覆盖层
starve	[staːv]	v.	急需,渴望(for),挨饿
dipstick	[ˈdipstik]	n.	(量)油尺,测深尺,测杆

Phrases and Expressions

flash point	(燃油等的)闪点(燃料上方的蒸气在空气中能被点燃而瞬间即熄灭的最低温度)
viscosity-index improver	黏稠度指数促进剂
pour-point depressant (PPD)	流点抗凝剂
oxidation inhibitor	抗氧化剂
corrosion inhibitor	防腐剂
rust inhibitor	防锈剂
foam inhibitor	泡沫抑制剂
extreme-pressure agent	极压添加剂
mounting pad	安装台,安装垫

Notes to the Text

1. The oil can form a good seal between the piston rings and cylinder walls.

机油在活塞环与汽缸壁之间形成密封油膜。
2. It must have proper viscosity and must resist oxidation, carbon formation, corrosion, rust, extreme pressures, and foaming.
它（润滑油）必须具有适当的黏稠度，并且必须具有抗氧化、防止积碳、防腐、防锈、抗极压和防泡沫等作用。

Exercises

I. Translate the following names of cars into Chinese.
1. Mitsubishi _____   2. Honda _____
3. Tommykaira _____   4. Acura _____
5. Daihatsu _____   6. Mazda _____
7. Autozam _____   8. Efini _____

II. Translate the following abbreviations into corresponding Chinese terms.
1. LO (lubricating oil) _____
2. OCV (oil control valve) _____
3. OFL (oil filter) _____
4. OPS (oil pressure sensor) _____
5. OL (oil level) _____
6. ODI (oil drain intervals) _____

Section C Henry Ford

Henry Ford (See Fig. 6-2) became something of a typical American folk hero during his lifetime.

Many people believe Henry Ford invented the automobile. But Henry Ford did not start to build his first car until 1896. That was eleven years after two Germans — Gottlieb Daimler and Karl Benz — developed the first gasoline-powered automobile.

What Henry Ford did was to use other people's ideas and make them better.

Others made cars. Henry Ford made better cars. And he sold them for less money. Others built car factories. Henry Ford built the biggest factory of its time. And he made the whole factory a moving production line.

Fig. 6-2 Henry Ford

Henry Ford, the son of a farmer, was born in Greenfield, Michigan, on 30th July, 1863. He left school at 15 to work on his father's farm but in 1879 he moved to Detroit where he became an apprentice in a machine shop.

Ford returned to Greenfield after his father gave him 40 acres to start his own farm. He disliked farming and spent much of the time trying to build a steam road carriage and a farm locomotive. Unable to settle at Greenfield, Ford returned to Detroit to work as an engineer.

During this period Ford read an article about how the German engineer, Nicholas Otto, had built an internal combustion engine. Ford now spent his spare time trying to build a petrol-driven motor car. His first car, finished in 1896, was built in a little brick shed in his garden. Driven by a two-cylinder, four-cycle motor, it was mounted on bicycle wheels. Named "Quadricycle," the car had no reverse gear or brakes (See Fig. 6-3).

Fig. 6-3　Henry Ford's first car — "Quadricycle" in 1896

By August, 1899, Ford had raised enough money to start his own company. His first group of investors withdrew after Ford had spent $86,000 without producing a car that could be sold. They might stop, but Henry Ford was just getting to start.

In the early days of the automobile, almost every car-maker raced his cars. It was the best way of gaining public notice. Henry Ford decided to build a racing car. After winning a race in 1901, his name appeared in newspapers and his fame began to spread.

Henry used what he learned from racing to develop a better engine. In 1903, he was ready to start building cars for the public. And also in this year the Ford Motor Company was founded with Henry Ford as vice-president and chief engineer. The infant company produced only a few cars a day with groups of two or three men working on each car.

Henry Ford realized his dream of producing an automobile that was reasonably priced, reliable, and efficient with the introduction of the Model T in 1908 (See Fig. 6-4). The Model T proved to be a huge success and had a tremendous influence on American life. The process by which Ford produced cars influenced the development of the means of production in other industries. The Model T's low cost made automobile transportation available to all but the poorest Americans, reducing isolation in rural areas. The popularity of the Model T also stimulated a demand for improved roads. The increase in automobile use was a huge stimulus to the petroleum industry. This vehicle initiated a new era in personal transportation. It was easy to operate, maintain, and handle on rough roads.

Fig. 6-4　Model T (1908)

By 1918, half of all cars in America were of Model T. To meet the growing demand for the Model T, the company opened a large factory at Highland Park, Michigan, in 1910. Here, Henry Ford combined precision manufacturing, standardized and interchangeable parts, a division of labor, and, in 1913, a continuous moving assembly line. Workers remained in place, adding one component to each automobile as it moved past them on the line. Delivery of parts by conveyor belt to the workers was carefully timed to keep the assembly line moving smoothly and efficiently. The introduction of the moving assembly line revolutionized automobile production by significantly reducing assembly time per vehicle, thus lowering costs. Ford's production of Model T made his company the largest automobile manufacturer in the world.

The company began construction of the world's largest industrial complex during the late 1910s and the early 1920s. By September 1927, all steps in the manufacturing process from refining raw materials to final assembly of the automobile took place at the vast plant, characterizing Henry Ford's idea of mass production.

Henry Ford said, "I will build a motor car for the great mass of people. It will be large enough for the family but small enough for one person to operate and care for. It will be built of the best materials. It will be built by the best men to be employed. And it will be built with the simplest plans that modern engineering can produce. It will be so low in price that no man making good money will be unable to own one."

Henry Ford was an ordinary man who found an extraordinary way of doing business. He learned from his mistakes, rose above his obstacles and ignored the critics to follow his dreams and become one of the most successful businessmen of the 20th century.

New Words

apprentice	[ə'prentis]	n.	学徒,徒工
shed	[ʃed]	n.	(当贮藏室用的)棚屋
withdraw	[wið'drɔː]	v.	(withdrew [wið'druː], withdrawn [wið'drɔːn])取回,撤回,收回,撤退,退出
component	[kəm'pəunənt]	a.	组成的,合成的
		n.	成分,部分
maintain	[mein'tein]	vt.	保持,维持,保养,维修
precision	[pri'siʒən]	n.	精确(性),精密(度)
standardize	['stændədaiz]	vt.	使符合标准,使标准化
complex	['kɔmpleks]	a.	复杂的,综合的
		n.	综合物,综合企业
refine	[ri'fain]	vt.	提炼,精炼

Phrases and Expressions

farm locomotive	农用机车
reverse gear	倒车挡
conveyor belt	传送带

Proper Names

Detroit 底特律(它是美国密歇根州最大的城市,1701年由法国毛皮商建立,是位于美国东北部,加拿大温莎以南,底特律河沿岸的一座重要的港口城市、世界传统汽车中心和音乐之都。)

Greenfield 格林菲尔德(位于美国马萨诸塞州西北部)

Notes to the Text

1. Henry Ford realized his dream of producing an automobile that was reasonably priced, reliable, and efficient with the introduction of the Model T in 1908.
1908年生产的T型汽车使亨利·福特制造价格合理、高效可靠的汽车梦想得以实现。

2. Here, Henry Ford combined precision manufacturing, standardized and interchangeable parts, a division of labor, and, in 1913, a continuous moving assembly line.
在这儿,亨利·福特将精密生产、标准的可互换零部件,以及劳动分工结合起来。1913年,一条流水线诞生了。

Questions for Discussion:

1. When did Henry Ford build his first car?
2. Can you describe Henry Ford's first car?
3. Why did Henry Ford's first group of investors withdraw from his first company?
4. When did Henry Ford gain his fame?
5. Why was Model T a huge success?

Unit Seven

Section A Engine Ignition System

Nowadays, there are three types of ignition systems. The mechanical (conventional) ignition system, used prior to 1975, was mechanical and electrical and used no electronics. The electronic ignition system became popular when better control and improved reliability became important with the advent of emission controls. Finally, the distributorless ignition system became available in the mid 1980s. This system was always computer controlled and contained no moving parts, so reliability was greatly improved.

Mechanical (Conventional) Ignition System

The ignition system on an internal combustion engine provides the spark to the correct cylinder at the correct time to ignite the combustible air-fuel mixture in the combustion chamber. Conventional systems consist of the battery, ignition coil, distributor, condenser, ignition switch, spark plug, resistor and the necessary low and high tension wiring (See Fig. 7-1).

The battery is the heart of the total electrical system. In regard to the primary circuit, its function is to supply voltage and current flow to the primary windings of the ignition coil, in order to produce an electromagnet.

The ignition coil is a pulse transformer designed to set up the primary voltage (received from the battery and generator) of 12V to approximately 20,000 V required to jump the spark plug gap in the combustion chamber. It is composed of a primary winding, secondary winding and core of soft iron.

The ignition distributor is the nerve center of the mechanical ignition system. It opens and closes the primary ignition circuit, and also distributes high tension current to the proper spark plug at the correct time.

The distributor cap transfers the high voltage from the distributor rotor to spark plug wires.

A distributor rotor is a conductor designed to rotate and distribute the high tension current to the towers of the distributor cap. The distributor rotor is provided with some sorts of spring connection to the center tower or terminal of the distributor cap.

The purpose of the ignition condenser is to reduce arcing at the breaker points, and prolong their life.

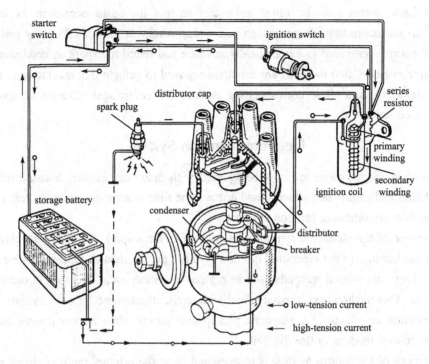

Fig. 7-1 The ignition system

The spark plug provides the gap in the combustion chamber across which the high tension electric spark jumps to ignite the combustible charge.

In most 12V systems, an ignition resistor is connected in series with the primary circuit of the ignition coil during normal operation. However, during the starting period, the resistor is cut out of the circuit so that full voltage is applied to the coil. This insures a strong spark during the starting period, and in that way quicker starting is provided.

The purpose of the ignition switch is to connect or disconnect the ignition system from the battery, so the engine can be started and stopped as desired.

With the ignition switch ON, and the ignition distributor contacts closed, current will flow from the battery, through the primary winding of the ignition coil, to the distributor contact (breaker) points, to the ground connection and back to the battery.

The current flowing through the primary winding of the ignition coil produces a magnetic field in the coil. When the distributor contact points open (break), the magnetic field collapses and the movement of the magnetic field induces current in the secondary winding of the coil. Since there are many more turns of wire in the secondary winding than those in the primary winding, the voltage is increased up to 20,000 V.

The distributor then directs this high voltage to the proper spark plug, where it jumps the gap. The heat of this spark ignites the air-fuel mixture in the combustion chamber. The burning fuel expands and forces the piston down. Downward motion of the piston, in turn, rotates the crankshaft.

The ignition system must be timed accurately so that the spark occurs in the combustion chamber at the correct instant. Incorrect ignition timing results in loss of efficiency and power.

A mechanism is provided to automatically advance and retard the spark as conditions require. On automotive engines, two methods are usually employed to actuate that mechanism, centrifugal force and engine vacuum. The corresponding devices are centrifugal advance components and vacuum advance units.

Electronic Ignition System

Electronic ignition systems are now being used with many car engines because they provide superior ignition and engine performance and at the same time require considerably less service and maintenance than conventional ignition systems.

The purpose of the electronic ignition system is to create a spark at each spark plug electrode gap at the right instant. In the electronic ignition system, the points and condenser are replaced by electronics. There are several methods used to replace the points and condenser in order to trigger the coil to fire. One method uses a metal wheel with teeth, usually one for each cylinder, which is called an armature or reluctor. A magnetic pickup coil senses when a tooth passes and sends a signal to the control module to fire the coil.

The purpose of the control module is to open and close the primary ignition circuit. When the reluctor tip moves a very short distance out of alignment with the pickup coil, the induced voltage in the pickup coil decreases. When this occurs, the control module closes the primary circuit and the primary current flow resumes.

The control module must keep the primary circuit turning on long enough to allow the magnetic field to build up in the ignition coil. This "on time" for the primary circuit is referred to as dwell time. In most electronic ignition systems, the dwell time is determined electronically by the control module.

The advantage of the electronic ignition system is that the control module can handle much higher primary voltage than the mechanical points. Voltage can even be stepped up before sending it to the coil, so the coil can create a much hotter spark, on the order of 50,000 volts instead of 20,000 volts that is common with the mechanical system.

The higher voltage that the system provided allows the use of a much wider gap on the spark plug for a longer, fatter spark. This larger spark also allows a leaner mixture for better fuel economy and still ensures a smooth running engine.

In the later systems, the inside of the distributor is empty and all triggering is performed by a sensor called crankshaft position sensor or camshaft position sensor. In these systems, the job of the distributor is solely to distribute the spark to the correct cylinder through the distributor cap and rotor. The computer handles the timing and any timing advance necessary for the smooth running of the engine.

Distributorless Ignition System

The distributorless ignition system, completely controlled by the on-board computer, is a completely solid state electronic system with no moving parts. In place of the distributor, there are multiple coils that each serves one or two spark plugs.

In systems with single-spark ignition coils, each cylinder has its own ignition coil with driver output stage, installed either directly above the spark plug or separately. This system, suitable for engines with any number of cylinders, provides the greatest latitude for adjustment, as there is only one spark per cycle. All these advantages mean that the single-spark ignition coil is being increasingly used and is taking over from the dual-spark ignition coil in spite of costing more.

In systems with dual-spark ignition coils, one ignition coil is required for every two cylinders. The crankshaft can be used for synchronization. The high-voltage end of each ignition coil is connected to the spark plugs for two cylinders whose operating cycles are 360° out of phase with each other.

As there is an additional spark during the exhaust stroke, it is important to ensure that residual mixture or fresh mixture is not ignited. Furthermore, the dual-spark system is only suited for use with even numbers of cylinders. Owing to its cost advantage relative to the single-spark unit, the dual-spark ignition system is the most common distributorless ignition in use today.

New Words

electronic	[ilek'trɔnik]	a.	电子的
distributor	[dis'tribjutə]	n.	分电器
condenser	[kən'densə]	n.	电容器
resistor	[ri'zistə]	n.	电阻器
voltage	['vəultidʒ]	n.	(电)电压,伏特数
electromagnet	[i,lektrəu'mægnit]	n.	电磁体,电磁铁
pulse	[pʌls]	n.	脉搏,脉冲,电流之突然增强或减弱
transformer	[træns'fɔ:mə]	n.	变压器
terminal	['tə:minl]	n.	(电)线接头,接线柱
arcing	['ɑ:kiŋ]	n.	电弧
turn	[tə:n]	n.	一圈,(线圈的)匝数
ground	[graund]	n.	接地,搭铁,路面
trigger	['trigə]	v.	触发
armature	['ɑ:mətjuə]	n.	电枢
reluctor	[ri'lʌktə]	n.	磁阻轮,变磁阻转子
module	['mɔdju:l]	n.	组件,模块,电子控制总成
resume	[ri'zju:m]	v.	恢复,重新开始,再继续

Phrases and Expressions

prior to   在……之前

with the advent of	随着……的出现(到来)
distributorless ignition system	无分电器点火系统
high tension wiring	高压电线,高压电路
In regard to (of)…	关于,相对于,就……而论
primary winding	初级线圈,初级绕组
secondary winding	次级线圈,次级绕组
distributor cap	分电器盖
distributor rotor	分火头
breaker point	断电器触点
in series	串联,连续地,逐次地
magnetic field	磁场
ignition timing	点火正时
centrifugal advance	离心式点火提前调节
vacuum advance	真空式点火提前调节
initial timing	初始点火正时
magnetic pickup	电磁传感器,电磁感应
pickup coil	传感线圈
control module(CM)	(电子)控制组件,控制模块
dwell time (DT)	延迟时间,延长时间,停歇时间(例如分电器的触电闭合时间)
lean mixture	稀混合气
on-board computer	车载电脑

Notes to the Text

1. The distributor rotor is provided with some sorts of spring connection to the center tower or terminal of the distributor cap.
   分火头借助弹簧的作用力连接到分电器盖的中心触头上。
2. With the ignition switch ON, and the ignition distributor contacts closed, current will flow from the battery, through the primary winding of the ignition coil, to the distributor contact (breaker) points, to the ground connection and back to the battery.
   如果点火开关闭合,而且点火分电器的断电器触点也闭合,则电流就从蓄电池经过点火线圈初级绕组,到断电器触点,再到搭铁,并回到蓄电池。
3. The control module can handle much higher primary voltage than the mechanical points.
   电子控制模块能够比机械式点火系统提供更高的初级电压。

Exercises on the Text

I. Answer the following questions according to the text.
  1. What's the function of the ignition system?

2. How many types of ignition systems have been used in the engine? What are they?
3. Please name the major parts that make up the conventional ignition system.
4. What's the function of the ignition coil?
5. What are the advantages of the electronic ignition system compared with the conventional ignition system?

II. **Fill in the table below (Tab. 7 – 1).**

Tab. 7 – 1

English	Chinese
	火花塞
pickup coil	
	点火线圈
distributor rotor	
	电阻器
secondary winding	
	磁场
transformer	
	点火正时
primary winding	

III. **Fill in the blanks with the words or phrases given below, and change the form where necessary.**

| distributorless | induce | transfer | time |
| battery | ignition coil | trigger | distribute |

1. The _____ ignition system was always computer controlled and contained no moving parts.
2. In regard to the primary circuit, the function of the _____ is to supply voltage and current flow to the primary windings of the ignition coil, in order to produce an electromagnet.
3. The _____ is a pulse transformer designed to set up the primary voltage of 12V to approximately 20,000 V.
4. The ignition distributor _____ high tension current to the proper spark plug at the correct time.
5. When the distributor contact points open, the magnetic field collapses and the movement of the magnetic field _____ current in the secondary winding of the coil.
6. There are several methods used to replace the points and condenser in order to _____

the coil to fire.

7. The distributor cap _____ high voltage from the distributor rotor to spark plug wires.
8. The ignition system must _____ accurately so that the spark occurs in the combustion chamber at the correct instant.

IV. **Reading comprehension: Read the following passage carefully and fill in the blanks with the words given below.**

temperatures	wear	electrical	plug	capacity
characteristics	low	wiring	dependent	ignition

Spark __1__ gaps do not remain constant, but increase in size. The amount of increase is __2__ on mileage, chemical __3__ of the fuel, combustion chamber __4__, and the action of the __5__ spark which tears off portions of the electrode. The electrical characteristics of the __6__ system also affect the rate of __7__ of the spark plug electrodes. The electrical capacity of the ignition coil and the __8__ is an important factor. Systems with high __9__ will cause more rapid gap wear than systems with __10__ capacity.

V. **Translate the following passage into Chinese.**

The current flowing through the primary winding of the ignition coil produces a magnetic field in the coil. When the distributor contact points open (break), the magnetic field collapses and the movement of the magnetic field induces current in the secondary winding of the coil. Since there are many more turns of wire in the secondary winding than those in the primary winding, the voltage is increased up to 20,000 V.

VI. **Translate the following sentences into English.**
1. 点火线圈由初级线圈、次级线圈和软磁铁铁心组成。
2. 有专门的机构来根据发动机工况需求自动提前和推后点火。
3. 点火电容器的作用是减少断电器触点间的放电,延长触点的使用寿命。
4. 点火开关的作用是把点火系统与蓄电池连接或断开,这样发动机才能根据要求启动或停止工作。
5. 电子点火系统提供更好的点火性能及发动机性能;同时,与传统的点火系统相比,只需相当少的维护。

Section B Battery and Its Maintenance

The battery is the main part of the electrical system in an automobile. Without the battery, the engine cannot be started with the starting motor. The battery supplies current for operation of the starting motor and the ignition system when the engine is being cranked for starting. It also supplies current for light, radio, heater and several other accessory units when the generator is not operating fast enough to handle the electrical load.

The battery is most often in the engine compartment. Most batteries are visible and accessible for inspection and service. If the battery and its large cable connections are not clearly visible, remote terminals are located under the hood for battery testing and jump-starting.

Most batteries today are the sealed, maintenance-free kind. These batteries are not completely sealed and airtight, however. They have small vents to release gases as the battery is charged or discharged. Maintenance-free batteries do not have removable caps or covers for their cells. Although maintenance-free batteries are more common today, the older style with removable cell covers is still in use on many vehicles.

Every automotive battery will eventually die. It's just a question of when. Proper battery maintenance can assure that its life is long and productive.

Visual Inspection

Examine the battery for signs of leakage, cracked case or top, corrosion, missing vent plugs, and loose or missing hold-down clamps. Leakage signs, which could indicate a cracked battery case, include white corrosion on the battery carrier, fender inner panel, or the car frame. If the top of the battery is covered with corrosion and the battery needs water frequently, the battery probably is being overcharged. Check the charging system.

The most common cause of a cracked top is improper installation. If the wrong wrench is used to remove or tighten the cable clamps, the battery top may be broken.

The most common cause of a cracked case is excessive tightening of the battery hold-down clamps. Also, a front-end crash, even if so minor that little damage is done to the sheet metal, may crack the battery case.

Cleaning Corrosion

Batteries work best when they're clean. Over time, an accumulation of dirt, battery acid and other stuff will build up on the top and sides of the battery. In addition to being an unsightly mess, this accumulation can provide a path to ground for the battery's stored voltage. While this may not represent a significant problem for a car that's driven regularly, a crusty battery can discharge more quickly than a clean one, possibly causing a no-start when the customer decides to drive a seldom-used vehicle.

Battery terminals and cable clamps will also develop corrosion over time. At least one source of the corrosion is the small amount of outgassing through the battery vents that takes place when the battery is in use. These gases condense into liquid form on the top of the battery, coating any unprotected surface. If this coating is not removed, large blossoms of corrosion on the terminal clamps are the end result. Corroded terminals and clamps cause a voltage drop at the connection, which reduces the available voltage flowing both to and from the battery. This can cause both charging and starting problems.

A mixture of baking soda and water can be used to neutralize and clean the corrosion accumulation from the top of the battery. Use a wire brush to clean a heavy accumulation on the clamps. To ensure a satisfactory electrical connection, remove the battery clamps, then clean them and the terminals with a tool designed for this purpose. After cleaning the terminals, coat them with an anti-corrosion compound to retard additional corrosion.

Rock Steady

The battery may be filled with lead, but that doesn't mean it's unbreakable. The hold-down brackets and rods must hold the battery firmly in place so it doesn't vibrate excessively or bounce around inside the engine compartment every time the vehicle hits a bump. Its internal plates may be dislodged or damaged due to inadequate battery mounting. This will shorten the battery's life.

Steady Voltage

The main job of the battery is to store power used by the starter motor to crank the engine. Once the engine starts, the alternator takes over to supply the vehicle's electrical needs, and the battery goes back to waiting for its next starting job. While it's waiting, the battery needs a steady voltage supply.

The voltage regulator assures that enough voltage is supplied to the battery to keep it as close as possible to a full charge at all times. Too much voltage will overheat and damage the battery, shortening its life span. If too little, the battery will not be able to provide enough power to the starter to crank the engine.

Properly Filled

Many maintenance-free batteries are sealed, but there are still plenty of conventional batteries that need to have the electrolyte level checked during routine maintenance. Simply unscrew the battery caps or remove the covers to check the level. On most batteries, the proper level will be indicated by a lip below the cap opening that's built into the battery's top cover.

Add distilled water to restore the proper level, if necessary. Don't overfill. Tap water should be avoided, as it may contain minerals that will shorten battery life. A battery that seems to be going through more electrolyte than normal may be giving you an early sign that it's on its last legs.

If your battery is the more common maintenance-free type, it may have an electrolyte indicator, or "eye," mounted in the top of the case. The eye indicates the general state of charge of the battery by indicating the approximate electrolyte level. A fully charged battery with electrolyte at the correct level will have a colored eye, usually green, sometimes red. A discharged battery will have a black or a clear eye. Do not try to recharge a maintenance-free battery if the indicator eye is clear. The electrolyte level is too low to safely charge the battery.

New Words

accessory	[əkˈsesəri]	n.	附件,附属品
generator	[ˈdʒenəreitə]	n.	发电机

vent	[vent]	n.	通风孔,透气口
charge	[tʃɑːdʒ]	v.	充电
discharge	[dis'tʃɑːdʒ]	v.	放电
cell	[sel]	n.	蓄电池单格,电池
acid	['æsid]	n.	酸
outgassing	[ˌautˈgæsiŋ]	n.	腐蚀性气体
coat	[kəut]	v.	涂上,覆盖
neutralize	['njuːtrəlaiz]	v.	使失效,抵消,使中和
dislodge	[dis'lɔdʒ]	v.	移出,移走
mounting	['mauntiŋ]	n.	托架,座架,衬垫物
electrolyte	[i'lektrəlait]	n.	电解液

Phrases and Expressions

starting motor	起动机
remote terminal	远置式接线柱
jump-starting	跨接启动
maintenance-free	免维护的
cable clamp	接线夹
baking soda	苏打水
rock steady	安装牢靠
properly filled	(保持)正常的电解液液面高度
electrolyte level	电解液液面高度
distilled water	蒸馏水
tap water	自来水

Notes to the Text

1. If the battery and its large cable connections are not clearly visible, remote terminals are located under the hood for battery testing and jump-starting.
   如果无法很清楚地看到蓄电池和与之连接的导线,则采用位于发动机罩下面的远置式接线柱进行蓄电池的检测和跨接启动。

2. Over time, an accumulation of dirt, battery acid and other stuff will build up on the top and sides of the battery. In addition to being an unsightly mess, this accumulation can provide a path to ground for the battery's stored voltage.
   随着时间的流逝,在蓄电池的顶部和侧面会形成一层聚集物,主要是灰尘、蓄电池酸液以及其他物质。这层聚集物不仅仅是一些看不见的污垢,而且还为蓄电池存储的电压提供了一条通往地下的通道。

3. A battery that seems to be going through more electrolyte than normal may be giving you an

early sign that it's on its last legs.

如果蓄电池耗用的电解液比正常情况下多,这意味着它接近了它的使用寿命。

Exercises

I. Translate the following names of cars into Chinese.
1. Subaru _____   2. Hino _____
3. Suzuki _____   4. Yelong _____
5. Eunos _____   6. Isuzu _____
7. SEAT _____   8. Picasso _____

II. Translate the following abbreviations into corresponding Chinese terms.
1. ICM (ignition control module) _____
2. DLI (distributorless ignition) _____
3. DI (distributor ignition) _____
4. IT (ignition timing) _____
5. C3I (computer controlled coil ignition) _____
6. PW (primary winding) _____

Section C   Dialogue   At the Auto Beauty Shop

The following dialogue took place at an auto beauty shop (See Fig. 7 – 2).

Fig. 7 – 2   Auto Beauty

Assistant(A): Good afternoon, Madam. Is there anything I can help you with?
Customer(C): Oh, I bought a car ten days ago. This is the first time that I have come to your

shop. What kinds of service do you offer?

A: We offer car washing (by hand or by machine) and waxing. Common maintenance of cars is also offered here. And we have various kinds of interior ornaments for customers to choose.

C: Do you guarantee quality?

A: Don't worry about it, Madam. Providing quality service is always our top priority. All our workers are experts in washing, waxing and common maintenance of cars. The materials used and the interior ornaments offered are of high quality.

C: Generally, how often should a car be washed?

A: Cars should be washed once every month at least. During the washing, pressure water is used to remove the dirt from all the areas where dirt and salt may be accumulated and wash is difficult to reach.

C: How about waxing?

A: You'd better have your car waxed at least once three or four months. Waxing helps to protect the paint from sun and chemicals. Besides, it can make your car look shiny.

C: How long will it take?

A: It will take you at least half an hour to have the whole car waxed. But the high quality car wax can stay on your car for three or four months.

C: Oh, I'm afraid I don't have much time to have my car waxed today. I'll come when I'm free. Now, just have my car washed, please.

A: OK. A complete clean-up?

C: No, just exterior, please.

A: Washing by hand or by machine?

C: I think a hand wash will do. When will it be ready?

A: In about fifteen minutes.

C: How much should I pay?

A: Fifteen yuan...

Useful Expressions and Sentences

1. At the Auto Beauty Shop
   在汽车美容店
2. Is there anything I can help you with?
   有什么我可以为您效劳的吗?
3. What kinds of service do you offer?
   您提供什么服务项目?
4. We offer car washing (by hand or by machine) and waxing.
   我们提供车子的清洗(手洗或机洗)和打蜡。

wax [wæks] *n.* 蜡 *v.* 打蜡

5. Common maintenance of cars is also offered here.
   我们这里还提供车子的常规保养。

6. We have various kinds of interior ornaments for customers to choose.
   我们有各种各样的内饰供顾客选用。
   interior [in'tiəriə] *a.* 内的,内部的   *n.* 内部,内景,内地
   ornament ['ɔːnəmənt] *n.* 装饰(物),修饰(品) *v.* 装饰,美化

7. Do you guarantee quality?
   你们保证质量吗?
   guarantee [ˌɡærən'tiː] *n.* 保证(书) *v.* 保证,担保
   quality ['kwɔliti] *n.* 质量

8. Providing quality service is always our top priority.
   提供优质的服务一向是我们的宗旨。
   priority [prai'ɔrəti] *n.* 重点,优先

9. All our workers are experts in washing, waxing and common maintenance of cars.
   我们的工人都是汽车清洗、打蜡及常规保养方面的专家。

10. The materials used and the interior ornaments offered are of high quality.
    所使用的材料和所提供的内饰都是优质的。

11. Generally, how often should a car be washed?
    一般多长时间洗一次车?

12. Cars should be washed once every month at least.
    每个月至少应该洗一次车。

13. During the washing, pressure water is used to remove the dirt from all the areas where dirt and salt may be accumulated and wash is difficult to reach.
    在洗车过程中,使用增压水把污垢和盐分可能堆积以及较难清洗的所有地方的污垢去除掉。

14. You'd better have your car waxed at least once three or four months.
    您最好至少每三四个月给车打一次蜡。

15. Waxing helps to protect the paint from sun and chemicals.
    打蜡有助于保护车漆不受阳光和化学物质的侵蚀。

16. Besides, it can make your car look shiny.
    此外,打蜡还能使你的车看起来有光泽。

17. How long will it take?
    打蜡要花多长时间?

18. It will take you at least half an hour to have the whole car waxed.
    整车打蜡至少需要半个小时。

19. But the high quality car wax can stay on your car for three or four months.
    但高质量的蜡能够在车上保持三四个月。

20. I'm afraid I don't have much time to have my car waxed today.

恐怕今天我没时间给车打蜡。
21. I'll come when I'm free。
    我有时间的时候再来。
22. A complete clean-up.
    彻底清洗（全套洗）
23. Just exterior, please.
    请只洗外部。
    exterior [eksˈtiəriə] a. 外部的,外面的,外表的 n. 外部,表面,外表
24. I think a hand wash will do.
    我想手洗就可以了。

Test (Unit 1 – Unit 7)

I. Vocabulary (10 points, 1 point for each).
   Directions: In each of the sentences below, there is one underlined word or phrase. Below each sentence are four other words or phrases, marked (A), (B), (C), and (D). You are to choose one word or phrase that best keeps the meaning of the original sentence if it is substituted for the underlined word or phrase.

1. There are several methods used to replace the points and condenser in order to trigger the coil to fire.
   (A) cure   (B) use   (C) cause   (D) relieve
2. For optimum engine operation, the cooling system must regulate engine temperature within a precise and narrow range.
   (A) control   (B) raise   (C) take   (D) lower
3. The No. 1 Auto Plant turned out the first batch of liberation automobiles for our country.
   (A) published   (B) produced   (C) sold   (D) advertised
4. The cooling system removes excessive heat from the engine components.
   (A) overdue   (B) oversize   (C) overmuch   (D) overweight
5. No engine can work well without suitable operating temperatures.
   (A) beautiful   (B) charming   (C) appropriate (D) elegant
6. The engine can work effectively only when the heat energy is equally handled so as to keep the engine temperature in balance.
   (A) controlled (B) put up with (C) improved   (D) coped with
7. The headmaster managed to compress ten pages of his speech into three paragraphs.
   (A) change   (B) condense   (C) produce   (D) extend
8. The amount of fuel delivered by the injector depends on the amount of time that the nozzle is open.
   (A) is keen on (B) is in need of (C) relies on (D) is in store for
9. The exhaust system also serves to silence the exhaust noise; and, in most cases, reduce the pollutants in the exhaust.
   (A) frighten   (B) quiet   (C) shock   (D) attract
10. The term "stroke" refers to piston movement within the cylinder.
    (A) action   (B) performance (C) operation   (D) motion

II. Word form (10 points, 1 point for each).
    Directions: Fill in the blanks with the words given in the brackets, and change the form where necessary.

1. There are several methods to test the _____ (operate) of the fuel injectors.
2. In the 4-stroke engine, four strokes of the piston in the cylinder _____ (require) to complete one full operating cycle.
3. The _____ (big) the exhaust pipes of an exhaust system are, the better, because exhaust gases can take their exit more freely that way.
4. The current _____ (flow) through the primary winding of the ignition coil produces a magnetic field in the coil.
5. A very important purpose of engine oil is to lubricate engine parts to _____ (reduce) friction and wear.
6. The cooling water _____ (use) in cooling systems is called coolant.
7. The purpose of the muffler is to reduce engine exhaust noise to an _____ (accept) level.
8. The tendency to form injector deposits _____ (vary) considerably depending on the fuel.
9. The origin of the automobile cannot _____ (attribute) to one person.
10. The fuel cap on the fuel tank is used to keep the fuel from _____ (splash) out.

III. Usage of prepositions (10 points, 1 point for each).

Directions: Fill in the following blanks with proper prepositions.

1. The main section of a piston is known _____ the piston skirts.
2. No engine can work well _____ suitable operating temperatures.
3. The ignition coil is composed _____ a primary winding, secondary winding and core of soft iron.
4. On January 29, 1886, Karl Benz from Germany applied _____ a patent for his tricycle.
5. _____ the event the filter gets clogged, a bypass valve is provided so that oil will continue to reach the bearings.
6. The body is generally divided _____ four sections — the front, the upper or top, the rear and the underbody.
7. The piston head or "crown" is the top surface _____ which the explosive force is exerted.
8. As fuel is burned in the engine, about one-third of the heat energy in the fuel is converted _____ power.
9. A plug in the bottom of the oil pan is used to drain the oil _____ required intervals.
10. Many parts of the engine are attached by fastening devices _____ the block.

IV. Reading Comprehension (20 points, 1 point for each blank).

Directions: Read the following passages carefully and fill in the blanks with the words and phrases provided below.

Passage One (10 points, 1 point for each blank)

    lowering   depend   choke   leaving   vital

  give off   obtained   stroke   case   dual

  The exhaust system is __1__ to any vehicle because the life and performance of the vehicle's engine __2__ on it. So, some vehicles run on __3__ exhaust systems. In a dual exhaust system, the engines of such vehicles can __4__ exhaust gases more freely, thereby __5__ the back pressure which is inherent in an exhaust system. An engine cannot function well if there is back pressure trapped in it. Trapped exhaust gases __6__ an engine and stop it from doing productive work. As a result, the vehicle cannot run smoothly and silently, or in the worst __7__, will not run at all. With a dual exhaust system, a sizable increase in engine horsepower can be __8__ because the "breathing" capacity of the engine is improved, __9__ less exhaust gases in the engine at the end of each exhaust __10__.

Passage Two (10 points, 1 point for each blank)

  cylinders   converting   mechanical   internal   perform
  term   propel   friction   transmission   motion

  The motor vehicle engine is basically a device for __1__ the internal energy stored in its fuel into __2__ energy. It is classified as an __3__ combustion engine by virtue of this energy conversion taking place within the engine __4__. Since the __5__ "energy" implies the capacity to __6__ work, the engine is thus able to __7__ the vehicle along the road and, within limits, overcome unwanted opposition to its __8__ arising from rolling __9__ and air drag. To facilitate this process, the engine is combined with a __10__ system.

V. Translation (40 points).
Part One (15 points)

  Directions: Translate the following passages into Chinese.

Passage One (7 points)

  The primary purpose of the suspension system is to support the weight of the vehicle. The basic job of the suspension system is to absorb the shocks caused by irregular road surfaces that would otherwise be transmitted to the vehicle and its occupants, thus helping to keep the vehicle on a controlled and level course, regardless of road conditions.

Passage Two (8 points)

  The automobiles now running on streets are so various in style and design that you can hardly imagine what the automobiles looked like one hundred years ago. With the development of auto industry, automobiles have been changed greatly and remodeled from time to time. But however different the auto models, automobiles are basically the same in structure. In other words, any automobile is composed of four sections such as the engine, chassis, body and electrical system.

Part Two (15 points, 3 points for each sentence)

Directions: Translate the following sentences into English.
1. 电器系统向汽车提供照明和驱动的电力。
2. 电子点火系统提供更好的点火性能及发动机性能;同时,与传统的点火系统相比,只需要相当少的维护。
3. 安装在散热器顶部的散热器盖被用来调节冷却系的压力。
4. 在发动机的所有工况下,电子燃油喷射系统均能提供一个正确的空燃比。
5. 进气预热阀用以在冷起动热机时限制废气。

Part Three (5 points, 0.5 point for each)

Directions: Translate the following names of cars into Chinese.
1. BMW　　　　　　　＿＿＿＿＿＿＿＿＿＿
2. Chevrolet　　　　　＿＿＿＿＿＿＿＿＿＿
3. Mazda　　　　　　＿＿＿＿＿＿＿＿＿＿
4. Porsche　　　　　＿＿＿＿＿＿＿＿＿＿
5. Bluebird　　　　　＿＿＿＿＿＿＿＿＿＿
6. General Motor　　＿＿＿＿＿＿＿＿＿＿
7. Mitsubishi　　　　＿＿＿＿＿＿＿＿＿＿
8. Lincoln　　　　　 ＿＿＿＿＿＿＿＿＿＿
9. Volkswagen　　　＿＿＿＿＿＿＿＿＿＿
10. Corolla　　　　　＿＿＿＿＿＿＿＿＿＿

Part Four (5 points, 1 point for each)

Directions: Translate the following abbreviations into corresponding Chinese terms.
1. VIN (vehicle identification number)　　＿＿＿＿＿＿＿＿＿＿
2. TDC (top dead center)　　＿＿＿＿＿＿＿＿＿＿
3. EFI (electronic fuel injection)　　＿＿＿＿＿＿＿＿＿＿
4. LLC (long-life coolant)　　＿＿＿＿＿＿＿＿＿＿
5. IT (ignition timing)　　＿＿＿＿＿＿＿＿＿＿

VI. Error correction (10 points, 2 points for each).

Directions: In each of the sentences below, there are four underlined words or phrases marked A, B, C, and D. You are to choose the one that is wrong, write it in the bracket and correct the word or phrase on the line.

1. The pump transfers the fuel oil from the fuel tank in the carburetor.
　　A　　　　　　B　　　　　C　　　　　　　　D

　　　　　　　　　　　　　　　　　　　　　　　　　(　　)＿＿＿＿＿＿

2. In spite of their priority, neither Daimler or Benz made cars in any significant numbers for
      A   B   C   D
   many years.
                                                                                                                        (   )

3. The auto industry in China did not start till the 1950s.
        A   B C D
                                                                                                       (   )

4. It is the up and down action of a piston in the cylinder which produces power in a reciprocating
       A   B   C   D
   engine.

5. The engine block is made up of cast iron or aluminum.
        A   B   C   D
                                                                                     (   )

Unit Eight

Section A Clutch

The function of the clutch when used in an automotive application is to connect or disconnect the power from the engine's crankshaft with or from the gearbox and transmission. A properly maintained clutch should perform this operation smoothly, positively, and quietly; a good clutch must slip while being engaged to allow gradual take-up of the load transfer, yet must not slip when it is fully engaged.

When the clutch is engaged (foot off the clutch pedal), the power from the engine can flow through the clutch to the transmission. However, the vehicle will not move unless the transmission is in gear. Engagement of the engine and transmission provides the necessary linkup of the engine and the drivetrain that permits power to transfer to the driving axles and wheels. After engagement, the clutch must continue to transmit all the engine torque to the transmission without slippage.

When the clutch is disengaged (foot on the pedal), it provides the means of disconnecting the engine from the drivetrain, and no power can flow through it to the transmission, therefore power transfer stops. This of course is required anytime when a gear selection or shift is desired.

The type of clutches that we will be discussing depends on friction for their operation; therefore, they are commonly called friction clutches.

The major parts of the clutch include the flywheel, clutch disc, cover assembly, pressure plate, release bearing, and clutch linkage. Other parts which make up the clutch assembly are the transmission input shaft and the clutch housing (See Fig. 8-1).

The flywheel provides a base for the starter ring gear, and also forms the foundation on which the other clutch parts are attached. The surface of the flywheel that mates with the clutch discs is machined smooth. For the clutch to work properly, the flywheel must be perpendicular to the crankshaft with very little allowable runout.

The clutch disc (or driven disc) contains a circular metal plate attached to a reinforced splined hub. Often the hub is mounted on coil springs to provide cushioned engagements. The splined hub is free to slide lengthwise along the splines of the transmission input shaft. When engaged, the clutch disc drives the input shaft through these splines. The clutch disc operates in

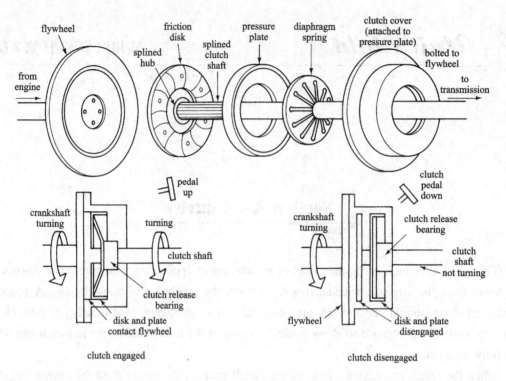

Fig. 8-1 A clutch

conjunction with a pressure plate or a clutch cover. In its operating position in the engine-transmission linkup, the clutch disc is sandwiched between the machined face of the flywheel and the clutch pressure plate.

The clutch cover assembly contains the pressure plate, springs, and other parts according to the design of the clutch. The cover is bolted to the flywheel and rotates with it at crankshaft speed.

The pressure plate is machined smooth on the side facing the engine and driven disc (or discs) and is itself driven by pins or lugs on the clutch cover. The plate is free to slide back and forth on the pins or lugs, and when spring pressure is applied to the plate, it meshes with the driven friction plates sandwiched between it and the flywheel. If the clutch has two driven discs, an intermediate, or center plate will separate the discs. The plate is machined smooth on both sides since it is pressed between two friction surfaces.

Between the cover and the pressure plate are springs. Depending on the design of the clutch, any number of coil springs might be used to force the plate against the driven discs, or the clutch might utilize a single diaphragm spring.

Engagement and disengagement of the clutch assembly are controlled by a foot pedal and linkage that must be properly adjusted and relatively easy to apply. The clutch linkage connects the clutch pedal to the clutch fork. The clutch fork and linkage provide the means of converting the up-and-down movement of the clutch pedal into the back-and-forth movement of the clutch release bearing assembly. The clutch release bearing, in most cases, is a ball bearing assembly with a machined face on one side that is designed to contact the pressure plate diaphragm release fingers during disengagement. Most clutches on heavy-duty vehicles are controlled by a mechanical linkage between the clutch pedal and the release bearing. Some vehicles have hydraulic clutch controls.

The transmission, pressure plate, flywheel, clutch disc, flywheel housing, and crankshaft must be properly aligned to prevent slippage, vibration, and noise.

Double Clutch

A double clutch is a driving procedure primarily used for vehicles with an unsynchronized manual transmission. The double clutching technique involves the following steps:

- The throttle (accelerator) is released, and the clutch pedal is pressed, and the gearbox is shifted into neutral.
- The clutch pedal is then released, and the driver matches the engine RPM to the gear RPM either using the throttle (accelerator) (when changing down) or waiting for RPM to decrease (when changing up) until they are at a level suitable for shifting into the next gear.
- At the moment when the revs between the engine and gear are closely matched, the driver then instantly presses the clutch again to shift into the next gear. The whole maneuver can, with practice, take no more than a fraction of a second, and the result is a very smooth gear change.

The purpose of the double-clutch technique is to aid in matching the rotational speed of the input shaft being driven by the engine to the rotational speed of the gear you wish to select (directly connected to rotating wheels). When the speeds are matched, the gear will engage smoothly and no clutch is required. If the speeds are not matched, the dog teeth on the collar will "crash" or grate as they attempt to fit into the holes on the desired gear. A modern synchromesh gearbox accomplishes this synchronization more efficiently. However, when the engine speed is significantly different from the transmission speed, the desired gear can often not be engaged even in a fully synchronized gearbox. An example is trying to shift into a gear while travelling beyond the gear's speed or directional range, such as accidentally into 1st from near the top of 2nd, or intentionally from reverse to a forward gear while still moving at speed.

Double clutching, although time consuming, eases gear selection when an extended delay or variance exists between engine and transmission speeds.

New Words

engagement	[in'geidʒmənt]	n.	连接,啮合
linkup	['liŋkʌp]	n.	连接,会合
drivetrain	['draivtrein]	n.	传动系统
slippage	['slipidʒ]	n.	打滑,滑动,空转
disengage	[disin'geidʒ]	v.	分离,脱离,解除
mate	[meit]	v.	(使)紧密配合
perpendicular	[ˌpəːpən'dikjulə]	a.	垂直的,成直角的

		n.	垂直,铅垂线
cushioned	[ˈkuʃənd]	a.	有弹性垫的
lengthwise	[ˈleŋθwaiz]	adv.	纵向地
spline	[splain]	n.	齿条,齿槽
sandwich	[ˈsænwidʒ]	v.	夹入
intermediate	[ˌintəːˈmiːdjət]	a.	中间的
diaphragm	[ˈdaiəfræm]	n.	隔膜,隔板,膜片
linkage	[ˈliŋkidʒ]	n.	联动装置
align	[əˈlain]	v.	排列,定位
synchronize	[ˈsiŋkrənaiz]	v.	(使)同步,(使)同时发生,(使)同速
maneuver	[məˈnuːvə]	n.	调动,演习
fraction	[ˈfrækʃən]	n.	(数学中的)分数,小数,(of)小部分,少量,一点儿
grate	[greit]	v.	发出刺耳的摩擦声,磨碎

Phrases and Expressions

clutch pedal	离合器踏板
in gear	啮合的,处于啮合的
driving axle	驱动桥,驱动轴,主动轴
gear selection	挡位选择
gear shift	换挡,换挡机构
clutch disc (or driven disc)	离合器盘,离合器从动盘
cover assembly	外壳总成
pressure plate	压盘,压力板
release bearing	分离轴承
clutch housing	离合器壳
input shaft	输入轴
starter ring gear	(与起动机啮合的)飞轮齿圈
reinforced splined hub	加强花键轮毂
coil spring	螺旋弹簧
in conjunction with	与……共同,连同
clutch cover	离合器盖
diaphragm spring	(离合器)膜片弹簧
clutch fork	离合器分离叉
ball bearing assembly	球轴承总成
machined face	已加工面
diaphragm release finger	膜片分离销

double clutch	双离合器
synchromesh gearbox	同步器换挡变速器
rev	转速,发动机的旋转

Notes to the Text

1. The clutch disc operates in conjunction with a pressure plate or clutch cover.
   离合器盘连同离合器压盘或离合器外壳一起工作。
2. Engagement and disengagement of the clutch assembly are controlled by a foot pedal and linkage that must be properly adjusted and relatively easy to apply.
   离合器总成的接合与分离由调节适当并易于使用的脚踏板及联动装置控制。

Exercises on the Text

I. Answer the following questions according to the text.

1. What's the function of the clutch?
2. Please name the major parts that make up the clutch.
3. What roles does the flywheel play in the clutch?
4. What's the function of the pressure plate?
5. What are the engagement and disengagement of the clutch assembly controlled by?

II. Fill in the table below (Tab. 8 – 1).

Tab. 8 – 1

English	Chinese
	离合器
drivetrain	
	联动装置
engagement	
	压盘
release bearing	
	弹簧
clutch disc	
	离合器踏板
cover assembly	

III. Fill in the blanks with the words or phrases given below, and change the form where necessary.

| make up | spring | require | flywheel |
| transmit | mount | connect | sandwich |

1. The _____ forms the foundation to which the other clutch parts are attached.
2. The clutch linkage _____ the clutch pedal to the clutch fork.
3. _____ are between the cover and the pressure plate.
4. When spring pressure is applied to the plate, it meshes with the driven friction plates _____ between it and the flywheel.
5. Other parts which _____ the clutch assembly are the transmission input shaft and the clutch housing.
6. The clutch must _____ all the engine torque to the transmission without slippage.
7. When the speeds are matched, the gear will engage smoothly and no clutch _____.
8. The hub _____ on coil springs to provide cushioned engagements.

IV. Reading comprehension: read the following passage carefully and fill in the blanks with the words given below.

| counterparts | torque | fuel | bathed | outputs |
| fundamental | losses | dry | generate | suitable |

There are two __1__ types of clutches used in dual-clutch transmissions: either two wet multi-plate clutches which are __2__ in oil (for cooling), or two __3__ single-plate clutches. The wet clutch design is generally used for higher torque engines which can __4__ 350 newton metres and more (the wet multi-plate clutch DCT in the Bugatti Veyron is designed to cope with 1,250 N·m), whereas the dry clutch design is generally __5__ for smaller vehicles with lower torque __6__ up to 250 N·m. However, whilst the dry clutch variants may be limited in __7__ compared with their wet clutch __8__, the dry clutch variants offer an increase in __9__ efficiency, due to the lack of pumping __10__ of the transmission fluid in the clutch housing.

V. Translate the following passage into Chinese.

The clutch disc (or driven disc) contains a circular metal plate attached to a reinforced splined hub. Often the hub is mounted on coil springs to provide cushioned engagements. The splined hub is free to slide lengthwise along the splines of the transmission input shaft. When engaged, the clutch disc drives the input shaft through these splines. The clutch disc operates in conjunction with a pressure plate or a clutch cover. In its operating position in the engine/transmission linkup, the clutch disc is sandwiched between the engine flywheel and the clutch pressure plate.

VI. Translate the following sentences into English.
1. 离合器是一种用以连接或分离发动机和手动换挡变速器的摩擦装置。
2. 发动机必须快速转动才能推动车辆前进。
3. 离合器的主要作用就是辅助车辆启动。
4. 离合器盘连同离合器压盘或离合器外壳一起工作。
5. 离合器分离叉和联动装置把离合器踏板的上下运动转变为离合器分离轴承总成的前后运动。

Section B Clutch Troubleshooting

Due to the variety of clutch models and manufacturers, a problem in one clutch may not necessarily reflect the same symptom in another. However, the majority of common clutch problems listed in the following table (See Tab. 8 – 2) can be applied to clutches generally.

Tab. 8 – 2

Chattering	
Problems	Remedies
Release levers not parallel	Adjust to correct height
Loose, broken, or worn engine mounts	Tighten or replace
Pedal linkage worn	Replace linkage
Oil or grease on facing	Install new facings
Improper disc facing thickness	Install correct disc assembly
Glazed facing	Replace disc assembly or facing
Warped or bent friction disc assembly	Replace driven disc
Loose rivet or rivets in disc facing	Replace disc facing or assembly
Worn pilot bearing	Replace pilot bearing
Misalignment	Realign
Loose or cracked clutch cover	Tighten or replace
Wrong spring pressure in cover	Replace with correct cover assembly
Grabbing	
Problems	Remedies
Worn or binding release levers	Replace or repair clutch assembly
Improper facing material	Install proper disc

To be continued

Grabbing	
Problems	Remedies
Warped friction disc, or hub splines worn	Replace driven disc assembly
Worn clutch shaft splines	Replace clutch shaft
Worn or loose pedal linkage	Replace or tighten
Loose engine mounts	Tighten or replace
Loose clutch assembly on flywheel	Tighten retaining bolts
Excessive backlash in powertrain	Adjust or replace worn parts
Slipping	
Problems	Remedies
Oil or grease on friction disc facings	Replace facings or install new driven disc assembly; correct oil leak
Loose, worn, or burned facings	Replace facings, or install new driven disc assembly
Flywheel burned, checked, or cracked	Replace or resurface
Insufficient pressure plate force	Weak or broken pressure springs
Improper adjustments	Adjust clutch and linkage
Binding release levers or pedal linkage	Adjust, lubricate, or repair
Improper facing material	Use correct facing, or replace friction disc assembly
Driver riding clutch pedal	Proper driver training
Dragging	
Problems	Remedies
Worn or loose pedal linkage	Replace or tighten
Loose, worn, or broken facing	Replace friction disc assembly
Friction facing too thick	Install proper driven disc assembly
Warped or bent disc or pressure plate assembly	Replace faulty components
Excessive pedal free-play	Adjust to correct free-play
Broken or loose engine mounts	Tighten or replace
Excessive engine idle speed	Adjust to correct rpm
Oil or grease on facings (gummy clutch)	Replace friction disc assembly
Release bearing sticking	Lubricate or replace
Worn friction disc hub splines	Replace friction disc assembly
Worn or rusty splines on clutch shaft	Repair or replace shaft
Improper pressure plate or driven member	Replace with correct assembly

To be continued

Hard Pedal	
Problems	Remedies
Worn pedal linkage	Replace worn parts
Binding pedal linkage	Lubricate, repair, or adjust
Excessive spring pressure in clutch cover assembly	Replace with correct assembly
Contact pad of release bearing carrier worn by the shifter yoke	Replace carrier and shifter yoke. Check for proper hookup to provide best linkage operating positions
Rattling Clutch	
Problems	Remedies
Damaged pressure plate	Repair or replace
Worn release bearing	Replace bearing
Dry or worn pilot bearing	Replace bearing
Unequal contact of release levers	Adjust to correct height
Excessive backlash in the transmission or propeller shaft	Repair or replace affected items
Warped driven member	Replace friction disc assembly
Incorrect friction disc	Replace with correct assembly
Vibration	
Problems	Remedies
Improper balance of clutch assembly	Ensure that clutch components are properly assembled and that balance marks are aligned
Improper clutch alignment	Check alignment
Worn clutch shaft splines	Replace clutch shaft
Badly worn crankshaft bearings	Replace bearings
Worn friction disc hub splines	Replace disc assembly
Worn or loose engine mounts	Tighten or replace

New Words

chatter	['tʃætə]	v.	振动,震颤
remedy	['remidi]	n.	补救(法),纠正(法)
		v.	补救,纠正,改善
bind	[baind]	v.	卡住,结合
grease	[gri:s]	n.	润滑脂,黄油,润滑油

rivet	[ˈrivit]	v.	铆,铆接
		n.	铆钉
misalignment	[misˈəlainmənt]	n.	未对准
grabbing	[ˈgræbiŋ]	n.	(汽车的)抖振,冲动现象(如猛抬离合器踏板时,汽车急剧抖动现象);抓住,钳住
backlash	[ˈbæklæʃ]	v.	发生后冲
		n.	后座,后冲
rattle	[ˈrætl]	v.	(使)发出咯咯声
		n.	咯咯声,吵闹声
dragging	[ˈdrægiŋ]	n.	拖,(离合器或液力传动分离不彻底引起的)缓慢拖带转动

Phrases and Expressions

release lever	(离合器压板)分离杆,放松杆
adjust to	调节,调整,校准,使适合
engine mount	发动机支座,发动机悬置
spring shackle	钢板弹簧吊环
pilot bearing	导向轴承
retaining bolt	定位螺栓,止动杆
ride clutch pedal	驾驶时脚一直踩在离合器踏板上,脱挡(踩离合器)滑行
hard pedal	制动踏板等的踩踏阻力过大过硬现象
free play	空转,空程,自由行程
shifter yoke	(换挡机构或变速器)换挡拨叉,变速叉

Exercises

I. Translate the following names of cars into Chinese.

1. Rolls-Royce _____   2. Jaguar _____
3. Aston Martin _____   4. Marcos _____
5. Triumph _____   6. Fooder _____
7. Vauxhall _____   8. MG _____

II. Translate the following abbreviations into corresponding Chinese terms.

1. CL (clutch) _____
2. CLSW (clutch switch) _____
3. CPC (clutch pressure control) _____
4. ACC (air conditioning clutch) _____

5. TCC (torque converter clutch) _____
6. CPU (central processing unit) _____

Section C General Motors Corporation

General Motors Corporation, also known as GM (Its logo is shown in Fig. 8 – 2.), is an American multinational automotive corporation headquartered in Detroit, Michigan (See Fig. 8 – 3). GM is the world's largest automaker and has been the global industry sales leader in each of the last 77 years.

Fig. 8 – 2   GM'S Logo

Fig. 8 – 3   GM headquarters in Detroit

The history of GM saw its beginning in 1908. The nucleus of the fledgling General Motors was the Buick Motor Car Company. It was formed in 1902 by David Buick in Detroit and later moved to Flint, Michigan, where William Crapo Durant, "king of the carriage makers," took control.

The shrewd businessman that he was, Durant realized that the future lay with cars and not carriages. Initially, the company was founded as a holding company for Buick. The latter part of the year saw the company acquiring Oldsmobile, followed by the possession of Cadillac in the very next year.

Many of the motor companies were in dire straits during the difficult years of the early 1900s. The stock market panic in 1907 put a lot of small companies into financial distress. Many of these companies were running on credit from various bankers. This was a golden opportunity for Durant, who proceeded to buy smaller car builders and companies that built car parts as well as car accessories. In 1908, these various companies were folded into a single unit, thus creating the new GM. This marked the exciting beginning of the true history of GM.

William Durant took GM both to its heights as well as plunged it into financial distress. In 1910, bankers were forced to step in to prevent financial collapse of GM, and Durant was removed from the company he had founded. But by 1911, the company had made enough advances into the international market and the General Motors Export Company was established to handle sales outside the US and Canada.

Durant managed to use another company he formed, Chevrolet, to come back to power in GM during 1915. The General Motors Company officially became General Motors Corporation on October 13, 1916. And the history of GM from 1915 to 1920 is full of successes.

During this time, the Cadillac became greatly successful. In 1918, GM bought the operating assets of Chevrolet Motors. But, soon America was hit by a power recession and in 1920, Durant again found himself out of the company.

During the financial boom in the 1920s, the history of GM glowed with success. Auto sales reached the 4.5 million Mark, and the auto industry now had three giants — GM, Ford and Chrysler. Alfred Sloan who was later acclaimed for his marketing genius had slowly worked his way up among the ranks of GM. His marketing genius breathed a new lease of life into GM that was beginning to get overshadowed by Ford.

Ford's philosophy was to give the public the best value for their money but it offered little variety, while Sloan and GM were interested in providing the public with more than a black box. Stylish colors, features and comfort became the new motto of the company. GM also made a path-breaking offer — the public could now buy a car on credit. The five brands of GM — Pontiac, Cadillac, Buick (See Fig. 8 - 4), Oldsmobile and Chevrolet (See Fig. 8 - 5) began changing every year with the focus being directed mainly at looks and styles. This strategy got rich dividends. Ford was pushed to the backseat again by GM.

Fig. 8 - 4 Buick — Riviera

Fig. 8 - 5 Chevrolet — Corvette

The great Wall Street crash in 1929 put an abrupt stop to all expansion plans at GM for the time being. Stocks of GM fell rather badly. But, by the early 1930s, GM bounced back and bought the Yellow Coach bus company. In 1930, GM bought Electro-Motive Corporation, the internal combustion engine railcar builder. The next 20 years saw GM powered diesel locomotives running on American railroads. December 31, 1955 is another landmark in the history of GM. GM became the first company to make more than a billion dollars in a year.

There was a time in the history of GM when it was the largest corporation in the US. The history of GM also shows that there was a time when GM was the single largest employer in the world. But, in recent times GM has been beset with financial woes. The late-2000s financial recession pushed the corporation into a period of crisis. In November, 2005 GM suffered from a $4 billion loss, about 30,000 employees were laid off and 12 plants were closed down. Two successive US presidential administrations chose intervention for GM in order to prevent collapse of the North American segment of the automotive industry. In December 2008, US President George W. Bush agreed to a $13.4 billion bailout for General Motors; within months, an additional $39 billion was added by the Barack Obama administration. GM has returned to profitability, even posting a record annual profit in 2011.

With common engineering and manufacturing systems and common components, GM will be able to offer a greater variety of vehicles tailored to the needs and tastes of the customers in the various worldwide markets and build them with lower costs.

As John F. Smith, Jr., GM chief executive officer and president stated, "GM is changing its ways and will continue changing."

New Words

multinational	[ˌmʌltiˈnæʃn(ə)l]	a.	多国的,跨国(公司)的
headquarter	[hedˈkwɔːtə]	n.	总部
		vt.	设总部于……
nucleus	[ˈnjuːkliəs]	n.	核心
fledgling	[ˈfledʒliŋ]	n.	刚会飞的幼鸟,无经验的人
shrewd	[ʃruːd]	a.	敏捷的,精明的,狡猾的
initially	[iˈniʃəli]	adv.	最初,开始
dire	[ˈdaiə]	a.	可怕的,悲惨的
strait	[streit]	n.	海峡,(pl.)困境,窘迫
panic	[ˈpænik]	n.	惊慌,经济上的恐慌
distress	[disˈtres]	n.	苦恼,痛苦
		v.	使痛苦,使苦恼
credit	[ˈkredit]	n.	贷款
accessory	[ækˈsesəri]	n.	附属,附件,零件
asset	[ˈæset]	n.	(usu. pl.)资产,财产
recession	[riˈseʃən]	n.	(经济)衰退,后退
glow	[gləu]	vi.	炽热,发红光
acclaim	[əˈkleim]	v./n.	欢呼,喝彩,称赞
overshadow	[ˌəuvəˈʃædəu]	vt.	遮蔽,使阴(暗),使失色,夺去……的光辉
stylish	[ˈstailiʃ]	a.	时髦的,漂亮的
motto	[ˈmɔtəu]	n.	标语,座右铭,箴言
dividend	[ˈdividend]	n.	红利,股息,债息
abrupt	[əˈbrʌpt]	a.	突然的,意想不到的

diesel	[ˈdiːz(ə)l]	n.	柴油机
landmark	[ˈlændmɑːk]	n.	突出事件,划时代的事件,(人生的)里程碑
beset	[biˈset]	vt.	(beset, beset)困扰,围攻,包围
woe	[wəu]	n.	悲痛,苦恼
bailout	[ˈbeilaut]	n.	(公司所受的)紧急援助
tailor	[ˈteilə]	vt.	缝制(衣服),配合,适应

Phrases and Expressions

holding company	控股公司
plunge into	跳入,冲进
step in	干预,介入,插手(棘手问题)
a new lease of /on life	(由于病愈或烦恼消除等而)重生,富于希望的新生,精神焕发
direct at	把……对准,针对
for the time being	暂时
bounce back	(受挫折后)恢复元气
lay off	解雇,停止工作

Proper Names

David Buick	大卫·别克(1855—1929)(大卫·别克在1899年开始研制汽油发动机,并于1900年造出了第一辆别克车。1903年5月19日,大卫·别克在布里斯·科施蒂的帮助下创建了别克汽车公司。)
Flint	弗林特(弗林特是美国的五大湖区工业城市,密歇根州第七大城市,位于密歇根州东南部。早期以木材工业为主,1904年始建汽车工厂,是著名的汽车工业中心,有美国通用汽车公司的工厂群。)
William Crapo Durant	威廉·杜兰特(1861—1947)(美国通用汽车公司的缔造者,世界汽车发展史上第一位传奇人物。)
Alfred Sloan	阿尔弗雷德·斯隆(1875—1966)(第一位成功的职业经理人,20世纪最伟大的CEO,通用汽车公司的第八任总裁,事业部制组织结构的首创人。)
Wall Street crash in 1929	1929年美国金融危机(1929年10月24日,美国爆发了资本主义历史上最大的一次经济危机。在历经10年的大牛市后,美国金融界崩溃了,股票一夜之间从顶巅跌入深渊。一周之内,美国人在证券交易所内失去的财富达100亿美元。)

Oldsmobile	奥兹莫比尔
Cadillac	凯迪拉克
Chevrolet	雪佛兰
Chrysler	克莱斯勒
Pontiac	庞蒂克

Notes to the Text

1. The shrewd businessman that he was, Durant realized that the future lay with cars and not carriages.
   杜兰特是个精明的商人,他意识到将来的主要交通工具将是汽车而不是马车。
2. The stock market panic in 1907 put a lot of small companies into financial distress. Many of these companies were running on credit from various bankers.
   1907 年的股市危机使许多小公司陷入了经济萧条。这些公司只得靠银行贷款维持运营。
3. William Durant took GM both to its heights as well as plunged it into financial distress.
   威廉·杜兰特使通用公司达到巅峰,而也正是他使公司陷入低谷。
4. Alfred Sloan who was later acclaimed for his marketing genius had slowly worked his way up among the ranks of GM.
   被后人称为市场天才的阿尔弗雷德·斯隆在 GM 逐步崭露头角。
5. His marketing genius breathed a new lease of life into GM that was beginning to get overshadowed by Ford.
   正当通用公司在福特公司的影响下黯然失色时,他的市场天赋为通用公司注入了新的活力。
6. With common engineering and manufacturing systems and common components, GM will be able to offer a greater variety of vehicles tailored to the needs and tastes of the customers in the various worldwide markets and build them with lower costs.
   为了适应全球不同客户的需要和品味,拥有普通工程制造体系和产品部件的 GM 将以优惠的价格推出品种多样的汽车。

Questions for Discussion:
1. What marked the beginning of the true history of GM?
2. How did Durant come back to power in GM during 1915?
3. What are the three giants in the auto industry in the 1920s?
4. What was GM's motto?
5. Why was December 31, 1955 another landmark in the history of GM?

Unit Nine

△ 实用汽车英语(第2版)

Section A Transmission

There are several different types of transmissions used on vehicles today: manual transmissions, semi-automatic transmissions and fully automatic transmissions (including continuously variable transmissions, CVTs).

Manual Transmission

A transmission is a speed and power changing device installed at some point between the engine and driving wheels of the vehicle. It is used to change the ratio between engine rpm (revolutions per minute) and driving wheel rpm to best meet each particular driving condition.

The transmission consists of a housing, an input shaft and gear, an output shaft and gear, an idler shaft, a reverse gear, a cluster of gears and a gear shift mechanism.

Given a level road, an automobile without a transmission could be made to move by accelerating the engine and engaging the clutch. However, a start under these conditions would be slow, noisy and uncomfortable. In addition, it would place a tremendous strain on the engine and driving parts of the automobile.

So in order to get smooth starts and have power to pass and climb hills, a power ratio must be provided to multiply the torque and turning effort of the engine. Also required is a speed ratio to avoid the need for extremely high engine rpm at high road speeds. The transmission is geared to perform these functions.

The transmission gears are shifted by means of a gear shift mechanism. In first gear, the engine turns much faster in relation to the drive wheels, while in high gear the engine is loafing even though the car may be going in excess of 70 mph. Depending on the number of forward speeds there are three, four, and five-speed transmissions. In addition to the various forward gears, a transmission also has a neutral position which disconnects the engine from the drive wheels, and reverse, which causes the drive wheels to turn in the opposite direction allowing you to back up. Finally, there is the park position. In this position, a latch mechanism is inserted into a slot in the output shaft to lock the drive wheels and keep them from turning, thereby preventing the vehicle from rolling.

Semi-Automatic Transmission

The semi-automatic transmission, also called clutchless manual transmission, is a manual gearbox on which all operations normally performed by the driver when changing gear is carried out by the electronically controlled actuator system. At the heart of this system is an electromechanical actuator, which converts signals received from an electronic control unit into angular displacement of the clutch withdrawal fork. It uses electronic sensors, processors and actuators to do gear shifts on the command of the driver. This removes the need for a clutch pedal which the driver needs to depress before making a gear change, since the clutch itself is actuated by the electronic equipment which can synchronize the timing and torque required to make gear shifts quick and smooth.

A dual-clutch transmission (DCT), sometimes referred to as a twin-clutch gearbox or double-clutch transmission, is a type of semi-automatic or automated manual automotive transmission. It uses two separate clutches for odd and even gear sets. It can fundamentally be described as two separate manual transmissions (with their respective clutches) contained within one housing, and working as one unit. They are usually operated in a fully automatic mode, and many also have the ability to allow the driver to manually shift gears, although still carried out by the transmission's electro-hydraulics.

A dual-clutch transmission eliminates the torque converter as used in conventional epicyclic-geared automatic transmissions. Instead, dual-clutch transmissions that are currently on the market primarily use two oil-bathed wet multi-plate clutches, similar to the clutches used in most motorcycles, though dry clutch versions are also available.

In dual-clutch transmissions (DCTs) where the two clutches are arranged concentrically, the larger outer clutch drives the odd numbered gears, while the smaller inner clutch drives the even numbered gears. Shifts can be accomplished without interrupting torque distribution to the driven roadwheels, by applying the engine's torque to one clutch at the same time as it is being disconnected from the other clutch. Since alternate gear ratios can pre-select an odd gear on one gear shaft while the vehicle is being driven in an even gear, (and vice versa), DCTs are able to shift more quickly than cars equipped with single-clutch automated-manual transmissions (AMTs), or single-clutch semi-automatics. Also, with a DCT, shifts can be made more smoothly than with a single-clutch AMT, making a DCT more suitable for conventional road cars.

Automatic Transmission

An automatic transmission, usually referred to as fully automatic transmission, performs the drive-engagement and ratio selection (shifting) operations with no additional driver input. Unlike a semi-automatic transmission system, an automatic transmission completely relieves the driver of the duty of changing gear. The only thing the driver has to do after engaging a gear is to press the accelerator to go and to press the brake to stop. Nothing could be easier!

An automatic transmission has four basic systems: a gear system, a torque converter, a hydraulic system and an electronic system. Operation of the automatic transmission is similar for both front wheel drive and rear wheel drive vehicles (See Fig. 9 – 1).

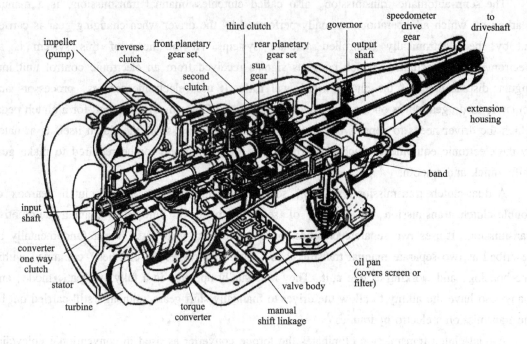

Fig. 9 – 1 An automatic transmission

Planetary Gear Set

Automatic transmissions contain many gears in various combinations. In a manual transmission, gears slide along shafts as you move the shift lever from one position to another, engaging various sized gears as required in order to provide the correct gear ratio. In an automatic transmission, however, the gears are never physically moved and are always engaged to the same gears. This is accomplished through the use of planetary gear sets, which are the mechanical systems that provide the various forward gear ratios as well as reverse.

There are three elements that make up one planetary gear system. The three elements are: an outer gear, with teeth cut into the inner surface; a sun gear, mounted on a shaft and located at the very center of the outer gear; and a set of four planet gears, meshing with both the sun gear and the outer gear. Either the outer gear or the sun gear may be held stationary, providing more than one possible torque multiplication factor for each set of gears. Also, if all three gears are forced to rotate at the same speed, the gear set forms, in effect, a solid shaft. Shifting is accomplished by changing the portion of each planetary gear set which is held to the case or to the shaft.

Torque Converter

On automatic transmissions, the torque converter replaces the conventional clutch. A torque converter consists of three internal elements that work together to transmit power to the transmission. The three basic elements of the torque converter are the pump (driving member), the turbine (driven member), and the stator (reaction member). The pump is mounted directly to the converter housing which in turn is bolted directly to the engine's crankshaft and turns at engine speed. The turbine is inside the housing and is connected directly to the input shaft of the transmission providing power to move the vehicle. The stator is mounted to a one-way clutch so that it can spin freely in one direction but not in the other. Each of the three elements has fins mounted in them to precisely direct the flow of oil through the converter.

With the engine running, transmission fluid is pulled into the pump section and is pushed outward by centrifugal force until it reaches the turbine section which starts it turning. The fluid continues in a circular motion back towards the center of the turbine where it enters the stator. If the turbine is moving considerably slower than the pump, the fluid will make contact with the front of the stator fins which push the stator into the one-way clutch and prevent it from turning. With the stator stopped, the fluid is directed by the stator fins to re-enter the pump at a "helping" angle providing a torque increase. As the speed of the turbine catches up with the pump, the fluid starts hitting the stator blades on the back-side causing the stator to turn in the same direction as the pump and turbine. As the speed increases, all three elements begin to turn at approximately the same speed.

Hydraulic System

The hydraulic system is a complex maze of passages and tubes that sends transmission fluid under pressure to all parts of the transmission and torque converter. Transmission fluid serves several purposes, including: shift control, general lubrication and transmission cooling. Every aspect of a transmission's functions depends on a constant supply of fluid under pressure. In fact, most of the components of a transmission are constantly submerged in fluid including the clutch packs and bands.

The transmission oil pump is responsible for producing all the oil pressure that is required in the transmission.

The valve body contains a maze of channels and passages that directs hydraulic fluid to the numerous valves which then activate the appropriate clutch pack or the band servo to smoothly shift to the appropriate gear for each driving situation.

Seals and gaskets are used to keep the oil where it is supposed to be and prevent it from leaking out.

Electronic Control System

Many new automatic transmissions are electronically controlled. On these units, electrical solenoids are used to better control the hydraulic fluid. Usually, the solenoids are regulated by an electronic control module. On modern cars, the line pressure, converter lockup, shift point and shift quality are all controlled by an electronic control unit (ECU).

Continuously Variable Transmission (CVT)

The continuously variable transmission (CVT) is a type of automatic transmissions that can change the gear ratio (gears are not generally involved) to any arbitrary setting within the limits. The CVT can respond instantly to throttle pressure, giving smooth and rapid acceleration. Its advantage over conventional fixed-ratio transmissions lies in the potential for enhancing performance and fuel economy while reducing exhaust emissions. The continuously variable transmission can operate mechanically (belt or friction-roller), hydraulically or electrically. Here, we give a brief introduction to the continuously variable mechanical transmission.

The major elements in the continuously variable mechanical transmission for passenger cars are: engagement mechanism for starting off, primary and secondary disks with axially adjustable taper-disk sections and power transfer via steel bands, electronic/hydraulic transmission control, reversing mode, and final drive unit with differential.

Instead of using gears, rotary motion can be transmitted from one shaft pulley to another by an endless flexible metal belt. It is the force of friction that compels the driving pulley to drive the belt and likewise the belt to rotate the driven pulley. This force of friction is derived from the contact pressure of the belt against the rims of the pulleys, which in turn is imposed by initial belt tension. The velocity ratio of a pulley drive is equal to the diameter of the driving pulley divided by the diameter of the driven pulley.

New Words

install	[in'stɔːl]	v.	安装,安置,装配
ratio	['reiʃiəu]	n.	比,比率
particular	[pə'tikjulə]	a.	特殊的,特别的,独特的
gear	[giə]	n.	齿轮
		v.	传动,使接上齿轮
reverse	[ri'vəːs]	v.	使倒退
accelerate	[ək'seləreit]	v.	加速,促进
strain	[strein]	n.	拉力,张力,应变
multiply	['mʌltiplai]	v.	成倍地增加,增加
loaf	[ləuf]	v.	游荡,运转
automate	['ɔːtəmeit]	v.	使自动化
odd	[ɔd]	a.	(数目)基数的,单数的
even	['iːvən]	a.	(数目)偶数的
mode	[məud]	n.	方式,样式
turbine	['təːbain]	n.	涡轮
stator	['steitə]	n.	定子,导轮
maze	[meiz]	n.	曲径,迷宫
submerge	[səb'məːdʒ]	v.	浸没,淹没
band	[bænd]	n.	带子,制动带子
servo	['səːvəu]	n.	伺服,伺服系统
coupling	['kʌpliŋ]	n.	耦合,耦合器,连接器

Phrases and Expressions

manual transmission	手动换挡变速器
automatic transmission (AT)	自动变速器
semi-automatic transmission	半自动变速器
fully automatic transmission	全自动变速器
continuously variable transmission (CVT)	无级变速器
clutch withdrawal fork	离合器分离叉
output shaft	输出轴
idler gear	惰轮,中间齿轮
reverse gear	倒挡齿轮
a cluster of gears	齿轮组
gear shift mechanism	换挡机构
driving parts	驱动部件
smooth start	平稳启动
in relation to	与……有关
in excess of	超过
neutral position	空挡挡位
park position	停车挡位
latch mechanism	锁止机构
manual gearbox	手动变速器
gear set	齿轮组,成套齿轮,变速器
oil-bathed	油浴式的
wet clutch	油浴式离合器,湿式离合器
dry clutch	干式离合器
vice versa	反之亦然
rely on	依赖,依靠
planetary gear set	行星齿轮机构
drive line	动力传动系统,驱动系统
gear arrangement	齿轮排列
hydraulic system	液压系统
one-way clutch	单向离合器
valve body	阀体总成
line pressure	主油路压力
electronic control unit (ECU)	电子控制模块
gear ratio	速比
continuously variable mechanical transmission	机械式无级变速器
multi-plate clutch	多盘离合器
throttle pressure	(自动变速器行星齿轮机构液压控制系统的)

final drive unit　　　　　　　　　加速踏板控制液压,节气门压力
metal belt　　　　　　　　　　　最终传动装置,主(轮边)减速器
velocity ratio　　　　　　　　　　金属带
　　　　　　　　　　　　　　　　速比,传动比

Notes to the Text

1. A transmission is a speed and power changing device installed at some point between the engine and driving wheels of the vehicle.
   变速器是一个安装在汽车发动机和驱动轮之间的速力变化装置。
2. Also required is a speed ratio to avoid the need for extremely high engine rpm at high road speeds.
   另外,还需要有个速度比以避免高速行驶中所需的极高的发动机转速。
3. In addition to the various forward gears, a transmission also has a neutral position which disconnects the engine from the drive wheels, and reverse, which causes the drive wheels to turn in the opposite direction allowing you to back up.
   除前进挡外,变速器还有一个将发动机和驱动轮断开的空挡和能驱动车轮反向返回的倒挡。
4. Seals and gaskets are used to keep the oil where it is supposed to be and prevent it from leaking out.
   密封圈和垫片被用来控制传动液的流动并防止其渗漏。

Exercises on the Text

I. Answer the following questions according to the text.

1. What's the function of a manual transmission?
2. What's the job of the reverse gear?
3. What are the three elements of a planetary gear set?
4. Please describe the principle of the torque converter.
5. Please describe the functions of the transmission fluid.

II. Fill in the table below (Tab. 9-1).

Tab. 9-1

English	Chinese
	变速器
output shaft	
	倒挡齿轮
neutral position	
	液压系统

To be continued

English	Chinese
planetary gear set	
	动力传动系统
valve body	
	变矩器
latch mechanism	

III. Fill in the blanks with the words or phrases given below, and change the form where necessary.

pressure	disconnect	make up	leak
in relation to	torque converter	rely on	shift

1. Many dual-clutch transmissions have the ability to allow the driver to manually _____ gears, although still carried out by the transmission's electro-hydraulics.
2. In first gear, the engine turns much faster _____ the drive wheels.
3. Neutral position _____ the engine from the drive wheels.
4. The majority of automatic transmissions _____ planetary gear sets to transfer power and generate torque from the engine to the drive line.
5. On an automatic transmission, the manually controlled clutch has been replaced with a _____.
6. There are three elements that _____ one planetary gear system.
7. Every aspect of a transmission's functions is dependent on a constant supply of fluid under _____.
8. Seals and gaskets are used to keep the oil where it is supposed to be and prevent it from _____ out.

IV. Reading comprehension: Read the following passage carefully and fill in the blanks with the words given below.

consumption	manual	technical	investments	reduction
connection	tests	transmissions	manufacturing	broad

In some comparative __1__, cars equipped with automatic transmissions have shown lower fuel __2__ in some cases than cars with five-speed __3__ transmissions. This was achieved by the use of lock-up converters for the third and fourth gear in __4__ with a "long" fourth gear and, of course, simultaneous __5__ of other internal losses. So, considering just the __6__ aspect, automatic transmissions will find __7__ acceptance in the future though the higher __8__ cost may still be considered a hindrance. Of course, in the situations where the market share for automatic __9__ is small, and where the manufacturer already has made large __10__ in manual transmissions, semi-automatic manual transmissions could be of interest.

V. Translate the following passage into Chinese.

The hydraulic system is a complex maze of passages and tubes that sends transmission fluid under pressure to all parts of the transmission and torque converter. Transmission fluid serves several purposes, including: shift control, general lubrication and transmission cooling. Every aspect of a transmission's functions depends on a constant supply of fluid under pressure. In fact, most of the components of a transmission are constantly submerged in fluid including the clutch packs and bands.

VI. Translate the following sentences into English.

1. 当今车辆上使用的变速器有多种：手动换挡变速器、半自动变速器、全自动变速器（包括无级变速器）。
2. 变速器被用以改变发动机转速与驱动轮转速间的比率关系，使之尽可能地适应每一个特定的行车条件。
3. 在自动变速器中，变矩器代替了传统的离合器。
4. 传动油具有多种作用，包括换挡控制、正常润滑和变速器冷却等。
5. 自动变速器油泵负责产生变速器内需要的所有油压。

Section B Checking and Servicing the Automatic Transmission

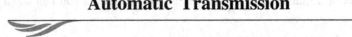

As with any other major parts of the automobile, routine service procedures for the automatic transmission must be learned before tackling any major repair work. The following describes the procedures for checking and servicing the automatic transmission.

Check the Automatic Transmission Visually

During the visual check, the vehicle should be raised on a hoist. Use a drop light to look for things that do not look or feel right. You will be looking for leaks, for looseness, and for damaged or missing parts. Use your hands in the areas where your sight is obstructed.

To check shift linkage, it may be necessary to lower the vehicle and look under the hood. The main areas to check for leaks or damage are: the transmission housing and linkage systems.

When you check the entire transmission housing for cracks or damage, please check where the slip joint enters the transmission housing for leaks. The rear portion of the transmission is called the extension housing. A leak in this area indicates a worn extension housing seal or bushing.

Sometimes a leak may appear in the transmission housing where it does not connect to a separate part. When there is a leak or a hole in the housing, it can be the result of casting porosity.

Shake the transmission linkage gently to be sure it is not excessively loose. Look at the places where the linkage pivots against another part. Also be sure that no retaining clips or nuts are missing from the linkage.

The shift linkage at the transmission may also be connected to the carburetor by a cable or rod. Check this linkage carefully from under the hood.

Check External Leaks

Transmission fluid can leak from any of the following places: the oil pan, transmission case, extension housing and converter housing.

Leaks from the oil pan can be the result of loose bolts, a bad gasket, or a hole in the pan. Check these areas and correct the condition. Loose bolts must be tightened to manufacturer's torque specifications. A bad gasket or oil pan must be replaced.

If any leaks are evident at the extension housing, they may be caused by a bad seal, gasket, or bushing. Leaking seals can be found anywhere around the transmission, including at the transmission case and converter housing. Replace seals, gaskets, and bushings if necessary.

Check all parts of the transmission for loose bolts, and tighten them.

Check Transmission Fluid Level

Automatic transmission fluid (ATF) levels must be checked at regular mileage or time intervals. Refer to the proper service manual.

The ATF level is checked from under the hood of the vehicle. A dipstick is located near the firewall. Be sure the dipstick hole leads to the automatic transmission.

In older vehicles, the ATF level must be checked only when the engine and transmission are at operating temperatures. If the engine and transmission are cold, start the engine and let it run until the transmission reaches the operating temperature. The fluid level can drop almost an inch when the transmission is cold. So, reading the dipstick at operating temperatures is critical.

Pull out the transmission dipstick and wipe it clean. Reinsert the dipstick in the dipstick hole. Remove the dipstick and note the reading. If the fluid level is between ADD and FULL, the fluid level is good. If fluid level reading is below ADD, at least 1 pint of fluid should be added.

Before adding ATF, first be sure the proper lubricant is used. Manufacturers differ as to the type of ATF that is required. Fluid is added through the dipstick hole. A special spout is used so that the ATF is not spilled over the engine and transmission. Never overfill the transmission. If too much fluid has been added, use a suction gun to remove the excess.

Diagnose Transmission Fluid

Inspecting the ATF should be routine whenever the fluid level is checked. The automatic transmission fluid is usually red in color. A special dye is added to the ATF so that transmission leaks can be easily identified. The two basic ways of telling the condition of the ATF are by sight and by smell.

If the ATF is dark brown in color, it may indicate overheating. Some fluids turn dark with age, so smell the fluid to determine if it has overheated. If it smells like burned food, the fluid has been overheated. Both an oil change and the filter change are necessary.

When a preliminary check for overheated fluid indicates a problem, the ATF should be checked more closely.

Check the cleaned dipstick. Any varnish or gum means that the ATF needs to be replaced, along with the filter.

If the ATF is pink or milky in appearance, it indicates that engine coolant has leaked into the transmission.

Bubbles appearing on the dipstick indicate that air has entered the transmission. If the fluid level is correct, this is usually caused by a high-pressure leak. Oil, under pressure, is sprayed into the oil in the reservoir. High-pressure oil aerates, or combines with air, to cause bubbles.

Remove the Oil Pan

Transmission fluid should be drained when the ATF is warm. Contaminants, such as varnish or sludge, flow out more easily when the fluid is warm. Be careful when draining the ATF, because it may still be hot enough to cause serious burns.

Most modern automatic transmissions do not have a drain plug. To drain the transmission, the oil pan must be removed.

Drain the Torque Converter

All of the ATF does not drain out when the transmission oil pan is removed. Some ATF remains in the torque converter. In some vehicles, a drain plug is used to empty the torque converter. Most vehicles, however, have no drain plug. Check the proper service manual for the correct procedure to drain the torque converter.

Service the Filter and Screen

Transmission fluid must be filtered to remove particles from the fluid. Otherwise, damage will result. To remove harmful particles, either a disposable filter or reusable screen is used. The filter must be replaced and the screen must be cleaned or replaced at regular service intervals, according to the manufacturer's recommendations. Be sure not to wipe the screen with a cloth. Any lint that may stick to the screen will enter the valve body, resulting in poor transmission operation.

Refill the Transmission

The amount of fluid that is to be added depends on the type of transmission being serviced and whether the torque converter was drained. An automatic transmission will hold between 5 and 8 quarts of ATF. If the torque converter was not drained, the transmission may only require 2 to 3 quarts. Check the proper service manual. Never overfill the transmission.

New Words

tackle	['tækl]	v.	着手处理,对付,解决

obstruct	[əbˈstrʌkt]	v.	阻(堵)塞,阻挡,阻止
crack	[kræk]	n.	裂缝,缝隙
bushing	[ˈbuʃiŋ]	n.	轴套,衬套,轴衬
porosity	[pɔːˈrɔsiti]	n.	(铸造件的)缩孔性,多孔性,孔,多孔结构
spout	[spaut]	n.	(水管等的)嘴,喷口,喷水孔
suction	[ˈsʌkʃən]	n.	吸,吸引,吸入
dye	[dai]	n.	染料,颜料
preliminary	[priˈlimənəri]	a.	初步的,开始的
varnish	[ˈvɑːniʃ]	n.	漆,清漆,光漆
gum	[gʌm]	n.	树胶,树脂
milky	[ˈmilki]	a.	乳白色的,乳状的
aerate	[ˈeəreit]	v.	加气于(液体)中
bubble	[ˈbʌbl]	n.	泡,气泡,水泡
sludge	[slʌdʒ]	n.	泥,淤泥
disposable	[diˈspəuzəbl]	a.	用后即可丢弃的,可自由处置的
lint	[lint]	n.	棉绒
stick	[stik]	v.	刺,戳,插于
		n.	棍,棒

Phrases and Expressions

drop light	活动吊灯
shift linkage	换挡杆系,变速杆系
transmission housing	变速器壳
linkage system	连动装置,杆系
slip joint	滑套接头,滑套连接
retaining clip	固定夹,卡夹
retaining nut	固定螺母
service manual	维修(保养)手册,使用说明书,售后服务手册

Notes to the Text

A special dye is added to the ATF so that transmission leaks can be easily identified.
自动变速器传动液中添加了一种特殊的颜料,以便易于识别变速器的渗漏。

Exercises

I. Translate the following names of cars into Chinese.

1. Lotus _____ 2. Bentley _____

3. Morgan _____   4. Leyland _____
5. Mini _____   6. Volvo _____
7. Scania _____   8. Saab _____

II. **Translate the following abbreviations into corresponding Chinese terms.**
1. AT (automatic transmission) _____
2. CVT (continuously variable transmission) _____
3. ATF (automatic transmission fluid) _____
4. SOL (solenoid) _____
5. ECU (electronic control unit) _____
6. HTC (hydraulic torque converter) _____

Section C Dialogue In the Auto Repair Shop

The following dialogue took place in an auto repair shop (See Fig. 9 – 2).

Fig. 9 – 2 Auto repair

Technician(T): Hello, sir. Can I help you?
Customer(C): I want to have my car repaired.
  T: What's wrong with your car?
  C: I heard some noise from my car several days ago.
  T: Oh, really? What kind of noise? Can you describe it in detail?
  C: As soon as I start the engine, I can hear a ticking noise from the engine. It sounds like a loud clock.
  T: I'll certainly check it out for you.
  C: When can I get my car back?
  T: The time depends on what the noise problem is.

C: You know, it's really inconvenient without a car. I hope I can get my car back as soon as possible.

T: I'll try my best. Please don't forget to write your name and phone number on the repairing report. I'll call you when it is done.

C: OK, thank you!

T: Oh, please wait a minute...

C: Is there something wrong?

T: I just looked at the car you gave me. I find there's a dent in the right fender of your car.

C: Is it serious?

T: No. I just don't want you to think that I did this.

C: Don't worry. I'll make a note here on your repairing report.

T: Thank you!

Useful Expressions and Sentences

1. In the Auto Repair Shop
   在汽车维修店

2. Hello, sir. Can I help you?
   您好,先生。有什么我可以帮忙的吗?

3. I want to have my car repaired.
   我想修车。

4. What's wrong with your car?
   您的车出什么毛病了?

5. Can you describe it in detail?
   您能详细地描述一下吗?
   in detail 详细地

6. I'll certainly check it out for you.
   我一定会为您查出故障的。
   check out 检查

7. It's really inconvenient without a car.
   没有车太不方便。

8. I'll try my best. Please don't forget to write your name and phone number on the repairing report. I'll call you when it is done.
   我会尽最大努力的。请不要忘记把您的名字和电话号码写在维修报告单上。修好车我就给您打电话。
   try one's best 尽某人最大努力

9. Is there something wrong?
   有什么不对劲儿吗?

10. I just looked at the car you gave me. I find there's a dent in the right fender of your car.
    我刚刚看了您交给我的车。我发现您的车的右侧挡泥板上有个凹痕。
11. I just don't want you to think that I did this.
    我只是不想让您认为这是我弄的。
12. Don't worry. I'll make a note here on your repairing report.
    别担心,我会在您的维修报告单上注明的。

Unit Ten

Section A Suspension System

Functions of a Suspension System

The functions of a suspension system are as follows:
- To prevent road shocks from being transmitted to the vehicle frame.
- To preserve the stability of the vehicle in pitching or rolling, while in motion.
- To safeguard the occupants from road shocks.
- To provide good road holding while driving, cornering and braking.
- To maintain proper steering geometry.

Types of Suspension system

The suspension system supports the weight of the engine, transmission, car body, and whatever the car body is carrying. There are two basic suspension systems in use today. One is the solid axle, leaf spring type; the other is the independent suspension using long and short swinging arms. There are various adaptations of these systems, but all use the same basic principle.

The **solid axle suspension** uses a solid steel dead axle (does not turn with wheels) with a leaf spring at each side. The wheels swivel on each end via a pivot arrangement between the axle and the wheel spindle.

With **an independent suspension**, each front wheel is free to move up and down with a minimum effect on the other wheel. In an independent suspension system, there is also far less twisting motion imposed on the frame than in a system with a solid axle.

Almost all modern **front suspension systems** are independent. A few off-road, four-wheel-drive vehicles and large trucks continue to use a solid axle front suspension. Types of front suspension systems include the conventional front suspension, coil spring front suspension, torsion bar front suspension, MacPherson strut front suspension and solid axle front suspension.

The **rear suspension** may be of the solid axle or independent design. Many cars have solid axle rear suspensions. Either design may have different kinds of springs. However, the coil spring and leaf spring types are most popular.

Components of Suspension System

Most suspension systems have the same basic parts — springs and shock absorbers and operate basically in the same way. They differ, however, in the type and arrangement of the linkages used to connect these parts to the frame and wheels.

Springs

In a suspension system, the major component is springs. Springs are vital to vehicles because they support the weight of your car and allow it to remain stable even in rough driving conditions. They have the ability to expand when you hit dips on the road and compress when you encounter bumps or cut into hard corners.

The springs used on today's vehicles are engineered in a wide variety of types, shapes, sizes, rates, and capacities for each kind of automobile and truck depending on your vehicle's suspension design. Leaf springs (both multiple and single leaf), coil springs, and torsion bars are the most commonly used springs. A certain kind of spring, called air spring, can also keep your truck off the ground and determine ride height, which in turn influences steering and suspension (See Fig. 10 – 1).

Springs are paired off in various combinations and are attached to vehicles by a number of different mounting techniques. Two different types of springs can be used on one vehicle.

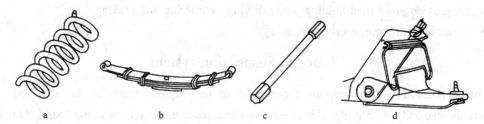

Fig. 10 – 1 Types of springs
a. coil spring; b. leaf spring; c. torsion bar; d. air spring

Front **leaf springs** are used in conjunction with solid axle beams in most truck applications. Rear leaf springs are used on trucks and some passenger cars. Single-leaf or multi-leaf springs are usually mounted longitudinally over the front axle beam or under the rear axle housing. The spring center bolt fastens the leaves together, and its head locates the spring in the front axle beam or saddle on the rear axle housing. U-bolts clamp the spring firmly in place and keep it from shifting. Eyebolts, brackets, and shackles attach it to the frame at each end. The main advantage of leaf springs is their ability to control vehicles' sway and lateral movement. For these reasons, leaf springs are often used on the rear suspension of rear drive vehicles.

A **coil spring** (also called helical spring) is a kind of torsion spring which can store energy and release it later when needed. It can also absorb shock and maintain the force between two contacting surfaces. Together with a shock absorber, coil springs are pre-assembled as one coil over shock unit before installation. While the coil spring compresses and stretches to keep you safe as you drive, the shock absorber keeps you from road noise, bumps, and vibrations that you might encounter while doing so. All in all, a coil over shock is essential in your vehicle's suspension because it gives you optimal damping, good handling and braking, and a comfortable ride.

A number of vehicles use a **torsion bar spring**. In the torsion-bar front-suspension system, two steel bars serve as the springs. The ends of the bars are locked to the cross member or to the body. The other ends of the bars are attached to the lower control arms. In operation, the lower control arms pivot up and down, twisting the torsion bars. The effect is very similar to the actions of the coil and leaf springs. Instead of the flexing action of a leaf spring, or the compressing-and-extending action of a coil spring, the torsion bar twists to exert resistance against up-and-down movement. Torsion bars that run across the car are called transverse torsion bars. When the torsion bars are installed and run from front to rear on the car, they are called longitudinal torsion bars.

Shock Absorbers

Under normal conditions, the springs support the body of the car evenly by compressing and rebounding with every up-and-down movement. This up-and-down movement, however, causes bouncing and swaying after each bump and is very uncomfortable to the passenger. These uncomfortable effects are reduced by the shock absorbers. Shock absorbers are mounted between the frame and the suspension by means of brackets and rubber bushings.

In the past, a wide variety of direct and indirect shock absorbing devices were used to control spring action of passenger cars. Today, direct, double-acting hydraulic shock absorbers and shock absorber struts have almost universal application.

The operating principle of direct-acting hydraulic shock absorbers is forcing fluid through restricting openings in the valves. This restricted flow serves to slow down and control repaid movement in the car springs as they react to road irregularities. Usually, the fluid flow through the pistons is controlled by spring-loaded valves. Hydraulic shock absorbers automatically adapt to severity of the shock. If the axle moves slowly, resistance to the flow of fluid will be light. If the axle movement is rapid or violent, the resistance is stronger, since more time is required to force fluid through openings. By these actions and reactions, the shock absorbers permit a soft ride over small bumps and provide firm control over spring action for cushioning large bumps. The double-acting units must be effective in both directions because spring rebound can be almost as violent as the original action that compressed the shock absorber.

Advanced Suspension System

The typical **electronic controlled suspension system** consists of several components in addition to the normal suspension components. The system includes sensors, switches, control unit and actuators. Sensors and switches provide input to the system control unit or the control module. The control unit is basically a small computer that receives input in the form of electrical signals from the sensors and switches and provides output electrical signals to the system actuators. The electrical signals cause the actuator to perform some mechanical action. Perhaps the most important component is the control unit (a small computer), which interprets input from various sensors that monitor such information as vehicle height or speed, whether the driver is accelerating or braking, or what switch position the driver has chosen for a console switch allowing a choice between certain suspension functions. The mechanical response of the actuator changes shock stiffness or spring rate.

Given the fact that electronic controlled suspension systems cost considerably more than conventional suspension systems, they are only found on expensive luxury-class automobiles, high-performance sports cars and racing cars.

New Words

pitch	[pitʃ]	v.	前后颠簸,纵摇(区别于roll横摇)
adaptation	[ˌædæpˈteiʃən]	n.	改造(物)
swivel	[ˈswivl]	v.	(使)旋转
twist	[twist]	v.	扭转,扭曲
bracket	[ˈbrækit]	n.	三角形的托架
impose	[imˈpəuz]	v.	把……强加于
strut	[strʌt]	n.	滑柱,支柱
bump	[bʌmp]	n.	撞击,肿块,凸起
engineer	[ˌendʒiˈniə]	v.	设计,建造
rate	[reit]	n.	标准
capacity	[kəˈpæsiti]	n.	负载
combination	[ˌkɔmbiˈneiʃən]	n.	组合
beam	[bi:m]	n.	梁,横梁
longitudinally	[ˌlɔndʒiˈtju:dinəli]	adv.	纵向地
clamp	[klæmp]	v.	(用夹钳)夹住,夹紧
sway	[swei]	n./v.	摇摆,摇动
lateral	[ˈlætərəl]	a.	侧面的,横向的
transverse	[ˈtrænzvə:s]	a.	横向的
rebound	[riˈbaund]	v./n.	回弹
stiffness	[ˈstifnis]	n.	刚度

Phrases and Expressions

steering geometry	转向系几何定位,转向几何结构,转向杆系几何布置
solid axle	整体式车桥
leaf spring	钢板弹簧
independent suspension	独立悬架
dead axle	非驱动桥,从动桥
wheel spindle	转向节轴,车轮轴头

off-road	越野的,在道路之外
coil spring	螺旋弹簧
torsion bar	扭杆弹簧
MacPherson strut front suspension	麦弗逊滑柱式前悬架
shock absorber	减震器
air spring	空气弹簧
pair off	使成对
U-bolt	U形螺栓,骑马螺栓
in place	在适当的位置上
coil over shock	(悬架)螺旋弹簧与减震器组件
electronic controlled suspension system	电控悬架系统
control module	控制模块
spring rate	弹簧刚度,弹簧刚度系数

Notes to the Text

1. The wheels swivel on each end via a pivot arrangement between the axle and the wheel spindle.
   通过安装在车桥和轮轴之间的驱动轴,两端的车轮可以转动。
2. The springs used on today's vehicles are engineered in a wide variety of types, shapes, sizes, rates, and capacities...
   在当今车辆上使用的弹簧被设计制造成许多不同的型号、形状、大小、标准及负载。
3. Hydraulic shock absorber automatically adapts to severity of the shock.
   液压减震器自动地适应剧烈的震动冲击。

Exercises on the Text

I. Answer the following questions according to the text.
   1. What are the functions of a suspension system?
   2. There are two basic suspension systems in use today, and what are they?
   3. What are the key components that make up the suspension system?
   4. List three types of springs in general use today.
   5. What's the function of the shock absorber?

II. Fill in the table below (Tab. 10-1).

Tab. 10-1

English	Chinese
	减震器
suspension system	
	后桥

To be continued

English	Chinese
independent suspension	
	钢板弹簧
dead axle	
	螺旋弹簧
solid axle	
	传感器
torsion bar	

III. Fill in the blanks with the words or phrases given below, and change the form where necessary.

in conjunction with	impose	pair off	swivel
by means of	transmit	rebound	twist

1. One function of the suspension system is to prevent road shocks from _____ to the vehicle frame.
2. The wheels _____ on each end via a pivot arrangement between the axle and the wheel spindle.
3. In an independent suspension system, there is also far less twisting motion _____ on the frame than in a system with a solid axle.
4. Springs _____ in various combinations on vehicles.
5. Front leaf springs are used _____ solid axle beams in most truck applications.
6. The torsion bar _____ to exert resistance against up-and-down movement.
7. The springs support the body of the car by compressing and _____ with every up-and-down movement.
8. Shock absorbers are mounted between the frame and the suspension _____ brackets and rubber bushings.

IV. Reading comprehension: Read the following passage carefully and fill in the blanks with the words given below.

expand	engineered	combinations	mounting	attached
stable	support	springs	depending	compress

In a suspension system, the major component is springs. Springs are vital to vehicles because they __1__ the weight of your car and allow it to remain __2__ even in rough driving conditions. They have the ability to __3__ when you hit dips on the road and __4__ when you encounter bumps or cut into hard corners.

The springs used on today's vehicles are __5__ in a wide variety of types, shapes, sizes, rates, and capacities for each kind of automobile and truck __6__ on your vehicle's suspension design. Leaf springs, coil springs and torsion bars are the most commonly used __7__. Springs are paired off in various __8__ and are __9__ to the vehicles by a number of different __10__ techniques.

V. Translate the following paragraph into Chinese.

The operating principle of direct-acting hydraulic shock absorbers is forcing fluid through restricting openings in the valves. This restricted flow serves to slow down and control repaid movement in the car springs as they react to road irregularities. Usually, fluid flow through the pistons is controlled by spring-loaded valves. Hydraulic shock absorbers automatically adapt to severity of the shock. If the axle moves slowly, resistance to the flow of fluid will be light. If the axle movement is rapid or violent, the resistance is stronger, since more time is required to force fluid through openings. By these actions and reactions, the shock absorbers permit a soft ride over small bumps and provide firm control over spring action for cushioning large bumps. The double-acting units must be effective in both directions because spring rebound can be almost as violent as the original action that compressed the shock absorber.

VI. Translate the following sentences into English.

1. 悬架系统的作用之一是防止路面震动传导至车架。
2. 悬架系统中的主要部件是弹簧。
3. 在当今车辆上使用的弹簧被设计制造成许多不同的型号、形状、大小、标准及负载。
4. 用不同的装配技术把弹簧安装在车辆上。
5. 钢板弹簧的主要优势是其有控制车辆摇摆及横向运动的能力。
6. 通常,弹簧负荷阀控制液体通过活塞。

Section B Leaf Spring Maintenance

The two main causes for failure of leaf-type spring suspensions are loose hold down bolts and fatigue. Due to the fact that leaf springs are deflected from compression to tension continuously while on the vehicle, eventual fatigue failures will result. A scratch, notch, or rust point can lead to cracks on the tension side of the leaf, usually near the corners of the leaf. These cracks become progressively larger as the spring flexes during operation.

Spring life is affected by the vehicle gross weight, the type of load, road conditions, speed, and maintenance.

Repairing a spring, although cheaper than a new one, does nothing to restore the fatigue life of the reused leaves. Therefore when spring leaf breakage occurs, it has to be established what is the best way to proceed. Items to consider would be the actual mileage or kilometers on the spring, the number of previous repairs, and the cost of the new springs, keeping in mind labor costs, and cost of down time.

When springs are replaced on a vehicle, the chassis/frame must be supported on stands before the technician attempts to remove the spring shackle pins and/or brackets. The easiest way to do this is to drive the vehicle onto a heavy-duty air, electric, or hydraulic hoist with individual lifting assemblies for both the front and rear axles.

The vehicle can be raised to a suitable working height, stands placed under the chassis for support, the spring-bolts and spring shackle pins removed, and the axle lowered slightly on the hoist to allow the spring assembly to be removed. When reinstalling the spring, it can be mounted and bolted to the saddle casting and spring hangers, the equalizing beams raised into position of the saddles by the use of the hoist, and the saddle caps installed. The torque rods attached to the axles will require removal initially and reinstallation once the spring is back into position.

If a hoist such as described is not available, then the vehicle should be parked on solid level ground and jacked up on either one or both sides to facilitate placing stands under the chassis. The axle can be raised or lowered with a floor jack, and the same basic procedure followed as with the drive on hoist.

If the spring U-bolts are not tight, spring movement will occur creating stability and steering problems, axle misalignment, abnormal tire wear, and spring breakage.

When the springs in the multi-leaf spring design are being replaced, the U-bolt nuts must have hardened washers under the bolt to obtain true tightening torque. (The U-bolts and nuts should be renewed at that time.) When new springs are installed, a small amount of settling will occur after they are in service, which will relieve the original tension on the U-bolts.

As part of a regular maintenance schedule, U-bolts must be checked for correct torque. The U-bolts should be rechecked after any service has been done to the suspension system within 805 km to 1,609 km. Subsequent re-torquing would depend on the severity of service. The torque applied to U-bolts will vary depending on whether an all steel locknut, all steel flange nut, or nylon insert nut is used.

Rusty joints must be disassembled, cleaned, and lubricated to assure a like-new condition prior to retorque. Check the applicable vehicle service manual for the recommended value.

New Words

fatigue	[fəˈtiːg]	n.	疲劳
notch	[nɔtʃ]	n.	凹口,刻痕
flex	[fleks]	v.	折曲,屈曲
hoist	[hɔist]	n.	起重机,吊车,升降机

jack	[dʒæk]	n.	起重器,千斤顶
		v.	用起重器举(或顶)
facilitate	[fə'siliteit]	v.	(不以人做主语)使容易,使便利
harden	['hɑːdn]	v.	变硬,变坚固
washer	['wɔʃə]	n.	垫圈
settling	['setliŋ]	n.	沉淀,沉淀物,渣滓

Phrases and Expressions

spring shackle pin　　　　　　　　　　　　（钢板）弹簧吊环销
spring hanger　　　　　　　　　　　　　　弹簧吊架
spring U-bolt　　　　　　　　　　　　　　钢板弹簧 U 形螺栓,钢板弹簧骑马螺栓

Notes to the Text

1. Spring life is affected by the vehicle gross weight, the type of load, road conditions, speed, and maintenance.
   弹簧的使用寿命受车辆总重量、装载类型、路况、车速及养护的影响。
2. If the spring U-bolts are not tight, spring movement will occur creating stability and steering problems, axle misalignment, abnormal tire wear, and spring breakage.
   如果没有拧紧钢板弹簧 U 形螺栓,就会发生弹簧移动,导致稳定性及转向问题、车轴不正、轮胎的异常磨损以及弹簧的毁损。

Exercises

I. Translate the following names of cars into Chinese.

1. Peugeot _____　　　　2. Renault _____
3. Venturi _____　　　　4. Citroen _____
5. Fiat _____　　　　　　6. Iveco _____
7. Abarth _____　　　　8. Lancia _____

II. Translate the following abbreviations into corresponding Chinese terms.

1. SUS (suspension) _____
2. IFS (independent front suspension) _____
3. AAS (automatic adjusting suspension) _____
4. LS (leaf spring) _____
5. FH (frame height) _____
6. GPS (global positioning system) _____

Section C Toyota

Toyota (Its logo is shown in Fig. 10 – 2 and its headquarters is shown in Fig. 10 – 3.) is a Japanese brand whose refined, well-designed vehicles have earned it a great deal of popularity. Toyota also has a superb record for reliability and durability, which goes a long way toward justifying their typically high purchase prices. For buyers who plan on owning their new vehicles for a long time, the Toyota marque is a very compelling choice.

Fig. 10 – 2 Toyota's logo

Fig. 10 – 3 The headquarters of Toyota in Toyota City, Japan

The automaker's name is a variation of the surname of its founder, Kiichiro Toyoda. His father founded Toyoda Automatic Loom Works. In 1933, Toyoda Automatic Loom Works created a new division devoted to the production of automobiles under the direction of Kiichiro Toyoda. He had traveled to Europe and the United States in 1929 to investigate automobile production and had begun researching gasoline-powered engines in 1930.

After years of research, Toyoda unveiled his first prototype, the A1, in 1935, marking the birth of the Toyota Motor Corporation. Early vehicles bore a striking resemblance to the Dodge Power Wagon and Chevrolet, with some parts actually interchanging with their American originals.

Toyota grew bigger in the 1950s and expanded its business with new small cars. The company also unveiled the BJ truck, the precursor to the Land Cruiser. By the end of the decade, Toyota had started exports to the US with the establishment of Toyota Motor Sales U S A, Inc. The first Toyota sold on American shores was the Crown; it held the distinction of being the first Japanese car sold in America.

Toyota began to expand in the 1960s with a new research and development facility. A presence in Thailand was established, and the 10 millionth model was produced. It introduced the Corolla (See Fig. 10 – 4), an immensely popular model that is still in production today. Vehicles like the home-market Publica, the 2000GT,

Fig. 10 – 4 Toyota Corolla, the best selling car in the world

Hiace and Miniace were also launched. By the end of the decade, Toyota had established a worldwide presence.

Japanese-market cars like the Carina, Light Ace and Publica Starlet were launched during the 1970s. In the United States, the Corolla grew in popularity and the Corona and Mk II models debuted as well. The successful Celica sports coupé was also rolled out and would remain in production for more than 30 years. Toyota's shadow had spread far beyond Japan by this point. The decade's oil crisis had made the manufacturer's compact, fuel-efficient models more popular than ever in the United States. By the time when the 1970s drew to a close, the automaker had exported more than 10 million vehicles.

Toyota expanded its presence in the U S market during the 1980s, with the introduction of popular models like the 4 Runner SUV and the MR2 sports car. The true high point of these years, though, was the birth of the Toyota Camry sedan. Originally known as the Celica Camry in Japan, the car went on to be a hit as America's best-selling car of the year time and time again.

During the 1990s, Toyota rolled out the Avalon full-size sedan and expanded its selection of SUVs with the compact RAV4. By the end of the decade, more than 100 million Toyota vehicles had been produced in Japan. The company also proved itself on the cutting edge of new technology with the rollout of the Prius, the world's first mass-produced hybrid. The car debuted in Japan in 1997; by 2001 it had made its way to American highways. Despite the presence of a growing number of competitors in its segment, the Prius continues to boast class-leading sales.

In 2002, Toyota managed to enter a Formula One works team and establish joint ventures with French motoring companies Citroen and Peugeot, a year after Toyota started producing cars in France. In 2007, Toyota released an update of its full size truck, the Toyota Tundra, produced in two American factories, one in Texas and the other in Indiana.

Toyota has grown to a large multinational corporation from where it started and expanded to different worldwide markets and countries by becoming the largest seller of cars in the beginning of 2007, the most profitable automaker ($11 billion in 2006) along with increasing sales in, among other countries, the United States.

Toyota's net profit slipped 13.5 percent for the first three months of 2011, hurt by the massive tsunami in Japan and flooding in the manufacturing center of Thailand. But Toyota also raised its annual profit forecast, as it rolls out new versions of its popular Prius gas-electric hybrid (See Fig. 10 – 5) and Lexus luxury vehicles in the United States and other important markets.

Fig. 10 – 5 Toyota Prius, flagship of Toyota's hybrid technology

The company says it hopes that the new models will help it regain some of the market share like General Motors last year, after the disasters in Japan and Thailand severely limited production for months.

Toyota's current lineup is relatively extensive, including minivans, cars, trucks and SUVs.

The brand remains extremely popular among consumers who place a high value on quality and dependability.

New Words

superb	[sjuːˈpɜːb]	a.	宏伟的,壮丽的,华美的, 极好的,超等的
marque	[mɑːk]	n.	商品(尤指汽车等)的型号(式样)
unveil	[ʌnˈveil]	v.	除去面纱使暴露,揭幕,公布
prototype	[ˈprəutətaip]	n.	原型(体),样机(品), 典型,样板,模范,标准
precursor	[priːˈkɜːsə(r)]	n.	前辈,先驱
debut	[ˈdebjuː]	n.	初次登场
coupé	[ˈkuːpei]	n.	带篷双座四轮轿式马车
compact	[kəmˈpækt]	a.	紧密的,紧凑的,结实的,简洁的
hit	[hit]	n.	(演出等)成功,走红
segment	[ˈsegmənt]	n.	段,片,部分,节
lineup	[ˈlainʌp]	n.	阵容,(用于同一用途的)一批东西
oval	[ˈəuvəl]	a.	卵形的,椭圆的
		n.	椭圆形

Phrases and Expressions

Land Cruiser	陆地巡洋舰
roll out	大量生产
draw to a close	结束
SUV (sports utility vehicle)	运动型多功能车
cutting edge	刀刃
hybrid technology	混合(电路)技术

Proper Names

Kiichiro Toyoda	丰田喜一郎
Toyoda Automatic Loom Works	丰田纺织株式会社
Crown	皇冠
Corolla	花冠
Hiace	海狮
Corona	光冠
Celica	司力架

Camry	凯美瑞
Avalon	亚洲龙
Prius	普锐斯
Formula One	一级方程式
Citroën	雪铁龙
Peugeot	标致

Notes to the Text

1. Toyota also has a superb record for reliability and durability, which goes a long way toward justifying their typically high purchase prices.
   丰田以其可靠耐用的品质创造了优异的销售记录,尽管价格高昂,但物有所值。
2. The first Toyota sold on American shores was the Crown; it held the distinction of being the first Japanese car sold in America.
   在美国销售的第一辆皇冠轿车使丰田保持了在美国销售第一辆日本汽车的殊荣。
3. A presence in Thailand was established, and the 10 millionth model was produced.
   随着丰田公司泰国新工厂的落成,第 1000 万辆汽车顺利下线了。
4. During the 1990s, Toyota rolled out the Avalon full-size sedan and expanded its selection of SUVs with the compact RAV4.
   20 世纪 90 年代,丰田公司大量生产亚洲龙大型轿车,同时用紧凑型 RAV4 拓展了 SUV 车型的选择面。
5. The company also proved itself on the cutting edge of new technology with the rollout of the Prius, the world's first mass-produced hybrid.
   普锐斯成为世界上第一辆批量生产的混合动力车,这证明了丰田公司在新技术领域的前沿地位。
6. Toyota has grown to a large multinational corporation from where it started and expanded to different worldwide markets and countries by becoming the largest seller of cars in the beginning of 2007, the most profitable automaker ($ 11 billion in 2006) along with increasing sales in, among other countries, the United States.
   丰田已经成长为一家大型跨国公司,产品远销海内外。在 2007 年年初其销售额继续上升,成为美国和其他国家最大汽车销售商和利润最高汽车生产商。

Questions for Discussion:
1. What's Toyota's feature introduced in the first paragraph?
2. Who is the founder of Toyota?
3. What marked the birth of Toyota Motor Corporation?
4. Which brand of Toyota is the first Japanese car sold in America?
5. According to Paragraph six, why were Toyota's compact, fuel-efficient models more popular than ever in the United States?

Unit Eleven

Section A Steering System

The function of the steering system is guiding the vehicle where the driver wants it to go. The steering system must deliver precise directional control. In a manual steering system, the driver's effort to turn the steering wheel is the primary force that causes the front wheels to swivel to the left or right on the steering knuckles. In a power steering system, power-assisted units are added so that the driver's effort is reduced.

Manual Steering System

The key components of the steering system are the steering wheel, steering column, steering shaft, steering gear, pitman arm, drag link, steering arm, ball joint, and tie-rod assembly. They enable the vehicle to change the direction by means of turning and moving forth and back.

The **steering wheel** is the driver's link to the entire system. Spokes extend from the wheel to the wheel hub, which is fastened securely at the top of the steering column. The driver's effort applied to the steering wheel at the rim becomes torque in the steering shaft. The larger the steering wheel diameter is, the more torque is generated from the same amount of the driver's effort.

The **steering column** is fastened to the cab at or under the instrument panel and contains bearings to support the steering shaft.

The **steering shaft** runs from the top of the steering column to the steering gear. U-joints in the shaft accommodate any angular variations between the steering shaft and the steering gear input shaft.

The **pitman arm** is a steel arm clamped to the output shaft of the steering gear. The outer end of the pitman arm moves through an arc in order to change the rotary motion of the steering gear output shaft into linear motion. The length of the pitman arm affects steering quickness.

The **steering arm**, sometimes called a steering lever, connects the drag link to the top portion of the driver's side steering knuckle and spindle. As the steering arm moves, it changes the angle of the steering knuckle.

The **drag link** connects the pitman arm to the steering arm. The drag link is connected at each end by ball joints. These ball joints isolate the steering gear and the pitman arm from axle motion.

The steering arm or lever controls the movement of the driver's side steering knuckle. There must be some methods of transferring this steering motion to the opposite, passenger side steering knuckle. This is done through the use of a **tie-rod assembly** that links the two steering knuckles together and forces them to act in unison.

The **steering gear** is the heart of the steering system. This gearbox multiplies steering torque and changes its direction as received through the steering shaft from the steering wheel. Two types of steering gears are widely used: the rack-and-pinion steering gear and the recirculating-ball steering gear.

The **rack-and-pinion steering gear** is used on many new smaller cars and on most cars with a transverse engine. This steering gear is small and lightweight. It provides good steering with the driver's minimum effort and gives more feedback and road feel to the driver.

In a rack-and-pinion steering gear, a pinion is attached to the steering shaft. This pinion meshes with the rack, and linkages are connected directly from the rack to the steering arms on the front wheels. Since the pinion is in direct contact with the rack in the rack-and-pinion steering gear, this type of steering gear is more responsive than the recirculating-ball steering gear. Most front-wheel-drive vehicles have rack-and-pinion steering gears.

The **recirculating-ball steering gear** is used on most large cars. This steering gear is durable, with good steering response and good road feel for the driver. In a recirculating-ball steering gear, the steering wheel and the steering shaft are connected to the worm shaft. A ball nut is mounted over the worm shaft and ball bearings run in grooves in the ball nut and worm shaft. When the worm shaft is rotated by the steering wheel, the ball nut is moved up or down. The gear teeth on the ball nut are meshed with the matching gear teeth on the pitman shaft sector. Therefore, movement of the ball nut causes rotation of the pitman shaft sector. Since the pitman shaft sector is connected through the pitman arm and steering linkage to the front wheels, the front wheels are turned by the pitman shaft sector.

Power Steering System

The power steering system is designed to reduce the effort required by the driver to turn the steering wheel. Actually, automobile power steering is "power assisted steering." In a power steering system, power-assisted units use either hydraulic or air assist setups to make steering effort easier. Nowadays, electric power aided steering is also adopted on some small cars. Here, we just discuss the hydraulic type, which is widely used on various kinds of vehicles.

The power steering system adds a hydraulic pump, a fluid reservoir, hoses, lines, and a power assist unit either mounted on, or integral with a steering wheel gear assembly. In addition, a control valve is incorporated somewhere in the hydraulic circuit (See Fig. 11-1).

The **power steering pump**, which is driven by a belt from the crankshaft pulley, sends fluid under pressure into the steering gear. This high-pressure fluid does about 80 percent of the work of steering. In operation, the pump produces a high pressure on the power-steering fluid, which is a

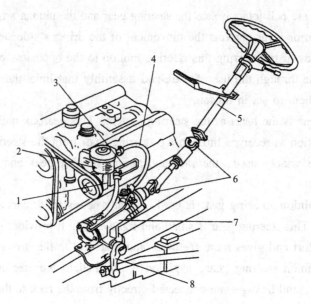

Fig. 11-1 A power steering system
1—power cylinder pump; 2—pump reservoir; 3—pressure hose; 4—return hose
5—steering column; 6—universal joints; 7—steering gear; 8—pitman arm

kind of special oil.

In the **power-assisted rack-and-pinion steering gear**, hydraulic fluid pressure from the power steering pump is used to reduce steering effort. A rack piston is integral with the rack and located in a sealed chamber in the steering gear housing. Hydraulic fluid lines are connected to each end of the chamber, and rack seals are positioned in the housing at the ends of the chamber. A seal is also located on the rack piston.

When a right turn is made, fluid is pumped into the right side of the fluid chamber, and fluid flows out of the left end of the chamber. Thus hydraulic pressure is exerted on the right side of the rack piston which assists the pinion gear in moving the rack to the left.

When a left turn is completed, fluid is pumped into the left side of the fluid chamber and exhausted from the right chamber area. This hydraulic pressure on the left side of the rack piston helps the pinion to move the rack to the right.

Since the steering gear is mounted behind the front wheels, rack movement to the left is necessary for a right turn, while rack movement to the right causes a left turn.

Fluid direction is controlled by a **rotary valve** attached to the pinion assembly. A rotary valve body contains an inner spool valve that is mounted over the torsion bar on the pinion assembly.

When the front wheels are in the straight-ahead position, fluid flows from the pump through the high-pressure hose to the center rotary valve body passage. Fluid is then routed through the valve body to the low-pressure return hose and the pump reservoir.

In the **recirculating-ball power steering gear**, the ball nut and pitman shaft sector are similar in both manual and power recirculating-ball steering gears. In the power steering gear, a torsion bar is connected between the steering shaft and the worm shaft. Since the front wheels resting on the road surface resist turning, the parts attached to the worm shaft also resist turning. This turning resistance causes torsion bar deflection when the wheels are turned. The extent of deflection is limited to a predetermined amount.

When the car is driven with the front wheels straight-ahead, oil flows from the power steering pump through the spool valve and the rotary valve body.

When the driver makes a left turn, deflection of the torsion bar moves the valve spool inside the rotary valve body so that oil flow is directed through the rotary valve to the upper side of the recirculating-ball piston. This hydraulic pressure on the piston assists the driver in turning the wheels to the left.

During a right turn, hydraulic pressure applied to the lower end of the recirculating-ball piston helps the driver to turn the wheels.

When a turn is being made and a front wheel strikes a bump which drives the wheel in the direction opposite to the turning direction, the recirculating-ball piston tends to move against the hydraulic pressure and force oil back out the pressure inlet port. This action would tend to create "kickback" on the steering wheel, but a poppet valve in the pressure inlet fitting closes and prevents kickback.

In the straight-ahead steering gear position, oil pressure is equal on both sides of the recirculating-ball piston. The oil acts as a cushion which prevents road shocks from reaching the steering wheel.

Many recirculating-ball power steering gears have a variable ratio which provides faster steering with fewer steering wheel turns.

New Words

knuckle	[ˈnʌkl]	n.	关节,转向节
spoke	[spəuk]	n.	轮辐
accommodate	[əˈkɔmədeit]	v.	容纳,提供
angular	[ˈæŋgjulə]	a.	有角的,成角的
linear	[ˈliniə]	a.	线的,直线的
spindle	[ˈspindl]	n.	轴,芯轴
isolate	[ˈaisəleit]	v.	隔离,分离,使脱离
unison	[ˈjuːnisən]	n.	和谐,一致
rack	[ræk]	n.	齿条
pinion	[ˈpinjən]	n.	小齿轮
recirculating	[riˈsəːkjuleitiŋ]	n.	再循环
transverse	[ˈtrænzvəːs]	a.	横向的,横断的
feedback	[ˈfiːdbæk]	n.	反馈,回授
groove	[gruːv]	n.	凹槽

		v.	开槽于
sector	['sektə]	n.	扇形
integral	['intəgrəl]	a.	构成整体所必需的,完整的
incorporate	[in'kɔːpəreit]	v.	把……合并,列入,包含
deflection	[di'flekʃən]	n.	偏转,变形,变位,弯曲
kickback	['kikbæk]	n.	转向盘反冲,急速回摆,逆转,回跳

Phrases and Expressions

steering wheel	转向盘,方向盘
steering column	转向管柱
steering gear	转向器,转向装置,转向齿轮机构
drag link	直拉杆
steering arm	转向臂
ball joint	球头节,球形节销
U-joint	万向节,万向节头
rack-and-pinion steering gear	齿轮齿条转向器
recirculating-ball steering gear	循环球转向器
mesh with	与……相啮合,紧密配合
steering linkage	转向转动杆系,转向转动机构
ball nut	球形螺母,循环球螺母
pitman shaft	转向摇臂轴
air assist setups	空气助力机构
electric power aided steering (EPAS)	电动助力转向
crankshaft pulley	曲轴皮带轮
rotary valve	转阀
spool valve	滑阀,滑柱阀(液压控制系中的液流方向控制阀),轴向滑动阀
inlet port	进入孔,进气孔,进气管道
poppet valve	菌形气门

Notes to the Text

1. Spokes extend from the wheel to the wheel hub, which is fastened securely at the top of the steering column.
   转向盘辐条从转向盘轮缘延伸到转向盘的轮毂,而轮毂则被紧紧地安装在转向管柱的顶端。

2. The steering arm, sometimes called a steering lever, connects the drag link to the top portion of the driver's side steering knuckle and spindle.

转向臂又被称为转向杆,它将转向直拉杆与驾驶员的侧转向节和转向轮的上端部分连在一起。

3. The power steering system adds a hydraulic pump, a fluid reservoir, hoses, lines, and a power assist unit either mounted on or integral with a steering wheel gear assembly.
动力转向系统增加了一个液压泵、一个油缸、油管和一个与转向机构制成一体的动力辅助装置。

Exercises on the Text

I. Answer the following questions according to the text.
1. What's the function of the steering system?
2. Please list the main components of the steering system.
3. What are the two widely used types of the steering gears?
4. How does the recirculating ball steering gear work?
5. What's the purpose of the power steering?

II. Fill in the table below (Tab. 11-1).

Tab. 11-1

English	Chinese
	转向系统
instrument panel	
	转向器,转向装置
steering column	
	方向盘
tie rod	
	转阀
pitman arm	
	直拉杆
steering knuckle	

III. Fill in the blanks with the words or phrases given below, and change the form where necessary.

incorporate	isolate	adopt	steering shaft
torque	deliver	integral	accommodate

1. The steering system must _____ precise directional control.

2. U-joints in the shaft _____ any angular variations between the steering shaft and the steering gear input shaft.
3. These ball joints _____ the steering gear and pitman arm from axle motion.
4. The larger the steering wheel diameter is, the more _____ is generated from the same amount of the driver's effort.
5. A rack piston is _____ with the rack and located in a sealed chamber in the steering gear housing.
6. Nowadays, electric power aided steering _____ on some small cars.
7. A control valve _____ somewhere in the hydraulic circuit.
8. In a rack-and-pinion steering gear, a pinion is attached to the _____.

IV. Reading comprehension: Read the following passage carefully and fill in the blanks with the words given below.

| responsive | attached | feedback | direction | contact |
| minimum | steering | rack | multiplies | wheel |

The steering gear is the heart of the __1__ system. This gearbox __2__ steering torque and changes its __3__ as received through the steering shaft from the steering __4__. The rack-and-pinion steering gear provides good steering with the driver's __5__ effort and gives more __6__ and road feel to the driver. In a rack-and-pinion steering gear, a pinion is __7__ to the steering shaft. This pinion meshes with the __8__, and linkages are connected directly from the rack to the steering arms on the front wheels. Since the pinion is in direct __9__ with the rack in the rack-and-pinion steering gear, this type of steering gear is more __10__ than the recirculating-ball steering gear.

V. Translate the following passage into Chinese.

The power steering pump, which is driven by a belt from the crankshaft pulley, sends fluid under pressure into the steering gear. This high-pressure fluid does about 80 percent of the work of steering. In operation, the pump produces a high pressure on the power-steering fluid, which is a kind of special oil.

VI. Translate the following sentences into English.
1. 通常用于汽车上的转向系统有两种：手动转向系统和动力转向系统。
2. 在手动转向系统中，驾驶员转动方向盘的所用之力就是使前轮左右转动的主要力量。
3. 手动转向系统中的零部件通过转动或前后移动能使汽车改变行驶方向。
4. 汽车动力转向实际上就是动力辅助转向。
5. 在动力转向系统中，油液的流向由安装在齿轮机构上的转阀控制。

Section B Causes of Steering Troubles

In addition to its vital role in vehicle control, the steering system is closely related to the front suspension, axle, and wheel/tire components. Improper steering adjustment can lead to alignment and tire wear problems, etc.

A variety of steering troubles will bring the driver to the mechanic, but it is rare that the driver will have a clear idea of what caused this trouble. He can detect an increase in hard steering, car wander or excessive play in the steering system. But he probably will not have a very good idea of what causes those conditions. Various steering troubles include the following:

Hard Steering

The possible causes of hard steering can be due to the following:

- Low or uneven tire pressure
- Too tight adjustments in steering gear and linkage
- Misaligned steering column to steering gear
- Bent or twisted suspension arms
- Insufficient or incorrect lubricant used
- Bound-up shock absorbers
- Shifted front axle on springs
- Excessive caster
- Overloaded front axle
- Bent steering knuckle
- Bent or broken frame

Excessive Play or Looseness in Steering

It means that there is excessive free movement of the steering wheel without corresponding movement of the front wheels. Some causes are responsible for it.

- Loose or worn steering gear connections
- Incorrectly adjusted or worn front wheel bearings
- Worn or loose worm steering shaft bearings
- Excessive pitman shaft or ball nut lash in the steering gear
- Loose pitman arm, tie rods, steering arms or steering linkage studs
- Worn ball joints
- Loose steering wheel on shaft
- Worn steering knuckle bushings
- Worn control arm bushings
- Soft shock absorbers

Car Pulls to One Side

You can find the possible causes from the following:

- Bent steering knuckle or knuckle support
- Rear wheels' not tracking with front wheels
- Too tight wheel bearings
- Weak or broken rear springs
- Incorrect or uneven caster or camber
- Incorrectly or unevenly adjusted brakes
- Low or uneven tire pressure
- Shifted rear axle
- Inoperative shock absorbers
- Incorrect toe-in
- Bent or broken frame

Rattle or Chuckle in Steering Gear

The following are the possible causes:

- Insufficient or improper lubricant in steering gear
- Worn or loose worm steering shaft bearings
- Loose pitman arm on shaft
- Excessive backlash in steering gear

Front Wheel Shimmy

The causes are the following:

- Low or uneven tire pressure
- Imbalanced wheels, tires or brake drums
- Incorrectly adjusted or worn steering connections
- Incorrectly adjusted steering gear
- Worn steering knuckle bushings
- Bent steering knuckle
- Incorrect toe-in
- Worn ball joints
- Incorrect or uneven caster
- Inoperative shock absorbers

Front Wheel Tramp

Front wheel tramp is also called high-speed shimmy. This condition causes the front wheels to move up and down alternately. The following are the possible causes for this condition:

- Imbalanced wheels, tires or brake drums
- Not concentric wheel or tire
- Inoperative stabilizer
- Inoperative shock absorbers

Car Wander

Car wander is experienced as difficulty in keeping the car moving straight ahead. Frequent steering-wheel movements are necessary to prevent the car from wandering from one side of the road to the other. An investigation should be made as soon as possible. The following are some of the causes for it:

- Too loose or worn steering gear or connections
- Too tight steering gear or connections
- Worn steering knuckle bushings
- Incorrect or uneven caster or camber
- Shifted rear axle
- Inoperative stabilizer
- Low or uneven tire pressure
- Excessive backlash in steering gear

If you are able to relate various steering complaints to the conditions that cause them, you are much better off than the fellow who seeks blindly to find what is causing the trouble. You will know what to check and correct to eliminate the trouble. You can save a great deal of time and effort when you know where to look.

New Words

alignment	[ˈəlainmənt]	n.	找正,(车轮/车门)对准(调整),(车轮/悬架)定位
uneven	[ʌnˈiːvən]	a.	不匀的,不稳定的,不平衡的
caster	[ˈkɑːstə]	n.	(转向节)主销纵倾,主销纵倾角
bound	[baund]	v.	跳跃,(球等)弹起
camber	[ˈkæmbə]	n.	(车轮)外倾,外倾角
inoperative	[inˈɔpərətiv]	a.	不起作用的
shimmy	[ˈʃimi]	n.	(机动车)不正常地振动
stabilizer	[ˈsteibəlaizə]	n.	稳定器(杆),稳压器

Phrases and Expressions

toe-in	前轮前束
front wheel tramp	前轮跳跃,前轮跳振
be better off	境况较好
hard steering	转向沉重

Notes to the Text

1. A variety of steering troubles will bring the driver to the mechanic, but it is rare that the driver will have a clear idea of what caused this trouble.
   转向机构的各种故障会迫使驾驶员去找机械师解决,但是驾驶员要做到清楚地了解引起故障的原因是很难的。

2. Car wander is experienced as difficulty in keeping the car moving straight ahead. Frequent steering-wheel movements are necessary to prevent the car from wandering from one side of the road to the other.
   汽车甩摆使司机感到保持汽车向前直线行驶很困难。为避免汽车从道路的一边到另一边的甩摆运动,必须频繁地转动方向盘。

Exercises

I. Translate the following names of cars into Chinese.

1. Ferrari _____
2. Piaggio _____
3. Lamborghini _____
4. Bugatti _____
5. Alfa-Romeo _____
6. Lada _____
7. Holden _____
8. Polonez _____

II. Translate the following abbreviations into corresponding Chinese terms.

1. PS (power steering) _____
2. PSP (power steering pressure) _____
3. 4WS (four-wheel steering) _____
4. VSA (vehicle stability assist) _____
5. SUV (sport utility vehicle) _____
6. RKE (remote keyless entry) _____

Section C Dialogue Auto Insurance

The following dialogue is about auto insurance (See Fig. 11 -2).

Fig. 11 -2 Dialogue about auto insurance

Assistant(A): Good morning, sir. Can I help you?
Customer(C): I'm looking for insurance from your company. May I ask you a few questions about insurance?
A: Certainly. Go ahead, please.
C: Generally speaking, what risks of the automobile must be covered?
A: Is your insurance aiming for a family car or a business car?
C: For a family car.
A: For a family car, it always covers vehicle loss, person in vehicle, the third party (indemnity) insurance, risk of breakage and insurance against theft, etc.
C: Generally, what risks will be covered for customers?
A: It is generally divided into two types: one is called All Risks; the other type is that customers can choose some of the risks according to their own requirements.
C: An All Risks policy covers every sort of hazard, doesn't it?
A: That's right. If your car is a new one, All Risks is a sensible choice.
C: Why?
A: Car troubles always seem to happen at the worst possible time. You cannot always prevent disasters, but you can insure against them. Protect yourself and your family with an All Risks for your car, so that large expenses cannot hit you all at once.
C: OK. I'll take it. Thanks for your advice.
A: You are welcome.

Useful Expressions and Sentences

1. Insurance 保险,保险额
   insurance company 保险公司
   insurance against responsibility 责任保险
   insurance against theft 失窃保险,窃盗保险
   insurance certificate 保险凭证
   insurance of unexpected injury of passenger 乘客意外伤害保险
   insurance period 保险期,保用期
   insurance policy 保险单
   insurance rate 保险费率
   insurance premium 保险费
   insurance rating 保险等级(评级)
   insurance tariff 保险价目表
   insurance coverage 保险范围
   insurance treaty 保险合同
   insurance claim 保险索赔
   insured person, the insured, insurant 被保险人,受保人
   insurer 保险人
   cover insurance 投保

2. I'm looking for insurance from your company. May I ask you a few questions about insurance?
   我是到贵公司来投保的。我可以问您几个关于保险的问题吗?

3. Certainly. Go ahead, please.
   当然可以,请讲。

4. Generally speaking, what risks of the automobile must be covered?
   一般来说,汽车需要承保哪些险种?
   risk n. (保险业用语)……险,保险金(额),保险对象
   risk of breakage 破碎险
   insurance against additional risks 附加险
   risk insured, risk covered 承保险项

5. Is your insurance aiming for a family car or a business car?
   你的保险是针对家用轿车还是商务用车?

6. For a family car, it always covers vehicle loss, person in vehicle, the third party (indemnity) insurance, risk of breakage and insurance against theft, etc.
   对于家用轿车,险种通常包括车损险、车上人员险、第三者责任险、玻璃破碎险以及盗抢险等。

7. Generally, what risks will be covered for customers?
   客户通常承保哪些险种呢?

8. It is generally divided into two types: one is called All Risks; the other type is that customers

can choose some of the risks according to their own requirements.

一般分为两种类型：一种叫做综合险；另一种是客户按他们自己的需求选择承保险项。

9. An All Risks policy covers every sort of hazard, doesn't it?

一份综合险保单承保所有的险,是吗?

10. That's right. If your car is a new one, All Risks is a sensible choice.

是的。如果您的车是新车,综合险是明智的选择。

11. Car troubles always seem to happen at the worst possible time. You cannot always prevent disasters, but you can insure against them. Protect yourself and your family with an All Risks for your car, so that large expenses cannot hit you all at once.

汽车问题似乎总是在最糟糕的时间发生。您不总能预防灾难,但是您可以投保。为了保护您自己和您的家人,为您的车上一份综合险,可使您不会立刻受到大量开支的突然冲击。

12. OK. I'll take it. Thanks for your advice.

好,我就保一份综合险。谢谢您的建议。

Unit Twelve

Section A Brake System

The brake system is vitally important in the running and control of the motor vehicle. The function of the brake system is to slow down or bring to rest a moving vehicle in a shortest possible distance, or to hold the vehicle stationary if already halted.

The brake is a friction device for converting the power of momentum or kinetic energy of the moving vehicle into heat by means of friction. In consistent with safety of the drivers, the passengers and the other road users, the brake must be strong enough to stop the vehicle during emergency within the shortest distance.

There are two completely independent brake systems used on a car: the service brake system and the parking brake system.

The service brake system allows the driver to reduce, directly or indirectly, the speed of a vehicle during normal driving or to bring the vehicle to a halt. It is foot-operated by the driver depressing or releasing the brake pedal. When the pedal is pushed, the brake assemblies of all four wheels operate simultaneously. It is also called running or foot brake.

The parking brake system allows the vehicle to be held stationary mechanically even on an inclined surface, and particularly in the absence of the driver. The parking brake is mechanically operated by the driver when a separate parking brake hand lever is set. A lever is pulled and the rear brakes are applied and locked in the "ON" position. The car may now be left without fear of its rolling away. The hand brake must also be able to stop the car in the event of the foot brake failing. For this reason, it is separated from the foot brake and uses cable or rods instead of the hydraulic system. So, it is also called the emergency or hand brake.

In terms of their power sources, brakes are basically of two types: mechanically actuated brakes and hydraulic brakes. However, hydraulic brakes have been universally used on cars. Mechanical brakes are mainly used in the parking brake system.

The typical hydraulic brake system consists of disk brakes on the front and either disk or drum brakes on the rear wheels connected by a system of tubes and hoses that link the brake at each wheel to the master cylinder. The master cylinder is fluid-filled and contains two separate sections. There is a piston in each section and both pistons are connected to a brake pedal in the driver's compartment. When the brake is pushed down, the brake fluid is sent from the master cylinder to the wheel cylinder. In the wheel cylinder, the fluid pushes the shoes or pads against the revolving drums or disks. The friction between the stationary shoes or pads and the revolving drums or disks slows or stops the revolving wheels, which, in turn, slow or stop the car (See Fig. 12-1).

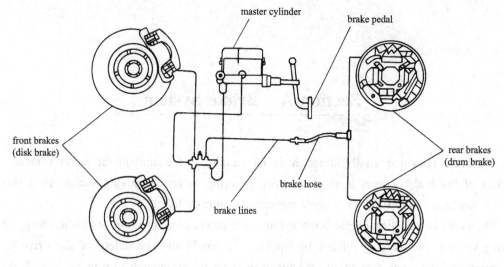

Fig. 12-1   The typical hydraulic brake system

In order to ensure the efficiency of the brake system, the dual master cylinder is designed for both front and rear brakes of most cars. The prominent advantage of the dual master cylinder is that it supplies separate hydraulic systems for the front and rear brakes. If a brake fluid leak should occur in one system, the other system would still operate, making it possible to stop the car.

Structurally, a drum brake contains several major parts such as a brake drum, a backing plate, a wheel cylinder, pull back springs, brake shoes with friction linings and an automatic or self-adjusting system.

The brake drum is bolted to the wheel hub between the hub and the wheel. It completely surrounds the brake shoe assembly and comes very close to the backing plate so that water and dust will be excluded. There is a clearance between the inner surface of the drum and the shoe lining. The stationary backing plate is what holds everything together. It is secured to the flange of the axle housing or to the steering knuckle and forms a solid surface for the wheel cylinder, brake shoes and assorted hardware. Most wheel brake assemblies use two brake shoes.

To apply brakes, the brake fluid is forced, under pressure, into the wheel cylinder which, in turn, pushes the brake shoes into contact with the machined surface on the inside of the drum. When the pressure is released, pull back springs, pull the shoes back to their rest position. A self-adjusting mechanism automatically reacts by adjusting the rest position of the shoes so that they are closer to the drum.

The disk brake has a metal disk instead of a drum, and a pair of pads, or flat shoes, instead of the curved shoes used with the drum brakes. The greatest advantage of the disk brake is that it provides significantly better resistance to "brake fade" compared with the drum brake. So, disk brakes, used for years for front wheel applications, are fast replacing drum brakes on the rear wheels of modern cars. There are three general types of disk brakes: fixed-calipers, sliding-calipers, and floating-calipers.

The main components of a disk brake include the brake pad, disk or rotor, and caliper.

The disk, or rotor, is a part of the wheel hub. The caliper and brake pads are positioned over the disk, and most calipers are bolted to the steering knuckle.

Since disk brakes do not have any servo action, the brake pads must be applied with higher pressure, which is obtained with the use of larger caliper pistons as compared with wheel cylinder pistons.

When the brakes are applied, the hydraulic pressure forces the piston against the brake pads. This action forces the linings against the disk friction surfaces to provide braking action. The brake action occurs very quickly because there is very small clearance between the brake linings and the disk surfaces. When two pistons are used in each side of the caliper, the application force is equal on each brake pad.

Many later model vehicles are equipped with single-piston floating calipers. When the brakes are applied with these calipers, the caliper piston movement forces the inner brake pad lining against the disk surface. Hydraulic pressure is applied equally to the piston and the bottom of the piston bore. Since the caliper is free to move laterally, the hydraulic force on the piston bore moves the caliper inward, which forces the outer brake pad lining against the outer disk surface. The force on each brake pad is equal.

New Words

depress	[di'pres]	v.	踩下,压下
release	[ri'li:s]	v.	放开,释放
simultaneously	[ˌsiməl'teinjəsli]	adv.	同时地,一齐地
actuate	['æktʃueit]	v.	开动,驱使
pad	[pæd]	n.	摩擦衬块
drum	[drʌm]	n.	鼓,制动鼓
disk	[disk]	n.	圆盘,制动盘
stationary	['steiʃənəri]	a.	静止的,固定的
lining	['lainiŋ]	n.	衬片,摩擦片
hub	[hʌb]	n.	轮毂
riveted	['rivitid]	a.	铆接的
bonded	['bɔndid]	a.	黏合而成的
resistance	[ri'zistəns]	n.	阻力
caliper	['kælipə]	n.	卡钳,测径器
		v.	用卡钳测量

Phrases and Expressions

brake pedal	制动踏板
hand brake	手制动器
in the event of	如果……发生
in terms of	根据,按照,从……方面(来说)
disk brake	盘式制动器
drum brake	鼓式制动器
master cylinder	制动主缸
brake fluid	制动液
brake pad	制动块
backing plate	制动底板,支承板
wheel cylinder	制动轮缸,车轮(液压)制动分泵缸
pull back spring	回位弹簧
in turn	依次,轮流
machined surface	已加工面
brake fade	制动衰减
disk rotor	制动盘,盘形转子
floating caliper	浮式制动钳

Notes to the Text

1. There are two completely independent brake systems used on a car: the service brake system and the parking brake system.
   车辆上有两套完全独立的制动系统:行车制动系统和驻车制动系统。
2. In the wheel cylinder, the fluid pushes the shoes or pads against the revolving drums or disks.
   在车轮的轮缸上,制动液推动制动蹄片或制动块阻止制动鼓或制动盘的转动。
3. If a brake fluid leak should occur in one system, the other system would still operate, making it possible to stop the car.
   尽管一个系统发生制动液渗漏,但另一个系统仍会运行,从而使车辆停止成为可能。

Exercises on the Text

I. Answer the following questions according to the text.

1. What is the function of the brake?
2. How is the service brake operated?
3. When is the parking brake used?
4. What does the typical hydraulic brake system consist of?
5. What is the prominent advantage of the dual master cylinder?

II. Fill in the table below (Tab. 12-1).

Tab. 12-1

English	Chinese
	制动主缸
brake pedal	
	制动盘
pull back spring	
	制动蹄片
fixed caliper	
	行车制动器
wheel cylinder	
	制动液
kinetic energy	

III. Fill in the blanks with the words or phrases given below, and change the form where necessary.

| resistance | brake fluid | convert | bolt |
| efficiency | in the event of | means | leak |

1. The brake is a friction device for _____ the power of momentum or kinetic energy of a moving vehicle into heat by means of friction.
2. When the brake is pushed down, _____ is sent from the master cylinder to the wheels.
3. The greatest advantage of the disk brake is that it provides significantly better _____ to "brake fade" compared with the drum brake.
4. The brake drum _____ to the wheel hub between the hub and the wheel.
5. Calipers must be replaced if they show signs of _____ brake fluid.
6. The dual master cylinder is designed for both front and rear brakes of most cars to ensure the _____ of the brake system.
7. The _____ of slowing down or bringing to rest a moving vehicle is called brakes.
8. The hand brake must be able to stop the car _____ the foot brake failing.

IV. Reading comprehension: Read the following passage carefully and fill in the blanks with the words given below.

| force | hydraulic | friction | slows | piston |
| connected | fail | pressure | dual | brake |

Modern master cylinders are actually two separated cylinders. Such a system is called a

___1___ circuit, because the front cylinder is ___2___ to the front brakes and the rear cylinder to the rear brakes. The two cylinders are separated, allowing for emergency stopping power should one part of the system ___3___. The entire hydraulic system from the master cylinder to the wheels is full of ___4___ brake fluid. When the ___5___ pedal is depressed, the ___6___ in the master cylinder are forced to move, exerting tremendous ___7___ on the fluid in the lines. The fluid has nowhere to go, but forces the wheel cylinder pistons or caliper pistons to exert ___8___ on the brake shoes or pads. The ___9___ between the brake shoe and wheel drum or the brake pad and rotor ___10___ the vehicle and eventually stops it.

V. Translate the following passage into Chinese.

The master cylinder is fluid-filled and contains two separate sections. There is a piston in each section and both pistons are connected to a brake pedal in the driver's compartment. When the brake is pushed down, brake fluid is sent from the master cylinder to the wheel cylinder. In the wheel cylinder, the fluid pushes the shoes or pads against the revolving drums or disks. The friction between the stationary shoes or pads and the revolving drums or disks slows or stops the revolving wheels, which, in turn, slow or stop the car.

VI. Translate the following sentences into English.

1. 汽车上使用两套完全独立的制动系统:行车制动和驻车制动。
2. 驻车制动机构的作用是防止已停车辆滑行或移动。
3. 液压制动器在汽车上已被普遍使用。
4. 行车制动系统用来使行驶中的车辆减速和停止。
5. 双制动主缸的主要优点是它为前后制动器提供分开的液压系统。

Section B Antilock Brake System (ABS)

An antilock brake system (ABS) is a closed-loop control device within the braking system which prevents wheel lock-up during braking and, as a result, retains the vehicle's steerability and stability. The purpose of ABS is to allow the driver to maintain steering control under heavy braking and, in most cases, in most situations such as wet road surface, to shorten braking distances by allowing the driver to hit the brake fully without the fear of skidding or loss of control. The main ABS components are: wheel-speed sensors, a hydraulic modulator, and an electronic control unit (ECU)(See Fig. 12-2).

The **wheel-speed sensors** sense the speed of rotation of the wheels, and this speed information is sent to the electronic control unit (ECU). They work in conjunction with a toothed wheel or a toothed ring. An electromagnetic sensor comprises a coil winding with a permanent magnet core and pole pin, the latter being accurately aligned in a radial or an axial position with a

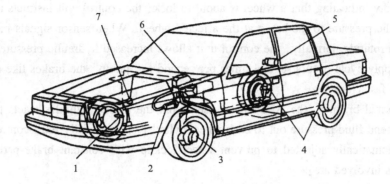

Fig. 12-2 Four-wheel antilock brake system
1—wheel speed sensor; 2—pump and motor; 3—wheel speed sensor; 4—wheel sensor;
5—anti-lock brake control module; 6—hydraulic assembly; 7—relays

toothed wheel, but separated from its teeth by a small although critical air gap. The teeth of the toothed wheel or the sensor ring act as a single generator, so that when each passing tooth faces the pole pin of the sensor, the changing magnetic field induces a voltage across the winding. Above walking pace this produces a frequency of signal that varies in proportion to road wheel speed and thus supplies the required input to the control system.

Some antilock systems use only three wheel sensors. One sensor is used at each front wheel, and one sensor is located near the drive shaft to sense lockup at both rear wheels.

Some light trucks have antilock brake systems that prevent lockup at the rear wheels only, which are called rear antilock brake systems (RABS). A single speed sensor in the differential-gear assembly senses rear-wheel lockup.

The **hydraulic modulator** assembly regulates the pressure to the wheel brakes when it receives commands from the control unit. The modulator assembly can maintain or reduce pressure over the level it receives from the master cylinder. The modulator assembly consists of three high-speed electric solenoid valves, two fluid reservoirs and a turn delivery pump equipped with inlet and outlet check valves. The modulator electrical connector and controlling relays are concealed under a plastic cover of the assembly.

The **electronic control unit** (ECU) monitors the rate of change in this frequency to determine impending brake lockup. It contains all the signal conditioning circuitry and the output circuits. The output circuits control the hydraulic unit to adjust the line pressure to each caliper. The unit is located under the dash panel on the left side, above the glove compartment and in the forward position of the electronic box in the engine compartment. If a problem is sensed, the control unit will light the instrument panel warning lamp.

The basic operating principle of antilock brake systems is quite simple. Antilock systems modulate brake application force several times per second to hold the tires at a controlled amount of slip; all systems accomplish this in basically the same way. One or more wheel-speed sensors generate alternating current signals whose frequency increases with the wheel rotational speed. An electronic control unit (ECU) continuously monitors these signals and if the frequency of a signal drops too rapidly indicating that a wheel is about to lock, the control unit instructs a modulator to reduce hydraulic pressure to the brake at the affected wheel. When sensor signals indicate that the wheel is again rotating normally, the control unit allows increased hydraulic pressure to the brake. This release-apply cycle occurs several times per second to "pump" the brakes like a driver might but at a much faster rate.

Under normal braking, the ABS is not used, and the master cylinder reacts to brake-pedal movement to send fluid pressure out to each wheel cylinder. During full, ABS-controlled braking, pressure is automatically adjusted to prevent wheel lockup with constant brake-pedal force. The three processes involved are:

- **Maintaining braking pressure** If the wheels are likely to lock up, the braking pressure at the wheel involved is initially kept constant as opposed to being further increased.
- **Reducing braking pressure** If the wheel still continues to decelerate, the pressure in the wheel brake cylinder is reduced so that the wheel is braked less heavily.
- **Increasing braking pressure** The wheel accelerates again as a result of the reduced braking pressure.

A modern antilock brake system makes braking safer and more convenient. It may be the greatest advance in vehicle safety since the seatbelt.

New Words

retain	[riˈtein]	v.	保留,保持
lockup	[ˈlɔkʌp]	n.	锁住
skid	[skid]	v.	滑动,打滑(空转),(侧向)滑移
toothed	[tuːθt]	a.	带齿的,锯齿状的
winding	[ˈwaindiŋ]	n.	绕组,线圈
magnet	[ˈmægnit]	n.	磁铁
axial	[ˈæksiəl]	a.	轴向的
magnetic	[mægˈnetik]	a.	磁的,有磁性的
generate	[ˈdʒenəreit]	v.	产生,发生
reservoir	[ˈrezəvwɑː]	n.	水库,蓄水池,储液器
decelerate	[diːˈseləreit]	v.	减速

Phrases and Expressions

antilock brake system	防抱死制动系统
wheel-speed sensor	轮速传感器
permanent magnet	永磁铁
impending brake	紧急制动
dash panel	仪表板
solenoid valve	电磁阀
fluid reservoir	储液室

hydraulic pressure　　　　　　　　液压,水压,油压

Notes to the Text

1. The hydraulic modulator assembly regulates the pressure to the wheel brakes when it receives commands from the control unit.
   当收到控制单元的指令时,液压调节总成就调节作用到制动轮缸上的油压。
2. If the wheel still continues to decelerate, the pressure in the wheel brake cylinder is reduced so that the wheel is braked less heavily.
   如果车轮仍然持续减速,制动轮缸内的压力便降低,这样车轮的制动力就会减轻。

Exercises

I. Translate the following names of cars into Chinese.
   1. Daewoo　_____　　2. Ssangyong　_____
   3. Hyundai　_____　　4. Kia　_____
   5. Skoda　_____　　6. Dacia　_____
   7. Proton　_____　　8. Smart　_____

II. Translate the following abbreviations into corresponding Chinese terms.
   1. ABS（anti-lock brake system）　_____
   2. AP（accelerator pedal）　_____
   3. BMC（brake master cylinder）　_____
   4. PKB（parking brake）　_____
   5. BTR（brake transmission ratio）　_____
   6. NPS（neutral position switch）　_____

Section C　FAW-VW

FAW-VW (First Automobile Works joint venture-Volkswagen) Automobile Co. Ltd. is a major passenger sedan joint venture of FAW Group Corporation and Volkswagen AG (Their logos are shown in Fig. 12 – 3.), Audi AG and Volkswagen Automobile (China) Investment Co. Ltd. It is China's first modern passenger sedan industrial base of considerable economic scale. The main FAW-VW factory is in Changchun, Jilin Province (Its headquarters is

Fig. 12 – 3　Logos of FAW-VW

Fig. 12 -4 The Headquarters of FAW-VW in Changchun, China

shown in Fig. 12 -4.).

In FAW-VW, Volkswagen AG has 20% stake, and Audi AG has 10% stake, and Volkswagen Automobile (China) Investment Co. Ltd. has 10% stake, and FAW has the remaining 60%.

FAW-VW manufactures some of the world's most famous brands — Jetta, Bora, Golf, Sagitar, Magotan and Audi. The establishment of the company heralds the entry of China's automotive industry into a new era of large-scale production.

FAW-Volkswagen Automobile Co. Ltd. was established in 1991, with the first Jetta automobile rolling off the assembly line on December 5 of that year. Audi AG became a member of the partnership in 1995, and full scale production commenced in July of 1996. Official government approval for the 150,000 annual unit project was received in 1997.

Through its continuous expansion, FAW-VW has become a company with a daily production capacity of over 1,000 motor vehicles, with additional capacity for export of assembled vehicles, powertrain and component parts.

Audi

In 1986, Audi AG made an initial official contact with China and together with FAW, began a joint feasibility study of certain technology in Changchun. Two years later, FAW was granted a manufacturing license by Audi. In the same year, a total of 499 Audi cars were assembled in Changchun.

In 1993, Audi joined the joint venture of FAW-VW. In 1996, Audi established an after-sales service division in Beijing. Audi technicians in FAW-VW provided training for the Chinese employees as well as technical support. In the same year, Audi established an expert team composed of professionals in automobile sales, marketing development, public relations and after-sales service, to improve the market development of Audi in China.

In 1999, the Audi A6, produced jointly by Audi and its partner, FAW Group, came off the production line at FAW-VW, Changchun. The Audi A6 made up for the absence of premium cars produced in China. Two years later the Audi A8 was officially launched in China. This symbolized the landing in China of Audi's flagship vehicle. Then, the new Audi A4 model and the Audi TT sports car were also launched in China, introducing more personalized choices for Chinese customers.

In 2003, the Audi A4, as the top range product of the world premium brands B-class vehicles, was put into production in China. In the next year, Audi launched the new Audi A4 model which offered not only more color choices, but also more personalized accessories. The new Audi A4 model became the ideal choice for the elites who pursue a high quality and individual life. In May the same year, the Audi A8L 6.0 quattro 4WD, the high-class flagship product of Audi, was launched in China. This model is the premium car with the most advanced technology and best performance in the global market. Its launch further strengthened Audi's leading position in the Chinese premium car market. China is currently the fourth largest market for the Audi A8.

In April 2005, the new China-made Audi A6L was launched (See Fig. 12 – 5). In October, the launch of the new Audi A4 further consolidated and completed the Audi product series in China. China became the third biggest market for Audi outside of Germany.

The latest-generation Audi A6L was launched on March 28, 2012 (See Fig. 12 – 6). Audi's executives said that the car marks a new milestone of the company's localization campaign in China. Specially developed for Chinese consumers who prefer roomy back seats, the long-wheelbase saloon is expected to further enhance Audi's competitiveness in the premium market. Passenger comfort is greatly improved in the latest Audi A6L with the new equipments like a panoramic sunroof, ion generator for air quality, backseat entertainment system and seats with a massage function.

Fig. 12 – 5   Audi A6L

Fig. 12 – 6   All-new Audi A6L

Audi will be bringing seven brand new models to China this year. In addition, FAW-VW plans to expand its dealer network for Audis from 237 outlets to 300, as well as make further strides in product localization.

New Words

stake	[steik]	n.	木桩,赌注,股份
herald	['herəld]	v.	预示,预报
entry	['entri]	n.	进入,入场,入口,通道
commence	[kə'mens]	v.	开始,着手
premium	['primjəm]	n.	高级,优质,奖金,奖励
elite	[ei'liːt]	n.	精英,精华,中坚
pursue	[pə'sjuː]	v.	追赶,追随,追求
milestone	['mailˌstəun]	n.	里程碑
localization	[ˌləukəlai'zeiʃən]	n.	定位
roomy	['ruːmi]	a.	宽敞的,宽大的
wheelbase	['wiːlbeis]	n.	轴距
saloon	[sə'luːn]	n.	双排座轿车
panoramic	[ˌpænə'ræmik]	a.	全景的,全貌的

sunroof	[ˈsʌnruːf]	n.	天窗
outlet	[ˈautlet]	n.	经销店

Phrases and Expressions

be located in	坐落于，位于
make up for	弥补
quattro 4WD	全时四轮驱动
ion generator	离子发生器

Proper Names

Volkswagen AG	德国大众公司（"AG"为德语"Aktiengesellschaft"的缩写，意为"股份制公司"）
Audi AG	奥迪公司
Volkswagen Automobile (China) Investment Co. Ltd.	大众汽车（中国）投资有限公司
Jetta	捷达
Bora	宝来
Golf	高尔夫
Sagitar	速腾
Magotan	迈腾

Notes to the Text

1. Official government approval for the 150,000 annual unit project was received in 1997.
   1997年，公司的年产量15万辆轿车工程项目通过了国家正式验收。

2. In the same year, Audi established an expert team composed of professionals in automobile sales, marketing development, public relations and after-sales service, to improve the market development of Audi in China.
   同年，奥迪公司为了加速其在中国市场的发展建立了一支由汽车销售、市场开发、公共关系和售后服务等方面的专业人士组成的专家团队。

3. In addition, FAW – VW plans to expand its dealer network for Audis from 237 outlets to 300, as well as make further strides in product localization.
   另外，一汽大众计划扩大奥迪的经销网络，将原来的237个经销商增加至300个，并且力争在产品的定位方面取得进展。

Questions for Discussion:

1. According to the text, what are the famous brands of FAW-VW?

2. When did Audi join FAW-VW?
3. What are the features of the new Audi A4?
4. What are the features of all-new Audi A6L?
5. According to the text, what are the plans of FAW-VW?

Unit Thirteen

Section A Automobile Navigation System

Presently, an automobile navigation system includes two parts: the global positioning system (GPS) and automobile automatic navigation system.

The global positioning system (GPS) is a satellite-based positioning system planned by the US Department of Defence in the early 1970s and has been operational in the traffic system since 1995. Magellan, a GPS navigation system manufacturer, claims it created the first GPS-based automobile navigation system in the US in 1995.

An automotive navigation system is a satellite navigation system designed for use in automobiles. Unlike other GPS, position data are used to locate the user on a road in the unit's map database. Using the road database, the unit can give directions to other locations along roads also in its database. Nestled in the front dash, the navigation screen can display road maps of the majority of the country. The maps are culled from data stored on a DVD in the car. The GPS locator can synchronize data on the car's whereabouts to cast the right maps onto the screen (See Fig. 13-1). The GPS can display specific traffic and travel information on a display screen. It can mark the location of the vehicle, plot out the best way of getting to the destination, and tell the driver how many miles have been traveled and how many miles are left before reaching the destination. It can also display traffic information regarding traffic backups due to congestion, and accidents; then it can display alternative routes so travel is not delayed.

Fig. 13-1 GPS

The global positioning system (GPS) consists of three segments: the space segment, the control segment, and the user segment. The space segment includes the satellites that broadcast navigation signals to receivers through carrier waves. The control segment traces and monitors the satellites through ground control stations to monitor their locations and check on their status. In this way, they can decide if a satellite goes out of its planned position. If it does, adjust it into the designed ideal position in the GPS satellite network. The user segment refers to the user-end

GPS receiver that calculates the time it takes to send and receive radio signals from satellites. By calculating the travel-time of signals from and to the satellites, a GPS receiver can find out the distance between the current position of the receiver and the satellites. The more satellites the receiver can "see," the more accurate the position fixing process will be.

Satellite technology is used in navigation, vehicle tracking, vehicle theft recovery, communication, and Internet access. The GPS forms a critical part of vehicle tracking systems, however many other components are required to keep track of the vehicle. Mountains, tunnels, large buildings and other objects can interfere with satellite communication and make it unreliable. Most vehicle tracking systems can work very accurately without satellites once their initial position has been determined. On-board sensors can be used to keep track of the exact vehicle location.

Satellite Navigation

Once a vehicle's position is determined via trilateration, software can be used to generate an accurate map of the area. The GPS continues to provide updated information to ensure accuracy of the map data. Trilateration is used to determine an initial vehicle position for reference. Once this has been determined, mapping software stored on a DVD can be used to generate an overlay map and data for the driver on a display screen. As the vehicle moves, the GPS continues to provide necessary information to allow for plotting of the position on the map.

Accurate and reliable navigation is still possible even when satellite signals become unavailable. This is achieved by using electronic sensors to monitor vehicle variables such as pitch, roll, yaw, road speed, steering angle, acceleration and deceleration. By using the information from these sensors, the navigation system is not continually and totally reliant on satellites. During normal operation, the computer program compares vehicle position data derived from the satellites and on-board sensor information to ensure a high level of accuracy. In addition, ground-based stations may be used in suitable locations as an absolute reference point.

The features of satellite navigation can include: multiple languages and journey destination plotting, where the most suitable route is provided and deviation from the recommended route causes the system to provide an alternate route. It can also include directional information provided with a combination of screen icons, maps and audible instructions; a self-learning route memory function; congestion avoidance, which can warn of the latest traffic bottlenecks and suggest alternative routes; infra red remote control; Trip Computer; speed dependent setting; and telephone mute for sound systems.

New Words

navigation	[ˌnævɪˈgeɪʃən]	n.	导航,航行,航海
satellite	[ˈsætəlaɪt]	n.	人造卫星
database	[ˈdeɪtəbeɪs]	n.	数据库,资料库
nestle	[ˈnesl]	v.	使紧贴,使舒适地安顿下来
dash	[dæʃ]	n.	仪表板

cull	[kʌl]	v.	挑选,收集,选用(尤指资料)
locator	[ləu'keitə]	n.	探测器,定位器
plot	[plɔt]	v.	在图上标绘……的位置,绘制……平面图
backup	['bækʌp]	n.	替代物,备用品,后备
congestion	[kən'dʒestʃən]	n.	拥挤
segment	['segmənt]	n.	部分;切片
trilateration	[trailætə'reiʃən]	n.	三维
variable	['vεəriəbəl]	n.	易变的事,可变因素
		a.	易变的,不稳定的
icon	['aikɔn]	n.	(计算机屏幕上显示的代表所指谓的事物的)图示,图符,记号
monitor	['mɔnitə]	v.	监视,监听
		n.	监视器
update	[ʌp'deit]	v.	更新,使现代化,使不过时
deviation	[diːvi'eiʃən]	n.	偏离,偏差

Phrases and Expressions

global positioning system (GPS)	全球定位系统
due to	由于
carrier wave / C/W	载波
on-board sensor	车载传感器
keep track of	跟踪
interfere with	干扰,妨碍
be reliant on	依赖,依靠
infrared remote control / IR remote control	红外线遥控
Trip Computer	行车电脑(美国 Cadillac 公司生产的驾驶员信息系统的商品名)
speed dependent	与速度有关的
speed dependent setting	设定车速
telephone mute for sound system	声音系统的电话静音

Notes to the Text

1. The global positioning system (GPS) is a satellite-based positioning system planned by the US Department of Defence in the early 1970's and has been operational in traffic system since 1995.

   全球定位系统是由美国国防部于20世纪70年代早期设计的基于卫星的定位系统,并且自

1995年开始已经应用于交通系统中。

2. It can mark the location of the vehicle, plot out the best way of getting to the destination, and tell the driver how many miles have been traveled and how many miles are left before reaching the destination.

它能够标定出车辆的位置,设计出到达目的地的最佳路线,并且告诉司机已经行驶了多少英里及还要行驶多少英里才能到达目的地。

3. This is achieved by using electronic sensors to monitor vehicle variables such as pitch, roll, yaw, road speed, steering angle, acceleration and deceleration.

这一目标的实现是通过使用电子传感器来监测汽车的变化的,例如俯仰、倾斜、偏航、车速、转向角、加速和减速。

4. In addition, ground-based stations may be used in suitable locations as an absolute reference point.

此外,还可将适当位置的地面车站作为绝对的参考点来使用。

5. It can also include directional information provided with a combination of screen icons, maps and audible instructions.

它还能包括由屏幕图标、地图及音响指示组合而成的定向信息。

Exercises on the Text

I. Answer the following questions according to the text.

1. What's the function of the global positioning system (GPS)?
2. What are the three segments of the global positioning system (GPS)?
3. What's the function of a GPS receiver?
4. In which fields can satellite technology be used?
5. Accurate and reliable navigation is still possible even when satellite signals become unavailable. How is this achieved?

II. Fill in the table below (Tab. 13 – 1).

Tab. 13 – 1

English	Chinese
	导航
GPS	
	人造卫星
on-board sensor	
	网络
carrier wave	
	监视器
database	
	定位器
dash	

III. Fill in the blanks with the words or phrases given below, and change the form where necessary.

| nestle | accurate | segment | update |
| create | cull | alternative | interfere with |

1. The GPS continues to provide _____ information to ensure accuracy of the map data.
2. The maps _____ from data stored on a DVD in the car.
3. Mountains, tunnels, large buildings and other objects can _____ satellite communication and make it unreliable.
4. The more satellites the receiver can "see," the more _____ the position fixing process will be.
5. _____ in the front dash, the navigation screen can display road maps of the majority of the country.
6. The global positioning system (GPS) consists of three _____.
7. Magellan claims it _____ the first GPS-based automobile navigation system in the US in 1995.
8. The GPS can display _____ routes so travel is not delayed.

IV. Reading comprehension: Read the following passage carefully and fill in the blanks with the words given below.

| database | updates | minimum | equipment | position |
| navigation | directs | destination | information | includes |

A system located in an automobile provides personalized traffic information and route planning capabilities. This system uses __1__ which is becoming standard in automobiles, such as on-board navigation systems and cellular telephones. On-board navigation systems use global positioning system (GPS) satellites to __2__ the automobile with respect to streets in a map database. As the automobile moves, the navigation system __3__ the location. A central database __4__ travel time information for each street segment and transition between street segments in the map __5__. Based upon the travel time __6__ in the database, a route from a current location to a desired __7__, or series of destinations, can be planned in order to have a __8__ travel time. The route can be provided to the on-board __9__ system, which then __10__ the driver in traveling the route.

V. Translate the following paragraph into Chinese.

Satellite technology is used in navigation, vehicle tracking, vehicle theft recovery, communication, and Internet access. The GPS forms a critical part of vehicle tracking systems, however many other components are required to keep track of the vehicle. Mountains, tunnels, large buildings and other objects can interfere with satellite communication and make it unreliable. Most vehicle tracking systems can work very accurately without satellites once their initial position has been determined. On-board sensors can be used to keep track of the exact vehicle location.

VI. Translate the following sentences into English.

1. 当前,汽车导航系统包括两部分:全球定位系统及车辆自动导航系统。
2. 如果一颗卫星偏离了它的既定位置,则调整它并使其进入设计好的全球定位系统卫星网络中的理想位置。
3. 车载传感器可以用来跟踪车辆的确切位置。
4. GPS 连续提供最新的信息,以便确保地图数据的精确。
5. 通过使用来自传感器的信息,导航系统并非连续完全地依赖卫星。

Section B　　Types of Vehicles

For classification purposes, automobile manufacturers have historically divided their light vehicle products into two categories: automobiles and light trucks.

Automobiles (cars, or motorcars in British English) include sedans, coupes, station wagons, convertibles and sports cars, etc.

A sedan (Saloon in British English) is one of the most common body styles of modern automobiles. Basically, a sedan has a separate hood (bonnet in British English) covering the engine in the front, and a separate trunk (boot in British English) for luggage at the rear. Most luxury vehicles are four-door sedans because they're more comfortable than most other body styles. The enclosed trunk offers security, while the rear doors allow easy entry for rear-seat passengers (See Fig. 13-2).

A coupe is an enclosed car with two doors and a sloping back (See Fig. 13-3). Many of them have a back hatch instead of a trunk, to allow large items to be carried for short distances. It has either 2 seats or 2+2 seats. The rear seats are difficult to access, as the front doors must be used.

Fig. 13-2　Sedan

Fig. 13-3　Coupe

A station wagon (an estate or estate car in British English) is a body style variant of a sedan with its roof extended rearward over a shared passenger/cargo volume with access at the back via a third or fifth door (the liftgate or tailgate), instead of a trunk lid. The body style transforms a standard three-box design into a two-box design. Station wagons feature flexibility to allow configurations to favor passengers or cargo volume, e. g., folding or removable back seats. So, station wagons remain the first choice for active families (See Fig. 13 – 4). Station wagons offer more stability, but they get horrible gas mileage, and their truck-like ride and handling are rough.

A convertible is a car with a roof that can be folded back or retracted (See Fig. 13 – 5). The collapsible roof section is made of flexible canvas or vinyl, although plastic, aluminium and steel have occasionally been used in elaborate folding designs. Most convertibles are sports cars, having two seats, high-performance engines and superior handling. When the weather is perfect, driving convertibles is great fun.

Fig. 13 – 4　Station wagon

Fig. 13 – 5　Convertible

A sports car (sportscar or sport car) is a fast car with a low body, usually having a roof which can be folded back or removed. Sports cars are designed for high speed driving and maneuverability, which have been either spartan or luxurious, but good handling, minimum weight, and high performance are requisite. Sports cars were originally European two-seat roadsters designed for both daily travel and week-end racing hobbyists. Later, a few manufacturers put permanent tops on their roadsters, resulting in the sports coupe. The term sports-sedan is a more recent term to describe a four-door vehicle that handles like a sports coupe or roadster. Sports cars are cool and fun to drive, but impractical for daily transportation (See Fig. 13 – 6).

Roughly, light trucks include vans, minivans, SUVs and pick-up trucks.

A van is a road vehicle, usually larger than a car but smaller than a truck, having an enclosed box-shaped body and used for carrying goods and sometimes people (See Fig. 13 – 7). It can transport large amounts of cargo (its payload capacity is of over one ton) or more than seven adult passengers (extended vans can seat up to 15 adult passengers).

Fig. 13 – 6　Sports car

Fig. 13 – 7　Van

Minivans including minibuses, multi utility vehicles (MUVs) or multi purpose vehicles (MPVs) are a type of vehicle which has a body that resembles a van, but which has rear side doors and rear side windows, and interior fittings to accommodate passengers similar to a station wagon. Minivans are higher than normal sedans and station wagons, and are designed for maximum interior room, often offering three seat rows which can provide comfortable seating for seven people or more. In addition, minivans' driving and handling are just like cars, with better visibility due to a higher center of gravity and an upright driving position (See Fig. 13 – 8).

The SUV (sport utility vehicle) is a truck-based station wagon equipped with either two-wheel or four-wheel drive. It features passenger car qualities such as bucket seats and optional DVD players in the rear passenger area. For versatility and durability on and off the road, the SUV is built on a light-duty pickup truck chassis. The SUV was the answer as a minivan and station wagon replacement with

Fig. 13 – 8　Minivan

truck qualities. It provided all the benefits of a masculine, large and tough vehicle with the amenities of a luxury car. But as gasoline prices began to climb in the mid-2000s, SUVs fell out of favor. The more economical CUV (crossover utility vehicle), based on a passenger-car chassis, became popular for its SUV looks, all wheel drive (AWD), smoother ride and high-ground clearance (See Fig. 13 – 9).

A pick-up truck is a light van having an open body with low sides (See Fig. 13 – 10). The smaller models now offer quad or crew-cab four-door versions, with seating for 5 adults. Full-size models offer extended cabs with smaller third and fourth doors giving access to the rear seats. Full-size 2-wheel and 4-wheel drive pickups get about 15 miles per gallon.

One continuing trend in pick-up trucks over the past few years is "bigger is better": Crew cabs are more spacious; there's more emphasis on heavy-duty models and features; compacts have grown to mid-size; and engines keep increasing power along with fuel efficiency. But size isn't everything, today's pickups are still purpose-built work vehicles. Many new models now feature the same improved safety and traction control systems (TCS) as the best-equipped passenger cars and SUVs. This includes head and side airbags, seatbelt pretensioners, and computer-guided traction and stability control, etc.

Fig. 13 – 9　SUV

Fig. 13 – 10　Pick-up truck

New Words

sedan	[si'dæn]	n.	轿车
coupe	[ku:p]	n.	双门小轿车
convertible	[kən'və:təbl]	n.	敞篷车,折篷汽车
saloon	[sə'lu:n]	n.	轿车
boot	[bu:t]	n.	[英]汽车行李箱
slope	[sləup]	v.	倾斜,成斜坡
hatch	[hætʃ]	n.	(门、地板等上的)开口,活板门
retract	[ri'trækt]	v.	(使)缩回(入),收起
collapsible	[kə'læpsəbl]	a.	可折叠的
canvas	['kænvəs]	n.	帆布
vinyl	['vainil]	n.	乙烯基(塑胶)
spartan	['spɑ:tn]	a.	简朴的
requisite	['rekwizit]	a.	需要的,必要的
roadster	['rəudstə]	n.	双座敞篷汽车
van	[væn]	n.	客货两用车,厢式载货汽车,厢式车
payload	['peiləud]	n.	(运输车辆的)净载重(量),酬载
fitting	['fitiŋ]	n.	(一般用复数)(房屋内的)固定装置,设备,器材
versatility	[ˌvə:sə'tiliti]	n.	多用途,多功能
durability	[ˌdjuərə'biləti]	n.	持久,耐用
masculine	['mɑ:skjulin]	a.	男性的,男子气概的
amenity	[ə'mi:nəti]	n.	(常用复数)娱乐(消遣)设施
cab	[kæb]	n.	驾驶室

Phrases and Expressions

station wagon	旅行车
sports car	跑车
ride and handling	乘坐与操控
bucket seat	(汽车或飞机上的)单人圆背座位
CUV (crossover utility vehicle)	跨界运动休旅车
all wheel drive (AWD)	全轮驱动
pick-up truck	皮卡,轻型货车,小卡车
quad cab	四门驾驶室
traction control system (TCS)	牵引力控制系统,驱动力控制系统,防滑装置
side airbag	侧面(安全)气囊
seatbelt pretensioner	安全带预紧器

Notes to the Text

1. Basically, a sedan has a separate hood (bonnet in British English) covering the engine in the front, and a separate trunk (boot in British English) for luggage at the rear.
   通常,轿车的前部有独立的引擎罩盖住发动机,后面有独立的行李箱(后备箱)。
2. A sports car is a fast car with a low body, usually having a roof which can be folded back or removed.
   跑车是车身较低,车速快,通常车顶可折叠或去掉的小汽车。
3. Minivans including minibuses, multi utility vehicles (MUVs) or multi purpose vehicles (MPVs) are a type of vehicle which has a body that resembles a van, but which has rear side doors and rear side windows, and interior fittings to accommodate passengers similar to a station wagon.
   包括小巴士及多功能车(MUV 或 MPV)在内的小型厢式车的车身和厢式车相似,但带有后门及侧后窗,内部载客装置与旅行车相似。
4. Full-size models offer extended cabs with smaller third and fourth doors giving access to the rear seats. Full-size 2-wheel and 4-wheel drive pickups get about 15 miles per gallon.
   大型皮卡有加大的驾驶室,第三及第四个车门(两个后车门)可进入后座。大型的两轮或四轮驱动皮卡每加仑油可行驶 15 英里。

Exercises

I. Translate the following types of vehicles into Chinese.

1. Minivan _____
2. Coupe _____
3. Sedan _____
4. Station wagon _____
5. Van _____
6. Pick-up truck _____
7. Sports car _____
8. Convertible _____

II. Translate the following abbreviations into corresponding Chinese terms.

1. SUV (sport utility vehicle) _____
2. TCS (traction control system) _____
3. GPS (global positioning system) _____
4. CUV (crossover utility vehicle) _____
5. C/W (carrier wave) _____
6. AWD (all wheel drive) _____

Section C Dialogue A Return Call Visit

The following dialogue is about a return call visit (See Fig. 13 – 11).

Fig. 13 – 11 A return call visit

Receptionist (R): Hello. Is this Mr. Wang?
Mr. Wang (W): Yes. Who is speaking?
R: This is after-sales receptionist in Wan Da Automobile Service Company. I'm calling to do a return call visit for our service.
W: OK. Go ahead.
R: How is it going with your car now?
W: It works very well.
R: How do you think about the maintenance for your car in our company last time?
W: Oh, I'm quite satisfied with it.
R: Thank you for saying so. By the way, would you please give us some suggestions to further improve our service?
W: Err, I hope there will be more comfortable place to rest, and more magazines and newspapers for us customers to read.
R: Thank you for your suggestions and warm-hearted reply. Please contact us at any time if there is something wrong with your car.
W: I will. Thanks.

Useful Expressions and Sentences

1. a return call visit
   电话回访
2. Hello. Is this Mr. Wang?

您好！是王先生吗？
3. Yes. Who is speaking?
   是。您是哪位？
4. This is after-sales receptionist in Wan Da Automobile Service Company. I'm calling to do a return call visit for our service.
   我是万达汽车服务公司的售后接待员。我打电话的目的是想对我们的售后服务做个回访。
5. How is it going with your car now?
   您的车现在怎么样？
6. How do you think about the maintenance for your car in our company last time?
   您认为我们公司上次给您的车维修得怎么样？
7. By the way, would you please give us some suggestions to further improve our service?
   顺便问一下，为进一步完善我们的售后服务，您能给我们一些建议吗？
8. Thank you for your suggestions and warm-hearted reply.
   谢谢您的建议及热心回答。
9. Please contact us at any time if there is something wrong with your car.
   如果您的车有什么问题，请随时与我们联系。

Test (Unit 8 – Unit 13)

I. **Vocabulary** (10 points, 1 point for each)

Directions: In each of the sentences below, there is one underlined word or phrase. Below each sentence are four other words or phrases, marked A, B, C, and D. You are to choose one word or phrase that best keeps the meaning of the original sentence if it is substituted for the underlined word or phrase.

1. Front leaf springs are used in conjunction with solid axle beams in most truck applications.
    A. in touch with   B. in communication with
    C. in association with   D. in cooperation with
2. The piston converts the potential energy of the fuel into the kinetic energy that turns the crankshaft.
    A. causes   B. turns   C. forms   D. takes
3. The bridge which was engineered in the 14th century remains sturdy in structure.
    A. measured   B. tested   C. planned   D. built
4. The street was so narrow that cars which entered it had to reverse out again.
    A. turn   B. drive   C. come   D. back
5. This situation needs to be tackled without delay. Otherwise, we'll suffer great loss in production.
    A. at once   B. at first   C. for a while D. with doubt
6. This group of chemicals is known to have harmful effects on people.
    A. damaging   B. helpful   C. offensive   D. physical
7. I am going to take the car to the garage to have it serviced this afternoon.
    A. washed   B. painted   C. repaired   D. adjusted
8. A transmission also has a neutral position which disconnects the engine from the drive wheels.
    A. separates   B. escapes   C. differs   D. withdraws
9. The next four or five years are likely to witness more automobile production in China.
    A. predict   B. ensure   C. see   D. expect
10. An automobile without a transmission would place a tremendous strain on the engine and driving parts of the automobile.
    A. very great   B. moderate   C. very small   D. medium

II. **Word Form** (10 points, 1 point for each).

Directions: Fill in the blanks with the words given in the brackets, and change the form where necessary.

1. Most luxury vehicles are four-door sedans because they're _____ (comfortable) than most other body styles.
2. There are various _____ (adaptation) of the suspension systems, but all use the same basic principle.
3. You'd better have your car _____ (wax) at least once three or four months.
4. The dual master cylinder is designed for both front and rear brakes of most cars to ensure the _____ (efficient) of the brake system.
5. The clutch disc _____ (sandwich) between the machined face of the flywheel and the clutch pressure plate.
6. The _____ (large) the steering wheel diameter is, the more torque is generated from the same amount of drive effort.
7. There are several different types of transmissions _____ (use) on the vehicles today.
8. One function of a suspension system is to prevent road shocks from _____ (transmit) to the vehicle frame.
9. The outside of the water jacket _____ (dissipate) some of the heat to the air surrounding it.
10. The clutch must _____ (transmit) all the engine torque to the transmission.

III. Usage of Prepositions (10 points, 1 point for each).

Directions: Fill in the following blanks with proper prepositions.

1. The clutch cover assembly contains the pressure plate, spring, and other parts according _____ the design of the clutch.
2. The flywheel provides a base _____ the starter ring gear.
3. When the clutch is disengaged, it provides the means of disconnecting the engine _____ the drivetrain.
4. The clutch disc operates in conjunction _____ a pressure plate or clutch cover.
5. The torsion bar twists to exert resistance _____ up-and-down movement.
6. The clutch linkage connects the clutch pedal _____ the clutch fork.
7. Seals and gaskets are used to keep the oil where it is supposed to be and prevent it _____ leaking out.
8. The transmission oil pump is responsible _____ producing all the oil pressure that is required in the transmission.
9. In first gear, the engine turns much faster _____ relation to the drive wheels.
10. The transmission gears are shifted _____ means of a gear shift mechanism.

IV. Reading Comprehension (20 points, 1 point for each blank).

Directions: Read the following passages carefully and fill in the blanks with the words and phrases provided below.

Passage One (10 points, 1 point for each blank).

| fluid-filled | connected | friction | against | link |
| revolving | consists | piston | brakes | fluid |

The typical hydraulic brake system __1__ of disk brakes on the front and either disk or drum __2__ on the rear wheels connected by a system of tubes and hoses that __3__ the brake at each wheel to the master cylinder. The master cylinder is __4__ and contains two separate sections. There is a __5__ in each section and both pistons are __6__ to a brake pedal in the driver's compartment. When the brake is pushed down, brake __7__ is sent from the master cylinder to the wheel cylinder. In the wheel cylinder, the fluid pushes the shoes or pads __8__ the revolving drums or disks. The __9__ between the stationary shoes or pads and the revolving drums or disks slows or stops the __10__ wheels, which, in turn, slow or stop the car.

Passage Two (10 points, 1 point for each blank).

| approximately | degree | turn | proportion | ratio |
| introduction | design | step | movement | wheels |

A major __1__ forward in steering gear design was accomplished with the __2__ of variable ratio steering. In conventional steering, the __3__ of turn of the front wheels is always in direct __4__ to the degree of turn of the steering wheel. In variable __5__ steering, the ratio remains constant for __6__ the first 40 degrees of steering wheel __7__. Then the ratio decreases and the response of the front __8__ quickens for every degree of __9__ of the steering wheel. The "variable" effect is made possible by the __10__ of the steering gear.

V. Translation (40 points).
Part One (15 points)
Directions: Translate the following passages into Chinese.

Passage One (7 points)

The clutch disc (or driven disc) contains a circular metal plate attached to a reinforced splined hub. Often the hub is mounted on coil springs to provide cushioned engagements. The splined hub is free to slide lengthwise along the splines of the transmission input shaft. When engaged, the clutch disc drives the input shaft through these splines. The clutch disc operates in conjunction with a pressure plate or clutch cover. In its operating position in the engine-transmission linkup, the clutch disc is sandwiched between the machined face of the flywheel and the clutch pressure plate.

Passage Two (8 points)

An automatic transmission selects gear ratios according to engine speed, powertrain load, vehicle speed, and other operating factors. Little effort is needed on the part of the driver, because both upshifts and downshifts occur automatically. A driver-operated clutch is not needed to change gears, and the vehicle can be brought to a stop without shifting to neutral. This is very convenient, particularly in stop-and-go traffic. The driver can also manually select a lower forward gear, reverse, neutral or park. Depending on the forward range selected, the transmission can provide engine braking during deceleration.

Part Two (15 points, 3 points for each sentence)

　　Directions: Translate the following sentences into English.
1. 悬架系统的作用之一是防止路面震动传导至车架。
2. 自动变速器油泵负责产生变速器内需要的所有油压。
3. 离合器盘连同离合器压盘或离合器外壳一起工作。
4. 行车制动系统被用来使行驶中的车辆减速及停止。
5. 通常用于汽车上的转向系统有两种：手动转向系统和动力转向系统。

Part Three (5 points, 0.5 point for each).

　　Directions: Translate the following names of cars into Chinese.

1. Volvo　　　　＿＿＿＿＿＿＿＿＿＿
2. Renault　　　＿＿＿＿＿＿＿＿＿＿
3. Bentley　　　＿＿＿＿＿＿＿＿＿＿
4. Ferrari　　　＿＿＿＿＿＿＿＿＿＿
5. Hyundai　　　＿＿＿＿＿＿＿＿＿＿
6. Mini　　　　＿＿＿＿＿＿＿＿＿＿
7. Peugeot　　　＿＿＿＿＿＿＿＿＿＿
8. Daewoo　　　＿＿＿＿＿＿＿＿＿＿
9. Lotus　　　　＿＿＿＿＿＿＿＿＿＿
10. Iveco　　　　＿＿＿＿＿＿＿＿＿＿

Part Four (5 points, 1 point for each)

　　Directions: Translate the following abbreviations into corresponding Chinese terms.

1. CVT (continuously variable transmission)　　＿＿＿＿＿＿＿＿＿＿
2. GPS (global positioning system)　　＿＿＿＿＿＿＿＿＿＿
3. PS (power steering)　　＿＿＿＿＿＿＿＿＿＿
4. ABS (anti-lock brake system)　　＿＿＿＿＿＿＿＿＿＿
5. AAS (automatic adjusting suspension)　　＿＿＿＿＿＿＿＿＿＿

VI. Error Correction (10 points, 2 points for each).

　　Directions: In each of the sentences below, there are four underlined words or phrases marked A, B, C, and D. You are to choose the one that is wrong, write it in the bracket and correct the word or phrase on the line.

1. The engine must gained speed before it moves a vehicle.
                    A   B   C   D

                                                                                    (   )＿＿＿

2. In a power steering system, power-assisted units add so that the driver's effort is reduced.
                                    A   B   C   D

                                                                                        (   )＿＿＿

3. The engine can't work if the temperature is either too high nor too low.
                 A   B   C   D

                                                                                        (   )＿＿＿

4. All power steering systems require a power steering pump attached in the engine.
      A   B   C   D

                                                                                        (   )＿＿＿

5. The main advantage of leaf springs are their ability to control vehicles' sway and lateral movement.
                                   A   B   C   D

                                                                                (   )＿＿＿

Final Exam

I. Vocabulary (10 points, 1 point for each).

Directions: In each of the sentences below, there is one underlined word or phrase. Below each sentence are four other words or phrases, marked A, B, C, and D. You are to choose one word or phrase that best keeps the meaning of the original sentence if it is substituted for the underlined word or phrase.

1. Any automobile is composed of four sections, such as the engine, chassis, body and electrical system.
   A. is made of   B. is joined by
   C. consists of   D. is organized by
2. The paper was heated to combustion point.
   A. warming   B. burning   C. firing   D. flying
3. I didn't know that there was a rear entrance to the post office.
   A. a back door   B. a side door   C. a front door   D. a double door
4. There has recently been fierce competition between the United States and Japan for world automobile market.
   A. rivalry   B. match   C. fight   D. war
5. The good news of a pay raise quickly circulated round the building of our company.
   A. passed through   B. passed by   C. passed round   D. passed down
6. The ignition system supplies the electric spark needed to ignite the air-fuel mixture in the cylinders, which initiates the power stroke.
   A. holds   B. gives   C. has   D. starts
7. A good range of cars are sold at reasonable prices at the 4S store.
   A. sensible   B. understanding C. acceptable   D. standard
8. In a dual exhaust system, the engines of such vehicles can give off exhaust gases more freely.
   A. different   B. double   C. multiple   D. similar
9. From then on, the transportation on land shifted from the age of coaches to the age of automobiles.
   A. placed   B. made   C. transferred D. put
10. The mechanical ignition system, used prior to 1975, was mechanical and electrical and used no electronics.
    A. after   B. for   C. in   D. before

II. Word Form (10 points, 1 point for each).

Directions: Fill in the blanks with the words given in the brackets, and change the form where necessary.

1. The clutch cover _____ (bolt) to the flywheel and rotates with it at crankshaft speed.
2. GM is the _____ (large) automaker and has been the global industry sales leader in each of the last 77 years in the world.
3. Changing the oil is an easy way to keep an engine _____ (work) well.
4. A transmission is a speed and power changing device _____ (install) at some point between the engine and driving wheels of the vehicle.
5. The steering system is used to control the driving direction of the vehicle as it _____ (move).
6. An electronic fuel injection system generally uses one or more injectors to _____ (spray) fuel.
7. The components of the manual steering system _____ (able) the vehicle to change the direction by means of turning and moving forth and back.
8. The parking brake system allows the vehicle to _____ (hold) stationary mechanically even on an inclined surface, and particularly in the absence of the driver.
9. The springs support the body of the car by _____ (compress) and rebounding with every up-and-down movement.
10. The SUV (sport utility vehicle) is a truck-based station wagon _____ (equip) with either two-wheel or four-wheel drive.

III. Usage of Prepositions (10 points, 1 point for each).

Directions: Fill in the following blanks with proper prepositions.

1. U-bolts clamp the spring firmly _____ place.
2. The fuel cap on the fuel tank is used to keep the fuel _____ splashing out.
3. The battery may be filled _____ lead, but that doesn't mean it's unbreakable.
4. Every aspect of a transmission's functions is dependent on a constant supply of fluid _____ pressure.
5. With better oil and better engines, the oil can be used longer _____ damaging the engine.
6. Each stroke is named _____ the action it performs — intake, compression, power, and exhaust.
7. These ball joints isolate the steering gear and pitman arm _____ axle motion.
8. The electronic ignition system became popular when better control and improved reliability became important with the advent _____ emission controls.
9. The engine oil has a cleaning effect _____ all the engine components that it contacts.
10. In terms _____ their power sources, brakes are basically of two types: the mechanically

actuated brakes and the hydraulic brakes.

IV. Reading Comprehension (20 points, 1 point for each blank).

Directions: Read the following passages carefully and fill in the blanks with the words and phrases provided below.

Passage One (10 points, 1 point for each blank).

| opposite | transmissions | means | rolling | excess |
| inserted | disconnects | relation | neutral | lock |

The transmission gears are shifted by __1__ of a gear shift mechanism. In first gear, the engine turns much faster in __2__ to the drive wheels, while in high gear the engine is loafing even though the car may be going in __3__ of 70 mph. Depending on the number of forward speeds there are three, four, and five-speed __4__. In addition to the various forward gears, a transmission also has a __5__ position which __6__ the engine from the drive wheels, and reverse, which causes the drive wheels to turn in the __7__ direction allowing you to back up. Finally, there is the park position. In this position, a latch mechanism is __8__ into a slot in the output shaft to __9__ the drive wheels and keep them from turning, thereby preventing the vehicle from __10__.

Passage Two (10 points, 1 point for each blank).

| influence | information | development | progress | significant |
| alternative | electronics | technologies | attention | closely |

Aside from product innovations, new __1__ such as electronics, the use of __2__ materials and new methods for __3__ and manufacture will substantially __4__ the future of the automobile. Any __5__ in these technologies will be reflected in the progress of the automobile. As is known to us, __6__ changes in the automobile of today are __7__ related to the introduction of __8__. An area that will receive increasing __9__ in the future will be the use of electronics for better driver __10__ regarding traffic conditions.

V. Translation (40 points).
Part One (15 points)

Directions: Translate the following passages into Chinese.

Passage One (7 points)

As fuel is burned in the engine, about one-third of the heat energy in the fuel is converted into power. Another third goes out through the exhaust pipe unused, and the remaining third must be handled by the cooling system. This means that the engine can work effectively only when the heat energy is equally handled so as to keep the engine temperature in balance.

Passage Two (8 points)

Nearly all vehicles on the road have electronic engine control systems. This is a system comprised of many electronic and electromechanical parts. The system is designed to monitor the operation of the engine continuously and make adjustments so the engine can run more efficiently. Electronic engine control systems have dramatically improved fuel mileage. The computer analyses data from the input sensors. Then, based on the inputs and the instructions stored in its memory, the computer directs the output devices to make the necessary changes in the operation of some engine systems.

Part Two (15 points, 3 points for each sentence)

Directions: Translate the following sentences into English.

1. 巨大的美国汽车市场曾被三大汽车制造商占据。
2. 车辆的排气系统用以把已燃气体传导至车辆后部并排放到空气中去。
3. 点火开关的作用是把点火系统与蓄电池连接或断开,这样发动机才能根据要求启动或停止工作。
4. 与老款相比,这款在外观设计和颜色色泽上有所改进。
5. 机油减压阀能够确保机油在适当的压力下在发动机各部件间循环。

Part Three (5 points, 0.5 point for each)

Directions: Translate the following names of cars into Chinese.

1. Cadillac _____
2. Opel _____
3. Citroen _____
4. Ssangyong _____
5. Fiat _____
6. Rolls-Royce _____
7. Golf _____
8. Hummer _____
9. Crown _____
10. Jaguar _____

Part Four (5 points, 1 point for each)

Directions: Translate the following abbreviations into corresponding Chinese terms.

PCV (positive crankcase ventilation) _____
MFI (multipoint fuel injection) _____
SUV (sport utility vehicle) _____
DTC (diagnostic trouble code) _____
CPU (central processing unit) _____

VI. Error Correction (10 points, 2 points for each).

Directions: In each of the sentences below, there are four underlined words or phrases marked A, B, C, and D. You are to choose the one that is wrong, write it in the bracket and correct the word or phrase on the line.

1. <u>Any</u> automobile <u>is consisted of</u> four sections, <u>such as</u> the engine, chassis, body and electrical <u>system</u>.
     A   B   C   D
                                                                                                                                                 (   )_____

2. <u>You'd</u> <u>better</u> have your car <u>wax</u> at least <u>once</u> three or four months.
     A   B   C   D
                                                                                                                               (   )_____

3. It is <u>important</u> that the oil temperature <u>is</u> kept below the flash point of the oil, <u>which</u> is the
            A   B   C
   temperature <u>at</u> which the oil will ignite and burn.
                   D
                                                                                                   (   )_____

4. What <u>else</u> does the lubrication system <u>contain</u> apart <u>of</u> the <u>lubricating</u> oil?
           A   B   C   D   (   )_____

5. The chassis is a framework <u>use</u> to <u>assemble</u> auto <u>components</u> <u>on</u> <u>it</u>.
                                    A   B   C D   (   )_____

Appendix

I. Key to the Exercises

Unit One

II. Fill in the table below.

English	Chinese
differential	差速器
propeller shaft	传动轴
steering wheel	方向盘
rear axle	后桥,后轴
clutch	离合器
cylinder	汽缸
torque	转矩
internal combustion engine	内燃机
power train	传动系统
power stroke	做功冲程

III. Fill in the blanks with the words or phrases given below, and change the form where necessary.

1. supplies   2. removes   3. conduct   4. assemble
5. retard   6. control   7. provides   8. is composed of

IV. Reading comprehension: Read the following passage carefully and fill in the blanks with the words given below.

1. chassis   2. engine   3. framework   4. case   5. functions
6. design   7. requirements   8. engineers   9. forces   10. body

V. Translate the following paragraph into Chinese.

悬架系统的主要目的是支撑车辆的重量。悬架系统的基本作用是吸收路面不平引起的冲击和振动,使其不会传递给车辆和乘客。这样,不管路况如何,都能使车辆具有可控制的、水平的行驶路线。

VI. Translate the following sentences into English.
1. Automobiles are basically the same in structure although they are quite different in design.
2. There are various types of engines, but the most common type is the internal combustion engine.
3. The steering system is used to control the driving direction of the vehicle.
4. The chassis includes the power train, suspension, steering, and brake system.
5. The electrical system supplies lighting and driving power for the automobile.

Unit Two

II. Fill in the table below.

English	Chinese
cylinder block	汽缸体
oil pan	油底壳
piston ring	活塞环
ignition distributor	点火分电器
automatic transmission	自动变速器
connecting rod	连杆
exhaust valve	排气阀
water jacket	冷却水套
compression stroke	压缩行程
spark plug	火花塞

III. Fill in the blanks with the words or phrases given below, and change the form where necessary.
1. converts... into   2. are secured   3. crankcase   4. coolant
5. reciprocating   6. crankshaft   7. stroke   8. is made of

IV. Reading comprehension: Read the following passage carefully and fill in the blanks with the words given below.
1. vast   2. reciprocating   3. spark   4. process   5. four-stroke
6. piston   7. compression   8. exhaust   9. applications   10. Petrol

V. Translate the following paragraph into Chinese.
　　根据发动机的类型,工作循环需要2~4个冲程来完成。四冲程发动机也叫奥托循环发动机,以此纪念德国工程师尼古拉斯·奥托博士,他于1876年首次运用了这一原理。在四冲程发动机中,需要汽缸中活塞的4个冲程来完成一个完整的工作循环。每个冲程都以其完成的工作来命名——进气冲程、压缩冲程、做功冲程以及排气冲程。

VI. Translate the following sentences into English.
1. The engine block forms the main framework, or foundation of the engine.
2. The piston is composed of the piston head, piston ring, piston land, piston skirt and piston pin hole.
3. The connecting rod is attached to the crankshaft at one end (big end) and to the piston at the other end (small end).
4. There are various types of engines such as electric motors, steam engines, and internal combustion engines.
5. The internal combustion engine burns fuel within the cylinders and converts the expanding force of the combustion into rotary force used to propel the vehicle.

Section C Questions for Discussion:
1. Karl Benz was a German engine designer and automobile engineer. He designed and built the world's first practical automobile powered by an internal combustion engine.
2. When he was in university.
3. Benz's fiancée, Bertha Ringer, bought out Ritter's share in the company.
4. In 1879.
5. His wife and two sons stole the car one night and drove it from Mannheim to Pforzheim.

Unit Three

II. Fill in the table below.

English	Chinese
fuel system	燃料系统
fuel injector	喷油器
sensor	传感器
throttle valve	节气门(化油器),油门
carburetor	化油器
fuel pressure regulator	燃油压力调节器
fuel filter	燃油滤清器
combustion chamber	燃烧室
fuel tank	燃油箱
multipoint fuel injection	多点燃油喷射

III. Fill in the blanks with the words or phrases given below, and change the form where necessary.

1. injector   2. camshaft   3. constant   4. clogged
5. protect   6. fuel lines 7. splashing   8. spray

IV. Reading comprehension: Read the following passage carefully and fill in the blanks with the words given below.

1. store   2. needed   3. rear   4. with   5. prevent
6. rounds   7. splashing 8. created 9. from   10. atmosphere

V. Translate the following passage into Chinese.

使用电动燃油泵和喷油器的燃油系统会采用燃油压力调节器来保持油压恒定。在多点燃油喷射系统中,燃油压力调节器在燃油管路处有一个进口连接,而出口用来使燃油返回油箱。控制膜片和弹簧压力决定出口的开度及可返回的燃油量。因此,压力弹簧的强度决定燃油管路中的燃油压力,并使油压保持固定值。

VI. Translate the following sentences into English.

1. The major parts of the fuel system include the fuel tank, fuel pump, fuel filter, carburetor and fuel lines.
2. A fuel tank is used to store the fuel oil.
3. The function of the fuel pump is to deliver the fuel oil from the fuel tank to the carburetor.
4. There are two types of gasoline engine pumps: mechanical fuel pumps and electric fuel pumps.
5. An EFI system supplies an accurate air/fuel ratio to the engine no matter what operating conditions are encountered.

Unit Four

II. Fill in the table below.

English	Chinese
exhaust system	排气系统
catalytic converter	催化净化器
exhaust pipe	排气管
burned gas	已燃气体
tail pipe	排气尾管
back pressure	回压,背压力
muffler	消声器
crossover pipe	交叉管
exhaust manifold	排气歧管
resonator	辅助消声器

III. Fill in the blanks with the words or phrases given below, and change the form where necessary.

1. assembly   2. silence   3. muffler   4. exhaust

5. absorb   6. exhaust pipe   7. depends on   8. performance

IV. Reading comprehension: Read the following passage carefully and fill in the blanks with the words given below.

1. function   2. reduce   3. made   4. body   5. pipe

6. absorb   7. noise   8. passed   9. slowly   10. amount

V. Translate the following passage into Chinese.

汽车上使用的排气管类型很多。有些排气管被设计成一定的形状,能越过后桥,这样可使后桥上下运动而不碰及排气管;有些排气管的形状使其能弯曲地安装在汽车地板下方,连接催化净化器和消声器。排气管的形状取决于发动机的构造和尺寸以及汽车底盘的构造。排气管还可以设计为单排气管或双排气管。排气系统的排气管越粗越好,因为那样废气排放会更通畅。

VI. Translate the following sentences into English.

1. The main function of the exhaust system is to conduct the burned gases to the rear of a vehicle and into the air.
2. The exhaust system mainly consists of the exhaust manifold, exhaust pipe, catalytic converter, muffler and tailpipe, etc.
3. The exhaust system serves not only to exhaust gases, but also to silence the exhaust noise.
4. The muffler is connected between the tail pipe and the catalytic converter.
5. In a dual exhaust system, the engines of such vehicles can give off exhaust gases more freely, thereby lowering the back pressure which is inherent in an exhaust system.

Section C   Questions for Discussion:

1. In 1917.
2. Because the 1919 Treaty of Versailles prohibited German companies from producing aircraft and aircraft engines.
3. In 1928.
4. The 328 roadster.
5. The "Efficient Dynamics" strategy.

Unit Five

II. Fill in the table below.

English	Chinese
cooling system	冷却系统
cooling agent	冷却介质
water pump	水泵
alternator	交流发电机
radiator	散热器
operating temperature	工作温度,运转温度

To be continued

English	Chinese
thermostat	恒温器
coolant	冷却液,冷却剂
water jacket	冷却水套
centrifugal fan	离心式风扇

III. Fill in the blanks with the words or phrases given below, and change the form where necessary.

1. melting   2. is converted   3. essential   4. coolant
5. circulate   6. radiator   7. thermostat   8. regulation

IV. Reading comprehension: Read the following passage carefully and fill in the blanks with the words given below.

1. operating   2. breakdown   3. seizure   4. cooling   5. efficient
6. temperature 7. degrees   8. combustion 9. engine   10. consumption

V. Translate the following passage into Chinese.

燃料在发动机中燃烧时,燃料中大约1/3的热能转化为动力,另外1/3的热能未经使用就从排气管排出,剩下的1/3的热能必须由冷却系来处理。这就意味着只有均等地处理热能以保持发动机温度的均衡,发动机才能有效地工作。

VI. Translate the following sentences into English.

1. No engine can work well without suitable operating temperatures.
2. There are two types of cooling systems used on vehicles: water-cooling systems and air-cooling systems.
3. A water-cooling system means that water is used as a cooling agent to circulate through the engine to absorb the heat and carry it to the radiator for dissipation.
4. A radiator cap mounted on the top of the radiator is used to control the pressure in the cooling system.
5. An air-cooling system means that air is used as a cooling agent to circulate through the engine to carry the heat away from the moving parts of the engine.

Unit Six

II. Fill in the table below.

English	Chinese
lubrication system	润滑系统
oil cooler	润滑油冷却器,机油散热器
regulator	调节器
jet nozzle	喷(油)嘴

To be continued

English	Chinese
oil pump	油泵
pick-up screen	集滤器
lubricating oil	润滑油
oil pan	油底壳,机油盘
oil filter	机油滤清器
oil pressure relief valve	机油减压阀

III. Fill in the blanks with the words or phrases given below, and change the form where necessary.

1. circulate   2. build up   3. is wound   4. wear
5. sump   6. regulate   7. bypass valve   8. drain

IV. Reading comprehension: Read the following passage carefully and fill in the blanks with the words given below.

1. hold   2. pressure   3. cleaning   4. control   5. circulate
6. splash   7. combined   8. filter   9. sent   10. lubricated

V. Translate the following passage into Chinese.

润滑系统中的机油滤清器被用来过滤掉机油中的污物及固体微粒。由于机油滤清器阻止了杂质微粒进入发动机,因此降低了发动机部件的磨损率。新型发动机普遍采用全流式离心机油滤清器。也就是说,所有机油都要先经过滤清器,再进入发动机各轴承。然而,如果机油滤清器被阻塞,就得起用分流阀,以使机油继续流向各轴承。

VI. Translate the following sentences into English.

1. Without the aid of friction, an automobile could not move itself.
2. The lubrication system of the engine is composed of mechanical parts such as the oil pump, the oil filter, and the oil pressure relief valve, etc.
3. The main function of the oil filter is to filter particles of foreign matter out of the oil.
4. The oil pressure relief valve can secure the oil circulation through engine parts under proper pressure.
5. The lubricating oil is fed to the moving parts of the engine by pump pressure, splashing, or a combination of both.

Section C   Questions for Discussion:

1. In 1896.
2. Driven by a two-cylinder, four-cycle motor, it was mounted on bicycle wheels. Named "Quadricycle," the car had no reverse gear or brakes.
3. Because Ford had spent $86,000, but didn't produce a car that could be sold.
4. When his racing car won a race in 1901.
5. It influenced the development of the means of production in other industries. The Model T's

low cost made automobile transportation available to all but the poorest American. The popularity of the Model T also stimulated a demand for improved roads. The increase in automobile use was a huge stimulus to the petroleum industry. This vehicle initiated a new era in personal transportation. It was easy to operate, maintain, and handle on rough roads.

Unit Seven

II. Fill in the table below.

English	Chinese
spark plug	火花塞
pickup coil	传感线圈
ignition coil	点火线圈
distributor rotor	分火头
resistor	电阻器
secondary winding	次级线圈,次级绕组
magnetic field	磁场
transformer	变压器
ignition timing	点火正时
primary winding	初级线圈,初级绕组

III. Fill in the blanks with the words or phrases given below, and change the form where necessary.

1. distributorless   2. battery   3. ignition coil   4. distributes
5. induces   6. trigger   7. transfers   8. be timed

IV. Reading comprehension: Read the following passage carefully and fill in the blanks with the words given below.

1. plug   2. dependent   3. characteristics   4. temperatures   5. electrical
6. ignition   7. wear   8. wiring   9. capacity   10. low

V. Translate the following passage into Chinese.

流经初级绕组的电流在线圈内产生磁场。当断电器触点打开时,磁场衰减,而磁场的变化在次级绕组中产生感应电流。由于次级绕组线圈的匝数远远大于初级绕组,因此电压高达 20 000 V。

VI. Translate the following sentences into English.

1. The ignition coil is composed of a primary winding, secondary winding and core of soft iron.
2. A mechanism is provided to automatically advance and retard the spark as conditions require.
3. The function of the ignition condenser is to reduce arcing at the breaker points, and

prolong their life.

4. The purpose of the ignition switch is to connect or disconnect the ignition system from the battery, so the engine can be started and stopped as desired.

5. Electronic ignition systems provide superior ignition and engine performance and at the same time require considerably less service and maintenance than conventional ignition systems.

Test(Unit 1 – Unit 7)

I. Vocabulary(每题1分,共10分).
1. C 2. A 3. B 4. C 5. C 6. D 7. B 8. C 9. B 10. D

II. Word Form(每题1分,共10分).
1. operation   2. are required   3. bigger   4. flowing   5. reduce
6. used   7. acceptable   8. varies   9. be attributed   10. splashing

III. Usage of Prepositions(每题1分,共10分).
1. as   2. without   3. of   4. for   5. In
6. into   7. against   8. into   9. at   10. to

IV. Reading Comprehension(每空1分,共20分).

Passage One：(每空1分,共10分)
1. vital   2. depend   3. dual   4. give off   5. lowering
6. choke   7. cases   8. obtained   9. leaving   10. stroke

Passage Two：(每空1分,共10分)
1. converting   2. mechanical   3. internal   4. cylinders   5. term
6. perform   7. propel   8. motion   9. friction   10. transmission

V. Translation(共40分).

Part One：Translate the following passages into Chinese. (共15分)

Passage One (7分)

悬架系统的主要目的是支撑车辆的重量。悬架系统的基本作用是吸收路面不平引起的冲击和振动,使其不会传递给车辆和乘客。这样,不管路况如何,都能使车辆具有可控制的、笔直的行驶路线。

Passage Two (8分)

如今行驶在街道上的汽车在风格和设计上是如此不同,以至于你很难想象一百年前的汽车是什么样子。随着汽车工业的发展,汽车已经发生了很大的变化,而且不时地得到了改造,但是无论汽车样式如何变化,汽车的基本构造是一样的。换句话说,任何汽车都由4部分构成,如发动机、底盘、车身及电气系统。

Part Two: Translate the following sentences into English. (每题 3 分,共 15 分)
1. The electrical system supplies lighting and driving power for the automobile.
2. Electronic ignition systems provide superior ignition and engine performance and at the same time require considerably less service and maintenance than conventional ignition systems.
3. A radiator cap mounted on the top of the radiator is used to control the pressure in the cooling system.
4. An EFI system supplies an accurate air-fuel ratio to the engine no matter what operating conditions are encountered.
5. The heat riser valve is used to restrict the exhaust gases during starting and warm-up periods.

Part Three: Translate the following names of cars into Chinese. (每题 0.5 分,共 5 分)
  1. 宝马 2. 雪佛兰 3. 马自达 4. 保时捷 5. 蓝鸟
  6. 通用 7. 三菱 8. 林肯 9. 大众 10. 花冠

Part Four: Translate the following abbreviations into corresponding Chinese terms. (每题 1 分,共 5 分)
  1. 车辆识别代码 2. 上止点 3. 电子燃油喷射 4. 长效冷却液 5. 点火正时

VI. Error Correction (每题 2 分,共 10 分)
1. D 改为:to
 (transfer... from... to 由……传导至……)
2. B 改为:nor
 (neither... nor 既不……也不,和……都不)
3. B 改为:until
 (not... until... 直到……才……)
4. B 改为:that
 ("It is... that..."为强调句结构)
5. C 改为:is made of (由……制造的)
 (is made up of 由……组成的)

Unit Eight

II. Fill in the table below.

English	Chinese
clutch	离合器
drivetrain	传动系统
linkage	联动装置
engagement	连接,啮合
pressure plate	压盘

to be continued

English	Chinese
release bearing	分离轴承
spring	弹簧
clutch disc	离合器盘
clutch pedal	离合器踏板
cover assembly	外壳总成

III. Fill in the blanks with the words or phrases given below, and change the form where necessary.

1. flywheel   2. connects   3. springs   4. sandwiched
5. make up   6. transmit   7. is required 8. is mounted

IV. Reading comprehension: Read the following passage carefully and fill in the blanks with the words given below.

1. fundamental 2. bathed   3. dry   4. generate   5. suitable
6. outputs   7. torque   8. counterparts 9. fuel   10. losses

V. Translate the following passage into Chinese.

离合器盘(从动盘)含有一个装于加强花键轮毂上的圆形金属板。螺旋弹簧通常安装在轮毂的弹簧座孔内,用以提供弹性结合。花键轮毂在变速器输入轴的花键上纵向地自由滑动。当离合器盘被连接时,它就通过花键驱动输入轴。离合器盘连同离合器压盘或离合器外壳一起工作。当离合器处于发动机与变速器接合状态时,离合器盘被夹在发动机飞轮与离合器压盘中间。

VI. Translate the following sentences into English.

1. The clutch is a friction device which provides the means of connecting or disconnecting the engine from the manual transmission.
2. The engine must gain speed before it moves a vehicle.
3. The main function of a clutch is to assist in starting a vehicle.
4. The clutch disc operates in conjunction with a pressure plate or a clutch cover.
5. The clutch fork and linkage provide the means of converting the up-and-down movement of the clutch pedal to the back-and-forth movement of the clutch release bearing assembly.

Section C   Questions for Discussion:

1. Durant bought smaller car builders, and companies that built car parts as well as car accessories. In 1908, these various companies were folded into a single unit, thus creating the new GM.
2. Durant managed to use Chevrolet, another company he formed.
3. GM, Ford and Chrysler.
4. It was to provide the public with stylish colors, features and comfort.
5. Because on that day GM became the first company to make more than a billion dollars in a year.

Unit Nine

II. Fill in the table below.

English	Chinese
transmission	变速器
output shaft	输出轴
reverse gear	倒挡齿轮
neutral position	空挡挡位
hydraulic system	液压系统
planetary gear set	行星齿轮机构
drive line	动力传动系统
valve body	阀体总成
torque converter	变矩器
latch mechanism	锁止机构

III. Fill in the blanks with the words or phrases given below, and change the form where necessary.

1. shift 2. in relation to 3. disconnects 4. rely on
5. torque converter 6. make up 7. pressure 8. leaking

IV. Reading comprehension: Read the following passage carefully and fill in the blanks with the words given below.

1. tests 2. consumption 3. manual 4. connection 5. reduction
6. technical 7. broad 8. manufacturing 9. transmissions 10. investments

V. Translate the following passage into Chinese.

液压系统是个复杂的弯曲管道，将一定压力的传动油输送到变速器和液力变矩器内的所有零部件上。传动油具有多种作用，包括换挡控制、正常润滑和变速器冷却等。变速器的各个方面的运转都离不开在一定压力下不断供给的传动油。实际上，多数变速器的组成部件都始终地浸在传动油中,包括多片式离合器和制动带。

VI. Translate the following sentences into English.

1. There are several different types of transmissions used on vehicles today: manual transmissions, semi-automatic transmissions and fully automatic transmissions (including continuously variable transmissions).
2. A transmission is used to change the ratio between engine rpm and driving wheel rpm to best meet each particular driving condition.
3. On automatic transmissions, the torque converter replaces the conventional clutch.

4. Transmission fluid serves a number of purposes, including shift control, general lubrication and transmission cooling.
5. The oil pump of the automatic transmission is responsible for producing all the oil pressure that is required in the transmission.

Unit Ten

II. Fill in the table below.

English	Chinese
shock absorber	减震器
suspension system	悬架系统
rear axle	后桥
independent suspension	独立悬架
leaf spring	钢板弹簧
dead axle	非驱动桥,从动桥
coil spring	螺旋弹簧
solid axle	整体式车桥
sensor	传感器
torsion bar	扭杆弹簧

III. Fill in the blanks with the words or phrases given below, and change the form where necessary.

1. being transmitted   2. swivel   3. imposed   4. are paired off
5. in conjunction with   6. twists   7. rebounding   8. by means of

IV. Reading comprehension: Read the following paragraph carefully and fill in the blanks with the words given below.

1. support   2. stable   3. expand   4. compress   5. engineered
6. depending   7. springs   8. combinations   9. attached   10. mounting

V. Translate the following paragraph into Chinese.

双向直接作用液压减震器的工作原理是推动液体从阀体的阻尼孔中流过。当汽车通过不规则的路面时,液体流动速度减慢,控制汽车快速移动。通常,弹簧负荷阀控制液体通过活塞。液压减震器自动地适应剧烈的震动冲击。如果车桥缓慢移动,对液流的阻尼会很小。如果车桥快速或剧烈运动,阻力就会变得很强,因为有更多的时间需要推动液体通过阻尼孔。通过这些作用和反作用,减震器在受到小的冲击时动作柔和,而在受到剧烈的冲击时则需要较强的弹簧作用控制。双向作用在两个方向上都是有效的,因为弹簧在从初始位置压缩减震器和弹簧反弹的作用一样剧烈。

VI. Translate the following sentences into English.
1. One of the functions of the suspension system is to prevent road shocks from being transmitted to the vehicle frame.
2. In a suspension system, the major component is springs.
3. The springs used on today's vehicles are engineered in a wide variety of types, shapes, sizes, rates, and capacities.
4. Springs are attached to vehicles by a number of different mounting techniques.
5. The main advantage of leaf springs is their ability to control vehicles' sway and lateral movement.
6. Usually, the fluid flow through the pistons is controlled by spring-loaded valves.

Section C   Questions for Discussion:
1. Reliability and durability.
2. Kiichiro Toyoda.
3. In 1935 the first prototype, the A1, was unveiled, which marked the birth of the Toyota Motor Corporation.
4. Crown.
5. Because of the decade's oil crisis.

Unit Eleven

II. Fill in the table below.

English	Chinese
steering system	转向系统
instrument panel	仪表盘
steering gear	转向器,转向装置
steering column	转向管柱
steering wheel	方向盘
tie rod	横拉杆
rotary valve	转阀
pitman arm	转向摇臂
drag link	直拉杆
steering knuckle	转向节

III. Fill in the blanks with the words or phrases given below, and change the form where necessary.

1. deliver
2. accommodate
3. isolate
4. torque
5. integral
6. is adopted
7. is incorporated
8. steering shaft

IV. Reading comprehension: Read the following passage carefully and fill in the blanks with the words given below.

1. steering   2. multiplies   3. direction   4. wheel   5. minimum
6. feedback   7. attached   8. rack   9. contact   10. responsive

V. Translate the following passage into Chinese.

由曲轴皮带轮通过皮带驱动的动力转向泵把压力油液送到转向器中。高压油液承担大约80%的转向工作。工作时，油泵对动力转向油液施以高压，这种液压油为专用油液。

VI. Translate the following sentences into English.

1. Two types of steering systems are commonly used on cars: manual steering systems and power steering systems.
2. In a manual steering system, the driver's effort to turn the steering wheel is the primary force that causes the front wheels to swivel to the left or right.
3. The components of the manual steering system enable the vehicle to change the direction by means of turning and moving forth and back.
4. Automobile power steering actually means power assisted steering.
5. In the power steering system, fluid direction is controlled by a rotary valve attached to the pinion assembly.

Unit Twelve

II. Fill in the table below.

English	Chinese
master cylinder	制动主缸
brake pedal	制动踏板
disk rotor	制动盘
pull back spring	回位弹簧
brake shoe	制动蹄片
fixed caliper	固定式制动钳
service brake	行车制动器
wheel cylinder	制动轮缸
brake fluid	制动液
kinetic energy	动能

III. Fill in the blanks with the words or phrases given below, and change the form where necessary.

1. converting   2. brake fluid   3. resistance   4. is bolted
5. leaking   6. efficiency   7. means   8. in the event of

IV. Reading comprehension: Read the following passage carefully and fill in the blanks with the words given below.
1. dual　　2. connected　　3. fail　　4. hydraulic　　5. brake
6. piston　　7. force　　8. pressure　　9. friction　　10. slows

V. Translate the following passage into Chinese.
　　制动主缸充满液体,并且它有两个独立的部分,每部分里面都有一个活塞,两个活塞都和驾驶室里的制动踏板相连。当制动踏板被踩下时,制动液被从主缸输送至车轮的轮缸。在车轮的轮缸中,液体推动制动蹄片或制动块阻止制动鼓或制动盘的转动。在固定的制动蹄片或制动块和转动的制动鼓或制动盘之间产生的摩擦使车轮减速或停止转动,从而使车辆减速或停止。

VI. Translate the following sentences into English.
1. There are two completely independent braking systems used on a vehicle: the service brake and the parking brake.
2. The function of the parking brake mechanism is to keep a parked vehicle from sliding or moving.
3. The hydraulic brakes have been universally used on cars.
4. The service brake system is used to decelerate and stop the moving vehicle.
5. The prominent advantage of the dual master cylinder is that it supplies separate hydraulic systems for the front and rear brakes.

Section C　　Questions for Discussion:
1. Jetta, Bora, Golf, Sagita, Magotan and Audi.
2. In 1993.
3. It offered more color choices and more personalized accessories. It also became the ideal choice for the elites who pursue a high quality and individual life.
4. It features roomy back seats, a panoramic sunroof, ion generator for air quality, backseat entertainment system and seats with a massage function.
5. FAW-VW plans to expand its dealer network for Audis from 237 outlets to 300, as well as make further strides in product localization.

Unit Thirteen

II. Fill in the table below.

English	Chinese
navigation	导航
GPS	全球定位系统
satellite	人造卫星
on-board sensor	车载传感器
network	网络

To be continued

English	Chinese
carrier wave	载波
monitor	监视器
database	数据库
locator	定位器
dash	仪表板

III. Fill in the blanks with the words or phrases given below, and change the form where necessary.

1. updated 2. are culled 3. interfere with 4. accurate
5. Nestled 6. segments 7. created 8. alternative

IV. Reading comprehension: Read the following passage carefully and fill in the blanks with the words given below.

1. equipment 2. position 3. updates 4. includes 5. database
6. information 7. destination 8. minimum 9. navigation 10. directs

V. Translate the following paragraph into Chinese.

卫星技术应用于导航、车辆跟踪、被盗车辆的追查、通信以及互联网接入。GPS 是车辆跟踪系统的重要组成部分。然而，跟踪车辆需要许多其他元件。山区、隧道、大型建筑物和其他物件可能干扰卫星通信，使卫星不可靠。一旦已经确定了车辆的初始位置，如果没有卫星，多数车辆跟踪系统也能很准确地工作。车载传感器可以用来跟踪车辆的确切位置。

VI. Translate the following sentences into English.

1. Presently, automobile navigation systems include two parts: the global positioning system (GPS) and automobile automatic navigation system.
2. If a satellite goes out of its planned position, adjust it into the designed ideal position in the GPS satellite network.
3. On-board sensors can be used to keep track of the exact vehicle location.
4. The GPS continues to provide updated information to ensure accuracy of the map data.
5. By using the information from the sensors, the navigation system is not continually and totally reliant on satellites.

Test (Unit 8 – Unit 13)

I. Vocabulary（每题1分，共10分）.
  1. D 2. B 3. D 4. D 5. A 6. A 7. C 8. A 9. C 10. A

II. Word Form（每题1分，共10分）.
  1. more comfortable   2. adaptations   3. waxed   4. efficiency

5. is sandwiched   6. larger   7. used   8. being transmitted
9. dissipates   10. transmit

III. Usage of Prepositions (每题 1 分,共 10 分).
1. to   2. for   3. from   4. with   5. against
6. to   7. from   8. for   9. in   10. by

IV. Reading Comprehension (每空 1 分,共 20 分).
Passage One:(每空 1 分,共 10 分)
1. consists   2. brakes   3. link   4. fluid-filled   5. piston
6. connected   7. fluid   8. against   9. friction   10. revolving

Passage Two:(每空 1 分,共 10 分)
1. step   2. introduction   3. degree   4. proportion   5. ratio
6. approximately   7. movement   8. wheels   9. turn   10. design

V. Translation (共 40 分).
Part One:Translate the following passages into Chinese. (共 15 分)
Passage One (7 分)

离合器盘(从动盘)含有一个装于加强花键轮毂上的圆形金属板。螺旋弹簧通常安装在轮毂的弹簧座孔内,用以提供弹性结合。花键轮毂在变速器输入轴的花键上纵向地自由滑动。当离合器盘被连接时,它就通过花键驱动输入轴。离合器盘连同离合器压盘或离合器外壳一起工作。当离合器处于发动机与变速器接合状态时,离合器盘被夹在发动机飞轮与离合器压盘中间。

Passage Two (8 分)

自动变速器根据发动机转速、动力机构的负荷、车速和其他的运行因素选择传动比。需要驾驶员做的工作很少,因为升挡和降挡都是自动完成的。换挡时无需驾驶员操作离合器,并且车辆停车时也无需换至空挡。这极为便利,尤其在停停走走的交通状况中。驾驶员也能手动选择低速前进挡、倒挡、空挡和驻车挡。依靠前进挡位的选择,变速器可以在减速过程中制动发动机。

Part Two:Translate the following sentences into English. (每题 3 分,共 15 分)
1. One of the functions of the suspension system is to prevent the road shocks from being transmitted to the vehicle frame.
2. The oil pump of the automatic transmission is responsible for producing all the oil pressure that is required in the transmission.
3. The clutch disc operates in conjunction with a pressure plate or clutch cover.
4. The service brake system is used to decelerate and stop the moving vehicle.
5. Two types of steering systems are commonly used on cars: manual steering systems and power steering systems.

Part Three: Translate the following names of cars into Chinese. (每题 0.5 分, 共 5 分)
1. 沃尔沃   2. 雷诺   3. 宾利   4. 法拉利   5. 现代
6. 迷你   7. 标致   8. 大宇   9. 莲花   10. 依维柯

Part Four: Translate the following abbreviations into corresponding Chinese terms. (每题 1 分, 共 5 分)
1. 无级变速器   2. 全球定位系统   3. 动力转向
4. 防抱死制动系统   5. 自动调整悬架

VI. Error Correction (每题 2 分, 共 10 分).
1. A 改为: gain   (情态动词 "must" 后接动词原形)
2. B 改为: are added   (此句应为被动语态)
3. D 改为: or   (either... or... 或者……或者……)
4. D 改为: to   (be attached to 把……装于……上)
5. B 改为: is   (此句主语为 advantage, 是单数)

Final Exam

I. Vocabulary (每题 1 分, 共 10 分).
1. C 2. B 3. A 4. A 5. C 6. D 7. C 8. B 9. C 10. D

II. Word Form (每题 1 分, 共 10 分).
1. is bolted   2. largest   3. working   4. installed   5. moves
6. spray   7. enable   8. be held   9. compressing   10. equipped

III. Usage of Prepositions (每题 1 分, 共 10 分).
1. in   2. from   3. with   4. under   5. without
6. after   7. from   8. of   9. on   10. of

IV. Reading Comprehension (每空 1 分, 共 20 分).

Passage One: (每空 1 分, 共 10 分)
1. means   2. relation   3. excess   4. transmissions   5. neutral
6. disconnects   7. opposite   8. inserted   9. lock   10. rolling

Passage Two: (每空 1 分, 共 10 分)
1. technologies   2. alternative   3. development   4. influence   5. progress
6. significant   7. closely   8. electronics   9. attention   10. information

V. Translation (共 40 分).
Part One: Translate the following passages into Chinese. (共 15 分)
Passage One (7 分)

燃料在发动机中燃烧时,燃料中大约有 1/3 的热能转化为动力,另外 1/3 的热能未经使用就从排气管排出,剩下的 1/3 的热能必须由冷却系统来处理。这就意味着只有均等地处理热能,以保持发动机温度的均衡,发动机才能有效地工作。

Passage Two（8 分）
几乎路上所有的车辆都采用电子发动机控制系统。这一系统由许多电子及机电部件组成。设计这一系统,是为了持续监控发动机的运行状况,并调整发动机,以使其更有效地运转。电子发动机控制系统已显著地改善了油耗。计算机分析输入传感器的数据,然后基于输入信号与储存的指令控制输出装置,对发动机系统的运行状况做出必要的调整。

Part Two：Translate the following sentences into English.（每题 3 分,共 15 分）

1. The massive market of the automobiles in America was dominated by the big three motor manufacturers.
2. The exhaust system of a vehicle is used to conduct the burned gases to the rear of the vehicle and into the air.
3. The purpose of the ignition switch is to connect or disconnect the ignition system from the battery, so the engine can be started and stopped as desired.
4. Compared with the old types, this type is improved in exterior design and tint.
5. The oil pressure relief valve can secure the oil circulation through engine parts under proper pressure.

Part Three：Translate the following names of cars into Chinese.（每题 0.5 分,共 5 分）

    1. 凯迪拉克   2. 欧宝   3. 雪铁龙   4. 双龙   5. 菲亚特
    6. 劳斯莱斯   7. 高尔夫   8. 悍马   9. 皇冠   10. 捷豹

Part Four：Translate the following abbreviations into corresponding Chinese terms.（每题 1 分,共 5 分）

    1. 曲轴箱强制通风   2. 多点燃油喷射   3. 运动型多功能车
    4. 诊断故障码   5. 中央处理器

VI. Error Correction（每题 2 分,共 10 分）.

1. B 改为：is composed of 或 consists of （由……组成）
2. C 改为：waxed （have sth. done 某事被别人做）
3. B 改为：be （此句为虚拟语气。在"important"后的 that 从句中的谓语动词应为动词原形或"should" + 动词原形）
4. C 改为：from （apart from 除……外）
5. A 改为：used （过去分词做定语,修饰先行词"framework"）

II. Abbreviations

Abbreviations	English	Chinese
AAS	automatic adjusting suspension	自动调整悬架
ABS	anti-lock brake system	防抱死制动系统
A/C	air conditioning	空调
AC	air cooling	风冷
ACC	air conditioning clutch	空调离合器
ACL	air cleaner	空气滤清器
ACT	air charge temperature	进气温度
A/F 或 AF	air fuel (ratio)	空燃比
AFC	air flow control	空气流量控制
AFS	air flow sensor	空气流量传感器
AI	(secondary) air injection	（二次）空气喷射
AIV	air injection valve	空气喷射阀
ALDL	assembly line diagnostic link	总装线诊断插座
ALT	alternator	交流发电机
ANT	antenna	天线
AP	accelerator pedal	加速踏板
APS	absolute pressure sensor	绝对压力传感器
ASSY	assembly	总成
AT 或 A/T	automatic transmission/transaxle	自动变速器/变速驱动桥
ATDC	after top dead center	上止点后
ATF	automatic transmission fluid	自动变速器油液
ATS	air temperature sensor	空气温度传感器
AWD	all wheel drive	全轮驱动
B+	battery positive voltage	蓄电池正极
BA	brake assist	辅助制动装置
BAT	battery	蓄电池
BDC	bottom dead center	下止点
BMC	brake master cylinder	制动主缸

To be continued

Abbreviations	English	Chinese
BPM	brake pressure modulator	制动压力调节器
BPMV	brake pressure modulating valve	制动压力调节阀
BTDC	before top dead center	上止点前
BTR	brake transmission ratio	制动传动比
C3I	computer controlled coil ignition	计算机控制线圈点火
CAC	charge air cooler	进气冷却器
CF	cooling fan	冷却风扇
CFI	central fuel injection	中央燃油喷射
CHG	charge	充电
CL	clutch	离合器
CL	closed loop	闭环
CLSW	clutch switch	离合器开关
CMFI	central multiport fuel injection	中央多点燃油喷射
CO	carbon monoxide	一氧化碳
CPC	clutch pressure control	离合器压力控制
CPU	central processing unit	中央处理器
CPS	crankshaft position sensor	曲轴位置传感器
CTS	coolant temperature sensor	冷却液温度传感器
CUV	crossover utility vehicle	跨界运动休旅车
CVT	continuously variable transmission	无级变速器
C/W	carrier wave	载波
CYL	cylinder	汽缸
DFI	direct fuel injection	直接燃油喷射
DI	distributor ignition	分电器点火
DIFF	differential	差速器
DLC	data link connector	数据传递插接器
DLI	distributorless ignition	无分电器点火
DS	detonation sensor	爆燃传感器
DTM	diagnostic test mode	诊断测试模式
DTC	diagnostic trouble code	诊断故障码
EATX	electronic automatic transmission	电控自动变速器
EC	engine control	发动机控制
ECA	electronic control assembly	电子控制总成

To be continued

Abbreviations	English	Chinese
ECL	engine coolant level	发动机冷却液液面
ECS	engine control system	发动机控制系统
ECT	engine coolant temperature	发动机冷却液温度
ECU	electronic control unit	电子控制模块,电脑
EEC	evaporative emission control	蒸发排放物控制
EFI	electronic fuel injection	电子燃油喷射
E/G	engine	发动机
EGOS	exhaust gas oxygen sensor	排气氧含量计
EGR	exhaust gas recirculation	排气再循环
EGRV	exhaust gas recirculation valve	排气再循环阀
EM	engine maintenance	发动机维护
EMD	engine monitor display	发动机监控显示器
EP	exhaust pipe	排气管
EX	exhaust	排气
FC	fan control	风扇控制
FH	frame height	车架离地高度
FI	fuel injection	燃油喷射
FIA	fuel injection air	燃油喷射进气
Fig.	figure	图,插图
FP	fuel pump	输油泵
GAS	gasoline	汽油
GPS	global positioning system	全球定位系统
HTC	hydraulic torque converter	液力变矩器
IA	intake air	进气
IAC	idle air control	怠速控制
IACV	idle air control valve	怠速空气控制阀
IATS	intake air temperature sensor	进气温度传感器
ICM	ignition control module	点火控制模块
IFS	independent front suspension	独立式前悬架
IMA	idle mixture adjustment	怠速混合比调整
IT	ignition timing	点火正时

To be continued

Abbreviations	English	Chinese
L/C	lock-up clutch	锁定离合器
LLC	long-life coolant	长效冷却液
LO	lubricating oil	润滑油
LS	leaf spring	钢板弹簧
LSD	limited slip differential	防滑差速器
MAP	manifold absolute pressure	歧管绝对压力
M/C	mixture control	混合气控制
MCU	microprocessor control solenoid	微处理控制单元
MF	maintenance free	免维护(的)
MFI	multipoint fuel injection	多点燃油喷射
MT 或 M/T	manual transmission/transaxle	手动变速器/变速驱动桥
NPS	neutral position switch	空挡开关
NOX	nitrogen oxides	氮氧化合物
OC	oil consumption	机油消耗
OCV	oil control valve	机油控制阀
ODI	oil drain intervals	换油周期
ODPSK	oil dipstick	(机)油尺,量油尺
OFL	oil filter	机油滤清器
OL	oil level	油位,油面(高度)
OPS	oil pressure sensor	油压传感器
PCV	positive crankcase ventilation	曲轴箱强制通风
PKB	parking brake	驻车制动器
PMR	pump motor relay	液压泵电动机继电器
PS	power steering	动力转向
PSC	power steering control	动力转向控制
PSP	power steering pressure	动力转向压力
PW	primary winding	初级线圈
RHD	right-hand drive	右侧驾驶
RKE	remote keyless entry	无线遥控门锁
RM	relay module	继电器模块
RWD	rear wheel drive	后轮驱动

To be continued

Abbreviations	English	Chinese
SBEC	single board engine control	单板发动机控制
SEFI	sequential electronic fuel injection	顺序电控燃油喷射
SFI	sequential fuel injection	顺序燃油喷射
SI	spark ignition	火花点火
SOL	solenoid	电磁阀,电磁线圈
SPI	single point injection	单点燃油喷射
SRS	supplemental restraint system	辅助约束系统(指安全带和安全气囊)
ST	scan tool	故障诊断仪
SUS	suspension	悬架
SUV	sport utility vehicle	运动型多用途车,运动型多功能车
SW	switch	切换开关
TB	throttle body	节气门体
TBI	throttle body fuel injection	节气门体燃油喷射
TCC	torque converter clutch	变矩器锁止离合器
TCS	traction control system	驱动力控制系统,防滑装置
TDC	top dead center	上止点
TP	throttle position	节气门位置
TPS	throttle position sensor	节气门位置传感器
TPS	throttle position switch	节气门位置开关
TR	transmission range	变速器挡位(范围)
TV	throttle valve	节气门
TWC	three way catalytic converter	三效催化转换器
VAT	vane air temperature	进气温度
VCM	vehicle control module	车辆控制模块
VIN	vehicle identification number	车辆识别号,车辆识别代码
VR	voltage regulator	电压调节器
VSA	vehicle stability assist	车辆稳定性控制装置
VSS	vehicle speed sensor	车速传感器
VSV	vacuum solenoid valve	真空电磁阀
VVIS	variable volume intake system	可变容积进气系统
4WS	four wheel steering	四轮转向

III. Names of Cars

America

Buick	别克
Cadillac	凯迪拉克
Chevrolet	雪佛兰
Chrysler	克莱斯勒
Cobra	眼镜蛇
Cougar	美洲狮
Dodge	道奇
Eagle	鹰
Ford	福特
General Motor (GM)	通用
General	上将
Hummer	悍马
Jeep	吉普
King	君主
Land Rover	路虎
Lincoln	林肯
Mack	马克
Mercury	水星
Mustang	野马
Oldsmobile	奥兹莫比尔
Panoz	帕诺兹
Phoenix	凤凰
Plymouth	普利茅斯
Pontiac	庞蒂克
Saturn	土星
Thunderbird	雷鸟
Viper	蝰蛇

Australia

Holden	霍尔顿

Britain

Aston Martin	阿斯顿马丁
Bentley	宾利
Foden	福登
Jaguar	捷豹
Leyland	利兰
Lotus	莲花
Marcos	玛柯斯
MG	名爵
Mini	迷你
Morgan	摩根
Rolls-Royce	劳斯莱斯
Rover	罗孚
Triumph	凯旋
Vauxhall	伏克斯豪尔

Czechoslovakia

Skoda	斯柯达

France

Citroen	雪铁龙
Peugeot	标致
Renault	雷诺
Venturi	文图瑞

German

Audi	奥迪
BMW	宝马
Golf	高尔夫
Grace	格拉塞
Mercedes – Benz	梅塞德斯 – 奔驰
Neoplan	尼奥普兰
Opel	欧宝
Porsche	保时捷
Volkswagen	大众

Italy

Abarth	阿巴斯

Alfa-Romeo	阿尔法罗密欧
Bugatti	布加蒂
Ferrari	法拉利
Fiat	菲亚特
Isorvolta	伊索
Iveco	依维柯
Lamborghini	兰博基尼
Lancia	蓝旗亚
Maserati	玛莎拉蒂
Piaggio	比亚乔
Pininfarina	平尼法尼那

Japan

Acura	讴歌
Autozam	奥图兰姆
Bluebird	蓝鸟
Cedric	公爵
Corolla	花冠
Crown	皇冠
Daihatsu	大发
Efini	仪飞尼
Eunos	优娜斯
Hino	日野
Honda	本田
Infiniti	无限
Isuzu	五十铃
Lexus	凌志
Mazda	马自达
Mitsubishi	三菱
Nissan	尼桑（日产）
Subaru	富士重工（斯巴鲁）
Suzuki	铃木
Tommykaira	龟牌
Toyota	丰田
Yelong	裕隆

Korea

Daewoo	大宇

Hyundai	现代
Kia	起亚
Ssangyong	双龙

Malaysia

| Proton | 宝腾 |

Poland

| Polonez | 波罗乃兹 |

Romania

| Dacia | 达西亚 |

Russia

| Lada | 拉达 |

Spain

| Picasso | 毕加索 |
| SEAT | 西特 |

Sweden

Saab	绅宝(萨博)
Scania	斯堪尼亚
Volvo	沃尔沃(富豪)

Switzerland

| Smart | 精灵 |

References

[1] John B. Rae. The American Automobile Industry[M]. Boston：Twayne Publishers,1984.

[2] Robert N. Brady. Electric and Electronic Systems for Automobiles and Trucks[M]. Virginia：Reston Publishing Company, Inc.,1982.

[3] Oldham, J. Auto Trouble Shooter[M]. New York：The Hearst Corporation, 1976.

[4] Heinz Heisler. Advanced Vehicle Technology[M]. Oxford：Butterworth Heinemann, 2002.

[5] Don Knowles. Automotive Principles, Theory and Fundamentals, Volume 1[M]. New Jersey：Prentice Hall, Inc., 1988.

[6] James D. Halderman, Chaes D. Mitchell, Jr. Automotive Brake Systems[M]. New Jersey：Prentice Hall, Inc., 2004.

[7] Robert N. Brady. On-Highway Trucks, Power Trains and Suspension[M]. Virginia：Reston Publishing Company, Inc., 1982.

[8] William L. Husselbee. Automotive Tune-up Procedures[M]. Virginia：Reston Publishing Company, Inc., 1983.

[9] Herbert E. Ellinger, Richard B. Hathaway. Automotive Suspension, Steering, and Brakes[M]. London：Prentice-Hall, Inc., 1990.

[10] Sheldon L. Abbott. Automobile Transmissions[M]. London：Glencoe Publishing Co, Inc., 1989.

[11] Dipl.-lng. (FH) Horst Bauer. Automotive Handbook, 5th Edition[M]. Stuttgart：Robert Bosch GmbH, 2000.

[12] 郑殿旺,陈庆新. 汽车英语阅读[M]. 哈尔滨：哈尔滨工业大学出版社,1998.

[13] 中国汽车技术研究中心. 英汉汽车综合词典[M]. 北京：北京理工大学出版社,2006.

[14] 陈坚林. 实用汽车英语[M]. 上海：上海外语教育出版社,1998.

[15] 王志华,朱晓晖. 实用公关英语[M]. 杭州：浙江大学出版社,2007.

[16] 赵燕飞. 用英语和客户交谈[M]. 广州：世界图书出版公司,2007.

[17] 宋进桂. 汽车专业英语读译教程[M]. 北京：机械工业出版社,2007.

[18] 大嘴英语工作室. 商务英语会话大全[M]. 北京：中国宇航出版社,2007.

[19] 陈勇,边明远. 汽车专业英语[M]. 北京：北京理工大学出版社,2007.

[20] 陈家瑞,等. 汽车构造(第二版)[M]. 北京：机械工业出版社,2005.